brilliant Home Computer book

P. K. MacBride

brilliant Home Computer book

WINDOWS VISTA EDITION

PEARSON
Prentice
Hall

Harlow, England • London • New York • Boston • San Francisco • Toronto • Sydney • Singapore • Hong Kong
Tokyo • Seoul • Taipei • New Delhi • Cape Town • Madrid • Mexico City • Amsterdam • Munich • Paris • Milan

Pearson Education Limited

Edinburgh Gate
Harlow
Essex CM20 2JE
England

and Associated Companies throughout the world

Visit us on the World Wide Web at:
www.pearsoned.co.uk

First published 2008

ISBN: 978-0-273-71573-3

British Library Cataloguing-in-Publication Data
A catalogue record for this book is available from the British Library

Library of Congress Cataloging-in-Publication Data
A CIP catalog record for this book can be obtained from the Library of Congress

10 9 8 7 6 5 4 3 2 1
13 12 11 10 09

Editorial management by McNidder & Grace, Alnwick
Printed and bound by Rotolito Lombarda, Italy

The publisher's policy is to use paper manufactured from sustainable forests.

Brilliant guides

What you need to know and how to do it

When you're working on your PC and come up against a problem that you're unsure how to solve, or want to accomplish something in an application that you aren't sure how to do, where do you look? Manuals and traditional training guides are usually too big and unwieldy and are intended to be used as end-to-end training resources, making it hard to get to the info you need right away without having to wade through pages of background information that you just don't need at that moment – and helplines are rarely that helpful!

Brilliant guides have been developed to allow you to find the info you need easily and without fuss and guide you through the task using a highly visual, step-by-step approach – providing exactly what you need to know when you need it!

Brilliant guides provide the quick, easy-to-access information that you need, using a detailed contents list and a troubleshooting guide to help you find exactly what you need to know, and then presenting each task in a visual manner. Numbered steps guide you through each task or problem, using numerous screenshots to illustrate each step. Boxed tips extend your knowledge, or direct you to related material on other pages.

In addition to covering all major office PC applications and related computing subjects, the **Brilliant** series also contains titles that will help you in every aspect of your working life, such as writing the perfect CV, answering the toughest interview questions and moving on in your career.

Brilliant guides are the light at the end of the tunnel when you are faced with any minor or major task.

Contents at a glance

Acknowledgements

The author and publisher would like to thank the web masters of the following sites for permission to reproduce the screenshots in this book:

Google UK, Web Museum, Real, Yamaha.

Microsoft product screenshot(s) reprinted with permission from Microsoft Corporation.

Every effort has been made to obtain necessary permission with reference to copyright material. The publisher apologises if, inadvertently, any sources remain unacknowledged and will be glad to make the necessary arrangements at the earliest opportunity.

About the author

P.K. MacBride spent 20 years at the chalkface in schools and technical colleges before leaving to work full-time as a writer, editor and typesetter. He has written over 120 books, mainly on computing topics, covering many aspects of computer programming, software applications and the Internet. He has been translated into over a dozen languages, including Russian, Portuguese, Greek, Chinese and American.

Contents

Contents

4   Communicating online   159

1 Getting to know your PC

I'm assuming that you have got your PC set up and that you have found the on/off switches. Turn it on now, and let's get started!

This chapter covers:

- The Vista Desktop and Start menu
- How to manage Windows
- How to use menus and set options
- Windows Explorer
- How to organise your files – you will see how to view, sort, rename, move, copy and delete them
- Tags and other properties of files
- How to personalise your Desktop by changing the colours and background
- How to set a screensaver
- Gadgets for your Desktop

The Desktop

The Desktop is the screen display that you see when you first turn on, and which sits there, behind your application windows, while you are working on your PC. Documents and tools can be laid out on here, just as paper documents, pens, calendars, clocks and other real tools can be laid out on a real desktop.

Everybody's Desktop looks different after they have been using their PC for a while, and even those of fresh-from-the-shelf PCs vary, because different manufacturers and retailers bundle different programs with the machines. However, all Desktops have the same basic features. Look at yours now and identify the ones labelled here.

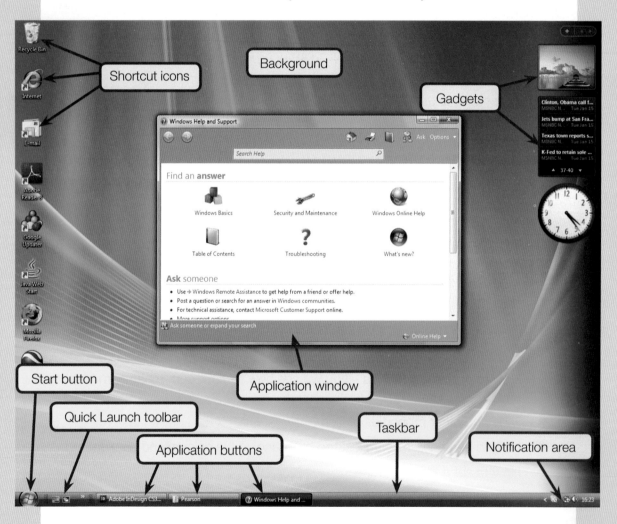

Desktop elements

- The **Background** is purely decorative. You can have plain or patterned colours, or a picture, and this can be one of those supplied with Vista or one of your own.

- Every **application** (also called a program) runs in its own **window**. This can be moved around the screen, resized or minimised out of the way. Windows can sit beside, behind or on top of other windows.

- **Gadgets** are mini applications that you can run on your Desktop – some of them can be useful, others are decorative or just for fun.

- **Shortcut icons** offer a quick way to start applications, or to open documents or the folders where you store documents.

- The **Taskbar** is used to start, to switch between and to control applications. Any application on your PC can be run from the Taskbar – one way or another.

- The **Start button** opens the Start menu, from where you can start any application on your PC.

- Every running **application** has a **button** on the Taskbar – if its window has been minimised, this is all that you can see of an application. Click the button to switch to an application, when you want to work on it.

- In the **Notification area** are icons for applications that are running in the background. For instance, if you have an Internet connection, there will be an icon here to tell you its status, when the printer is active, you'll see an icon in this area. The volume control and clock are usually present here too.

The Start menu

From the Start menu you can:

- run any application on your PC
- open the folders where you store your documents, pictures and music
- search for files
- get Help
- and much more.

The right half of the Start menu carries links to your main folders and to utilities that are part of the Vista system. The left half of the Start menu has two display modes. When it first opens, it will list the programs you use most.

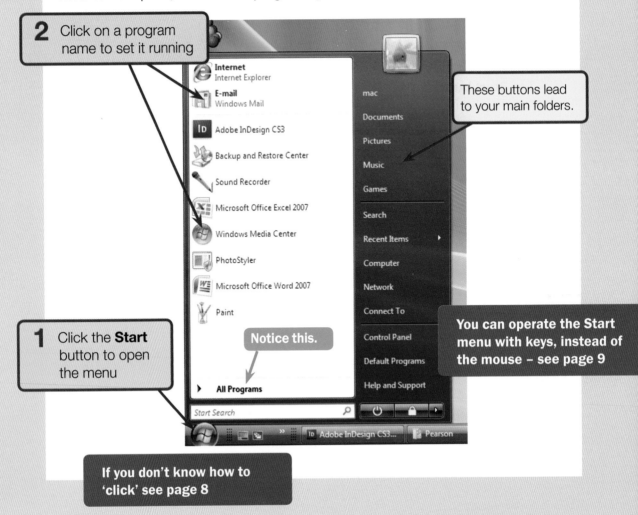

2 Click on a program name to set it running

These buttons lead to your main folders.

1 Click the **Start** button to open the menu

Notice this.

You can operate the Start menu with keys, instead of the mouse – see page 9

If you don't know how to 'click' see page 8

Start menu buttons

Let's have a look at the right half of the Start menu. What we've got here are links to things that the Vista designers think we will find useful. When you click these, some will open a menu, but most open a folder. Both menus and folders can contain either your own documents, or programs from Windows' core set.

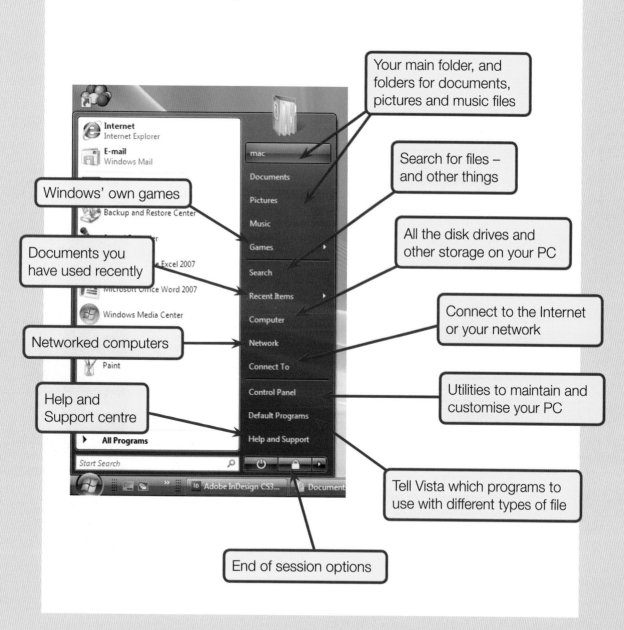

Your main folder, and folders for documents, pictures and music files

Search for files – and other things

Windows' own games

All the disk drives and other storage on your PC

Documents you have used recently

Connect to the Internet or your network

Networked computers

Utilities to maintain and customise your PC

Help and Support centre

Tell Vista which programs to use with different types of file

End of session options

All programs

At the bottom left of the Start menu is a bar marked **All Programs** (you did notice it, didn't you). If you click this, the menu lists all the programs on your PC. Some are listed by name at the top, and below this are folders where groups of programs are stored. At first, you may not have much here, but each time you install another piece of software, a new folder will be created for its programs.

The actual applications are not listed here, just links to them.

Some good applications come free with Windows Vista – we will be exploring them later.

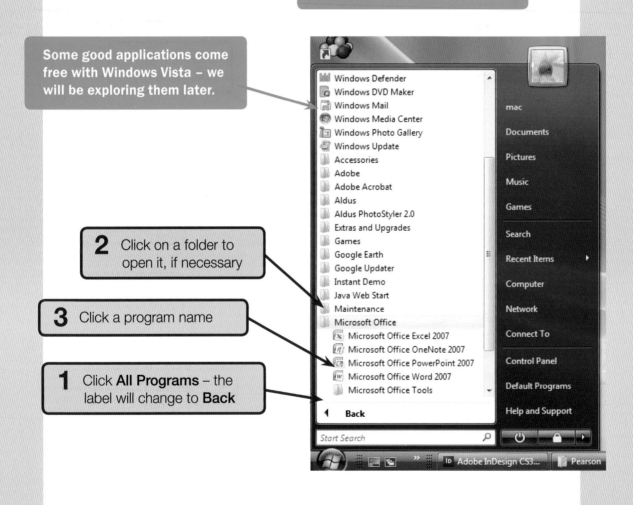

2 Click on a folder to open it, if necessary

3 Click a program name

1 Click **All Programs** – the label will change to **Back**

The Taskbar

The Taskbar comes into its own once you have got your applications running. It is normally present along the bottom of the screen, no matter what else is going on. (It is possible to move it to the side, or to hide it, but you need a special reason for changing what works best!)

The Taskbar's main job is to hold the buttons which are used for switching between open applications.

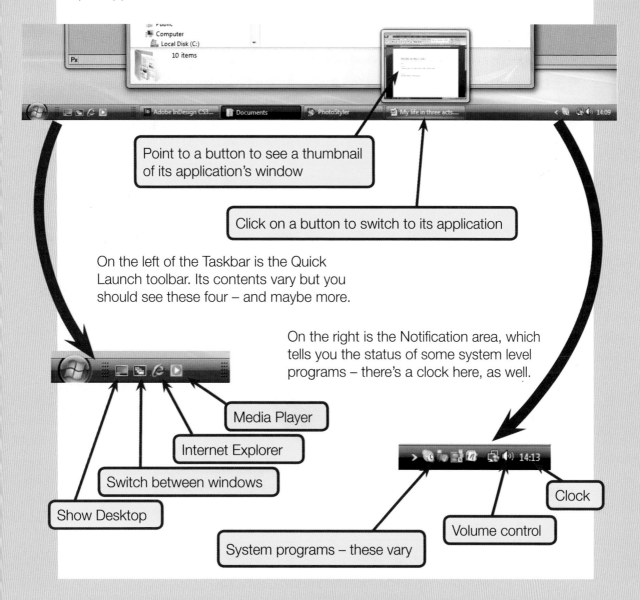

Point to a button to see a thumbnail of its application's window

Click on a button to switch to its application

On the left of the Taskbar is the Quick Launch toolbar. Its contents vary but you should see these four – and maybe more.

On the right is the Notification area, which tells you the status of some system level programs – there's a clock here, as well.

Media Player

Internet Explorer

Switch between windows

Show Desktop

Clock

Volume control

System programs – these vary

The mouse

It is possible to use a Windows PC without a mouse, but it's much simpler with one.
There are seven mouse actions you should master:

- **Point** – move the mouse to locate the pointer on the screen
- **Click** – press the left button once
- **Double-click** – press the left button twice, in quick succession
- **Right-click** – press the right button once
- **Drag** – hold down the left button while you move the mouse
- **Drag and drop** – used for moving things around on screen. Drag the object to where you want it, then release the mouse button to drop it into place.
- **Scroll** – use the wheel between the buttons to move the display within a window. (Not all mice have these wheels, but don't worry – they are not essential.)

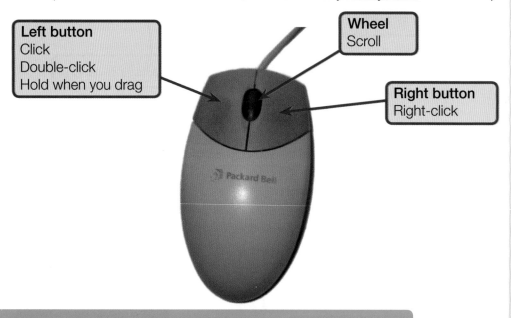

Left button
Click
Double-click
Hold when you drag

Wheel
Scroll

Right button
Right-click

Packard Bell

If you cannot use the mouse, or do not want to, you can set up the keyboard to do the mouse's work. Click the Control Panel button on the Start menu and open the Ease of Access centre. Follow the link to Change the way the mouse works and Turn on Mouse Keys. You can then move the cursor, 'click' and 'right-click' using the number pad.

The keyboard

The keyboard is primarily there for typing in text and numbers, but it is also used for controlling the PC. There are four main sets of keys, plus other special ones:

- The **character set** produce letters, digits and symbols. As with a typewriter, you hold down [Shift] to get capitals or symbols.

- The **arrows** and other **movement** keys move the insertion point around when you are working with text.

- The **number pad** is for when you are entering lots of numbers – perhaps when doing the accounts. The same keys can instead be used for **movement** – the Num Lock key toggles the keys between numbers and movement.

- The **function keys** can be set up to do different jobs in different applications, but some things are usually the same, e.g. F1 always starts the Help system.

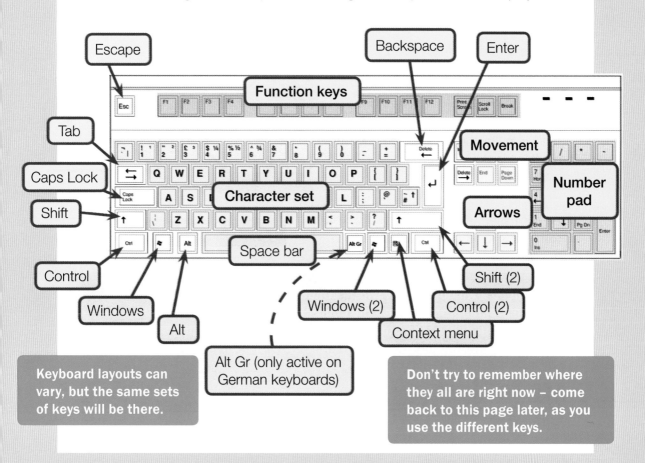

Keyboard layouts can vary, but the same sets of keys will be there.

Alt Gr (only active on German keyboards)

Don't try to remember where they all are right now – come back to this page later, as you use the different keys.

Windows

Every application runs in its own window – in fact, everything in Windows happens in a window – and you can have any number of things going on at once, and so any number of windows open at once. You need to know how to keep on top of them! It's not hard – there are only four basic operations: resize, move, switch and close, and the controls are all built into the window frame.

Window modes

Windows have three modes:

- **Maximised**, filling the whole screen
- **Restore**, in which the window can be moved and its size varied
- **Minimised**, where the only sign of the window is its button on the Taskbar.

You can switch between them using the buttons at the top right.

When the window is maximised, you have these buttons:

When it is in Restore mode, the buttons look like this.

> **Close** shuts the window and exits the application.

When minimised, all you see is the Taskbar button – click to reopen the window.

You need a window to play with – Windows Explorer will do nicely. This is the program that displays the contents of your disks. Most of the buttons on the right of the Start menu run Explorer, but starting at different points in the system. We'll get an overview of the whole computer.

1 Click the **Start** button

2 Click **Computer** on the right of the menu.

The frame contains all the controls you need for adjusting the display.

Title bar – drag to move a window. This usually shows the name of the applications, but not in Computer.

Mode and **Close**

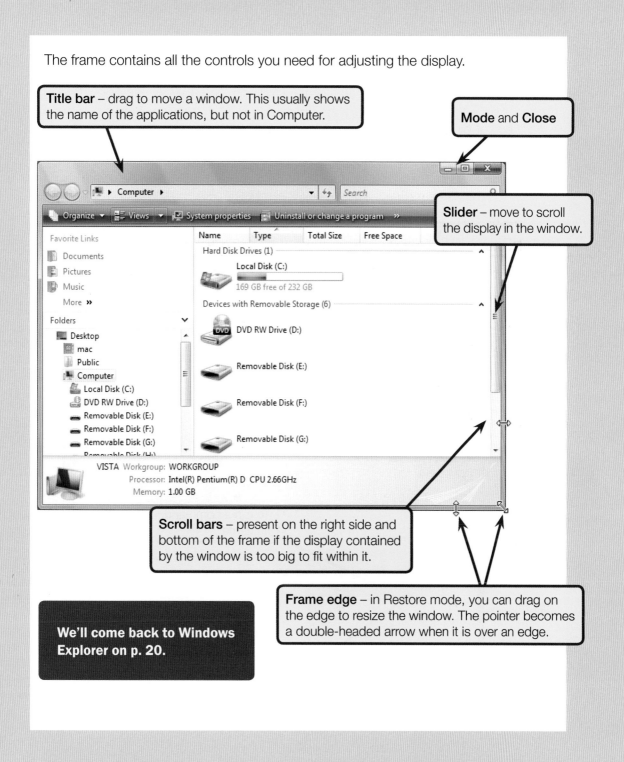

Slider – move to scroll the display in the window.

Scroll bars – present on the right side and bottom of the frame if the display contained by the window is too big to fit within it.

We'll come back to Windows Explorer on p. 20.

Frame edge – in Restore mode, you can drag on the edge to resize the window. The pointer becomes a double-headed arrow when it is over an edge.

Menus

Every program has a set of commands and options. There may be not many more than Start and Stop, or there may be a huge range of features. You can normally reach these through a system of menus which drop down from the headings in the Menu bar.

We will explore menus using WordPad.

To start WordPad:

1 **Click the Start button**

2 **Point to All Programs**

3 **Click on the Accessories bar to open its folder**

4 **Click the WordPad entry.**

To open a menu, click its heading

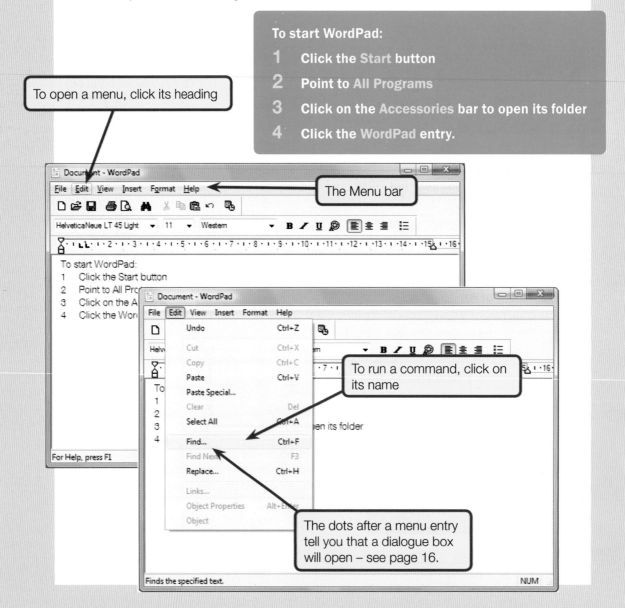

The Menu bar

To run a command, click on its name

The dots after a menu entry tell you that a dialogue box will open – see page 16.

Menus from the keyboard

Menus can also be controlled through the keyboard. You might want to do this all the time because you do not like using the mouse, but it is also very useful to be able to run commands from the keyboard when you are typing.

Some commands and options have keyboard shortcuts but they can all be reached using the [Alt] key.

> Many commands have keyboard shortcuts. They may be function keys or you may need to hold down [Ctrl] or press [Alt] and then press a letter key to run the command. The shortcuts are normally shown on menus.

1 Press **[Alt]** – an underline will appear beneath one letter in each of the menu headings

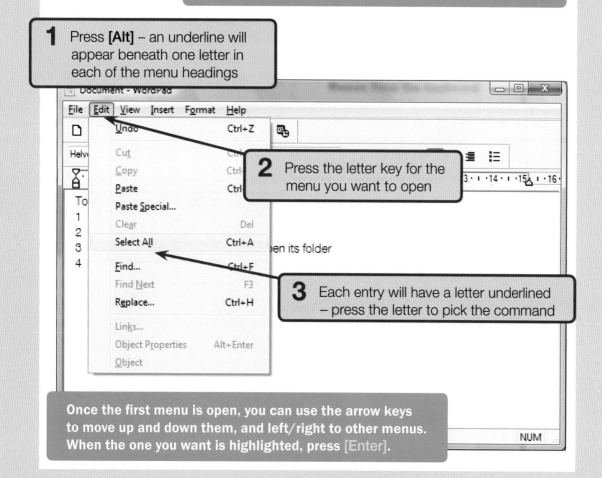

2 Press the letter key for the menu you want to open

3 Each entry will have a letter underlined – press the letter to pick the command

> Once the first menu is open, you can use the arrow keys to move up and down them, and left/right to other menus. When the one you want is highlighted, press [Enter].

Context menus

If you right-click on an object – an image, a window, a selected block of text, or just about anything – a context menu appears. This carries a set of commands that may be relevant to that object at that time. It's clever stuff! Nine times out of ten, the menu will contain the command you want. The menus vary hugely, of course. They even vary for the same kind of object, because it depends upon the context that it's in. (Hence the name. These are also called 'right-click menus' or 'shortcut menus'.)

Here are some examples. Notice that sometimes the first item is in bold – this is the one you are most likely to want. Press **Enter** or click on it to select it.

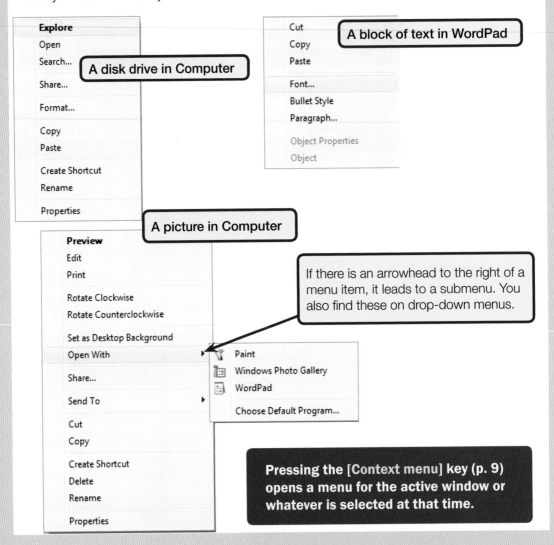

A disk drive in Computer

A block of text in WordPad

A picture in Computer

If there is an arrowhead to the right of a menu item, it leads to a submenu. You also find these on drop-down menus.

Pressing the [Context menu] key (p. 9) opens a menu for the active window or whatever is selected at that time.

Toolbars

In most applications, the most commonly used commands can also be reached through toolbars. These have sets of buttons or drop-down lists that you can click to start routines or set options.

If you point at a toolbar button and wait, a tooltip should appear to tell you what the tool does.

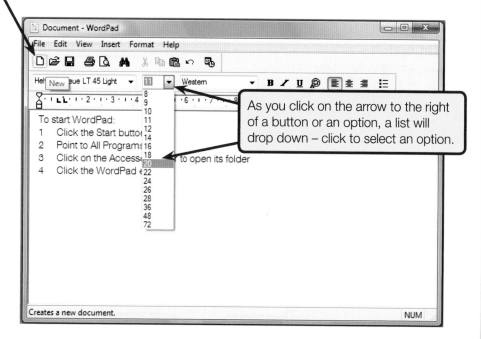

As you click on the arrow to the right of a button or an option, a list will drop down – click to select an option.

Some programs have only one toolbar, some have lots – WordPad has two. If you would like more working room on your screen, you can usually turn off any toolbars that you are not using.

In WordPad, open the **View** menu and click on a toolbar name to turn it off or on – the tick tells you it's there.

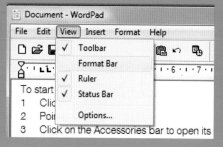

Dialogue boxes

When a Windows application needs to get some information from you, such as what to call a file and where to save it, or how to format some text, it usually does this through a dialogue box. These vary, depending upon the sort of information, but they have many features in common.

- **Radio button** – only one of this set of options can be selected at a time
- **Checkbox** – a tick means it's on
- **Drop-down list** – click the arrow to open the list
- **Text box** – type the text or values here
- **OK button** – click when you have finished to save your choices and typed information, and to close the box
- **Cancel** – click to close the box without saving the data
- **Close** button – click to exit without saving any changes.

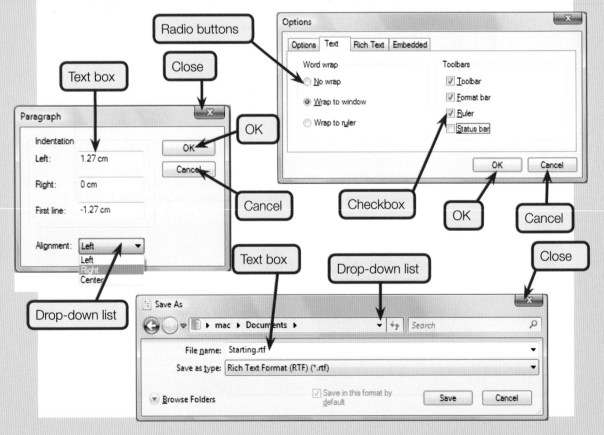

Properties

Files, folders, screen elements and other objects have **Properties**. Some of these are just descriptive, others define how an object works or how it can be used. You can see an object's properties in its Properties dialogue box – the last item on its context menu will open this.

Try right-clicking on different objects on screen. If there is a Properties entry in the menu, select it and have a look to see what it tells you about the object.

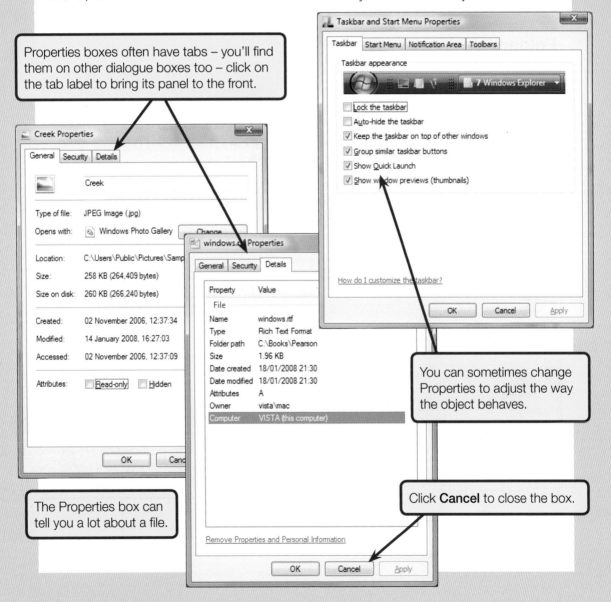

Properties boxes often have tabs – you'll find them on other dialogue boxes too – click on the tab label to bring its panel to the front.

You can sometimes change Properties to adjust the way the object behaves.

The Properties box can tell you a lot about a file.

Click **Cancel** to close the box.

Files and folders

The hard disks supplied on new PCs are typically 120 gigabytes or larger. 1 gigabyte is 1 billion bytes and each byte can hold one character (or part of a number or of a graphic). That means that a typical hard disk can hold nearly to 25 billion words – enough for about 120,000 hefty novels! More to the point, if you were using it to store letters and reports, it could hold many, many thousands of them. Even if you are storing big audio or video files you are still going to get hundreds of them on the disk. It must be organised if you are ever to find your files.

Folders

Folders provide this organisation. They are containers in which related files can be placed to keep them together, and away from other files. A folder can also contain subfolders – which can themselves by subdivided. You can think of the first level of folders as being sets of filing cabinets; those at the second level are drawers within the cabinets, and the next level are equivalent to divisions within the drawers. (And these could have subdividers – there is no limit to this.)

Windows creates a basic set of folders for every user – Documents, Pictures, Music, Downloads, etc. – and you could use just these, but they will get terribly crowded! You need a separate folder for each type of file or area of work or interest, sub-dividing as necessary, so that no folder holds more than a few dozen files.

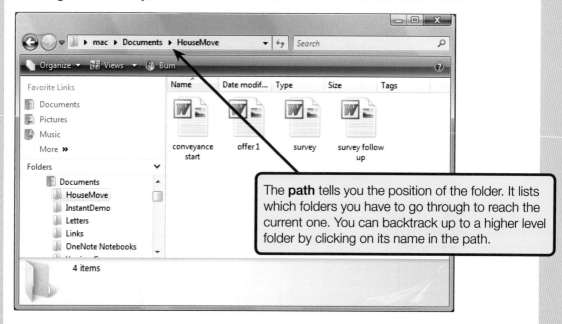

The **path** tells you the position of the folder. It lists which folders you have to go through to reach the current one. You can backtrack up to a higher level folder by clicking on its name in the path.

Files: names and types

Filenames

A filename has two parts – the **name** and an **extension**.

The **name** can be as long as you like, and use almost any characters – including spaces. But don't overdo it. The longer it is, the greater the opportunity for typing errors. The most important thing to remember is that the name must mean something to you, so that you can find the file easily next time you want to use it.

The **extension** is typically 3 or 4 characters, and is separated from the rest of the name by a dot. It identifies the type of file. Windows uses the extensions COM, EXE, SYS, INI, DLL to identify special files of its own – handle these with care!

Most applications also use their own special extensions. Word files are marked DOC or DOCX; spreadsheet files are usually XLS; web pages are often HTM.

When you save a file, and are asked for a filename, you normally only have to give the name part. The application will take care of the extension. If you have to give an extension, make it meaningful. BAK is good for backup files; TXT for text files.

File types and icons

Windows tries to associate every type of file with an application, so that it knows which application to run when you open a file. When it does know the file type – and it generally does – then it hides the extension in the Computer display. Instead, it shows an icon, which helps us to identify the type of file.

The icons change with the display style – as you will see shortly – and when large icons are used, there is often a thumbnail preview of the file to help you identify it.

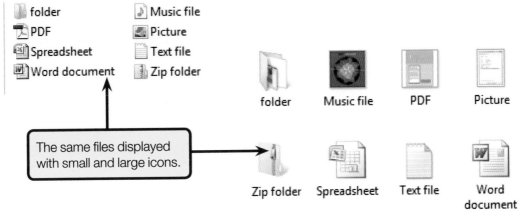

folder Music file
PDF Picture
Spreadsheet Text file
Word document Zip folder

The same files displayed with small and large icons.

folder   Music file   PDF   Picture

Zip folder   Spreadsheet   Text file   Word document

Windows Explorer

Windows Explorer (or just Explorer for short) is the tool that we use for managing the files on our disks. You can start Explorer from Computer, Documents, Pictures and several other of the links on the Start menu – each gets Explorer to open at a different part of your system. Click the Computer button.

The Explorer display is highly variable. Some elements can be turned on or off, and some change in response to the material that is currently displayed.

Current Folder box – shows you where you are now.

Toolbar – the buttons vary according to the type of folder, and type of file selected.

Search box – used to find files.

Favorite Links – open most-used folders with a click.

Folders – shows the structure of folders.

Contents Pane – shows what is in the folder, or on the disk, or in the computer.

Details Pane – shows information about the selected file or folder.

Navigation Pane

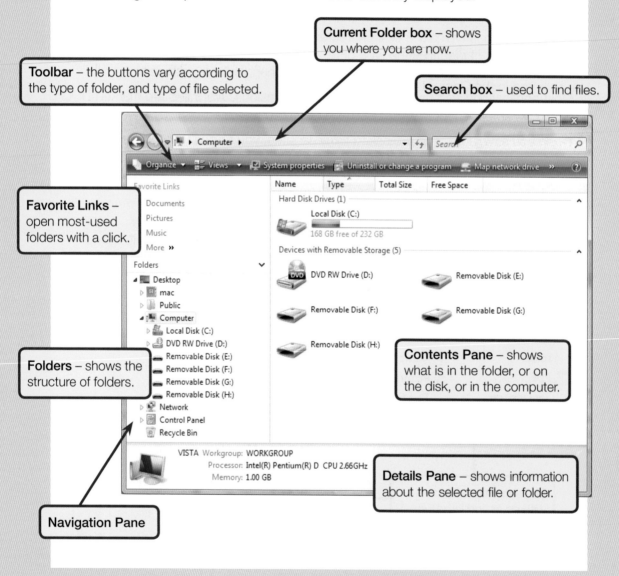

The Explorer window can also have:

- The **Preview Pane** – which shows a small version of an image or the first page of other documents, if a preview is available.
- The **Search Pane** – which opens when you run an advanced search (see p. 45).
- The **Menu bar** – which gives another way to reach the commands and options – this is a fuller set, and they are always there, while the Toolbar buttons change as you work.

These three and other elements are options. You will see shortly (p. 26) how to turn them on and off. The **Toolbar** contents vary. This is what you see when a document is selected in the Contents Pane.

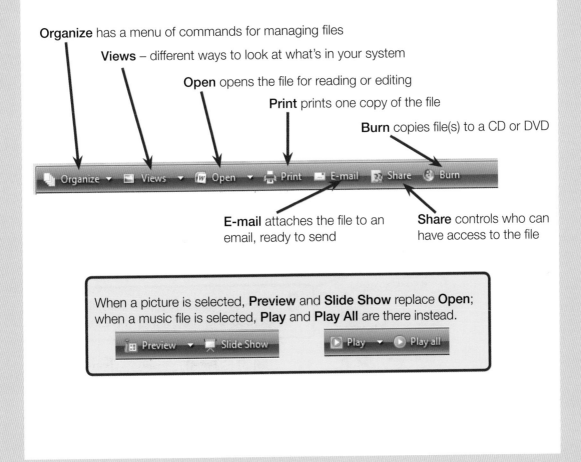

Organize has a menu of commands for managing files

Views – different ways to look at what's in your system

Open opens the file for reading or editing

Print prints one copy of the file

Burn copies file(s) to a CD or DVD

E-mail attaches the file to an email, ready to send

Share controls who can have access to the file

When a picture is selected, **Preview** and **Slide Show** replace **Open**; when a music file is selected, **Play** and **Play All** are there instead.

Favorite Links

Favorite Links, at the top left of the Explorer window, provides a quick way to get to those folders that you use most often.

At first, there will be links to some of the folders that were created for you:

- **Documents**, **Pictures** and **Music** – the default folders for those types of files
- **Recently Changed** – which has links to files that you have been working on
- **Searches** – where the results of searches are stored. (See p. 44 for more on searches.)

You can add other folders to the Favorites Links, if you like.

1 To open a folder, click on its name

2 To add a link to a folder, you must be able to see it in the main pane

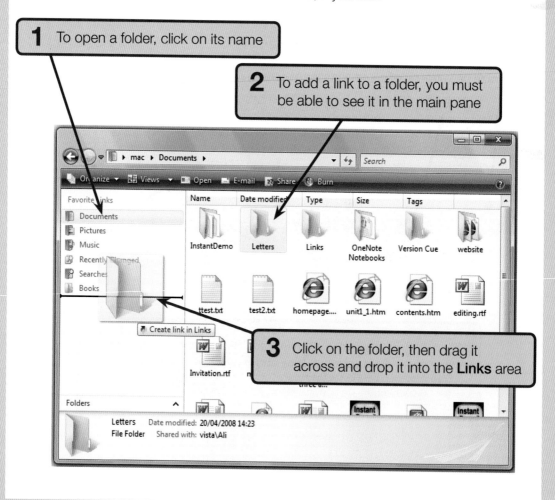

3 Click on the folder, then drag it across and drop it into the **Links** area

The Folders list

The Folders list provides an easier way to switch between folders, and to move files between them. It shows the disk drives, folders and network connections in a branching structure.

1 At the bottom of the Navigation Pane, you will see a bar labelled **Folders** – click on this to open up the Folders display

2 ▷ to the left of a folder name shows that the folder has subfolders – click this to open up the branch

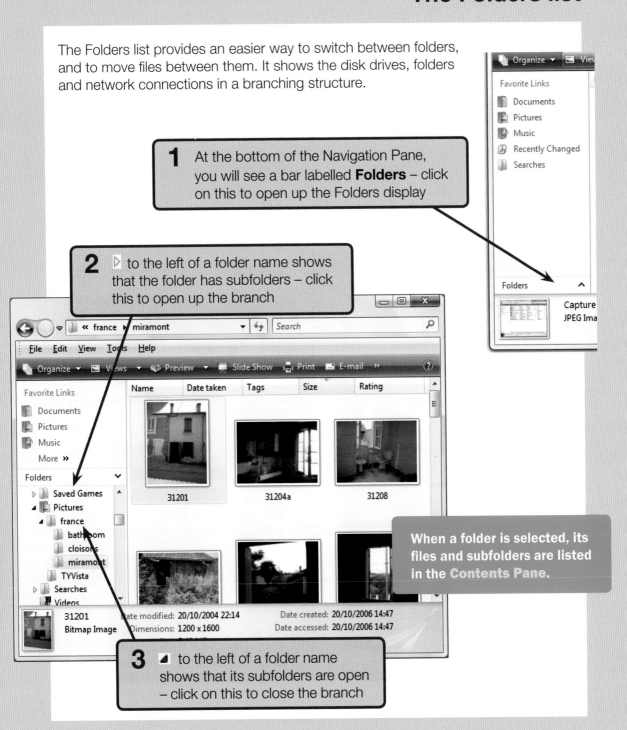

When a folder is selected, its files and subfolders are listed in the Contents Pane.

3 ◢ to the left of a folder name shows that its subfolders are open – click on this to close the branch

Viewing files

Files can be displayed in different ways. When you open a folder for the first time, Windows Explorer chooses the view it thinks is best for the types of files that are in the folder. It is not necessarily right, and you can change the view easily.

The display is controlled from the **Views** button. You can select one of the preset views, or use the slider to get an in-between size.

1 Click the Views button

2 Click on an option

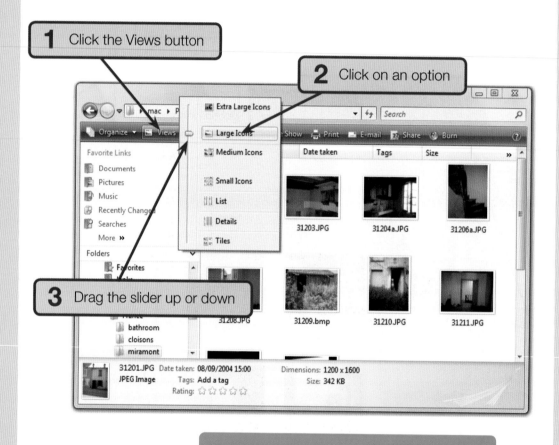

3 Drag the slider up or down

The **Large Icons** view is good for pictures as it shows thumbnails – use **Extra Large Icons** if you need to see more detail.

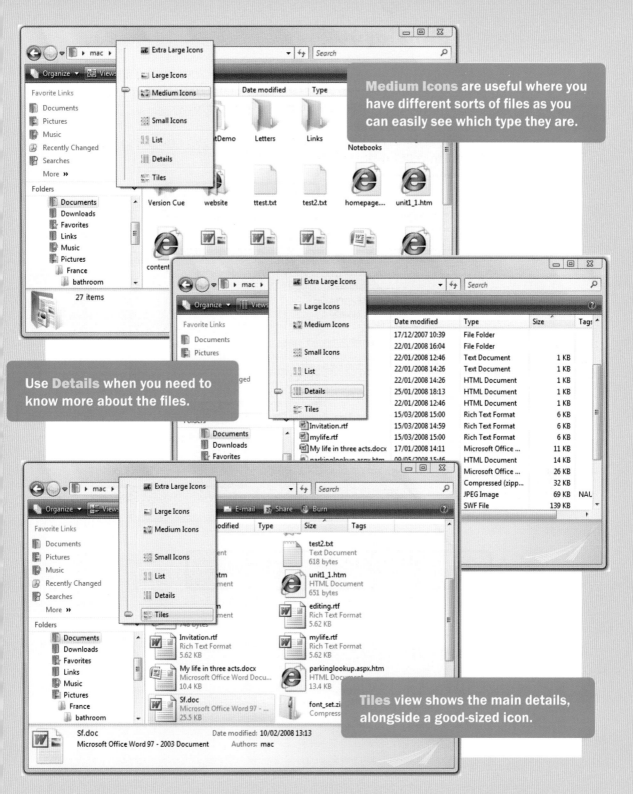

Medium Icons are useful where you have different sorts of files as you can easily see which type they are.

Use Details when you need to know more about the files.

Tiles view shows the main details, alongside a good-sized icon.

Customising the layout

The Search, Details, Preview and Navigation panes and the Menu bar are all optional. You can turn them on or off from the Organize menu.

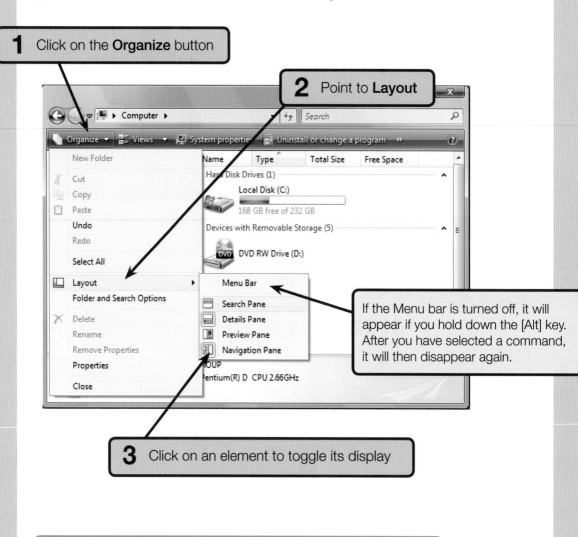

1 Click on the **Organize** button

2 Point to **Layout**

If the Menu bar is turned off, it will appear if you hold down the [Alt] key. After you have selected a command, it will then disappear again.

3 Click on an element to toggle its display

Explorer remembers your settings, and will show the same set of optional items when you next turn on the PC.

The Preview Pane

If you turn on the Preview Pane in Computer, there will be nothing to see. Let's find something. Click Documents in the Favorite Links list.

1 If the Preview Pane is not present, set the Organize Layout options to turn it on now

2 Select a file and see if it has a preview

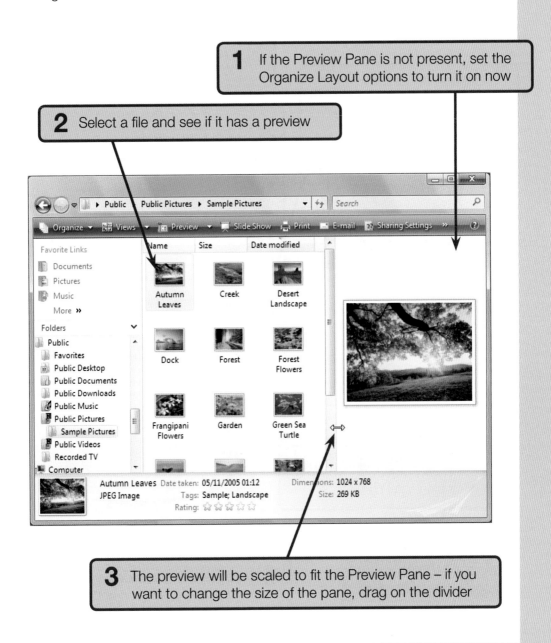

3 The preview will be scaled to fit the Preview Pane – if you want to change the size of the pane, drag on the divider

Creating folders

A new folder can be created at any time, and at any point in the folder structure.

1 In Explorer, select the folder which will contain the new one, or select the drive letter for a new top-level folder

2 Open the **File** menu, point to **New** and select **Folder**

You can also start to create a folder from the **Organize** button – click it and select **New Folder**.

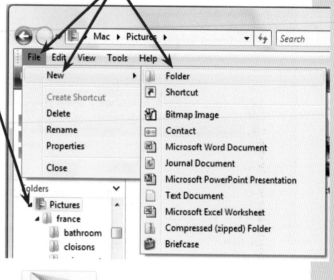

3 Delete the highlighted **New Folder** and type in a meaningful name

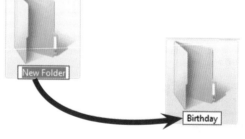

See p. 36 for more on moving files and folders.

4 If you decide the folder is in the wrong place, select it and drag it into place in the Folders list

Renaming folders

Folders can be renamed, if you decide that the original name is not clear enough. As with many jobs in Windows, there are several ways to do it. Here's one of the simplest.

1 Select the folder in the main pane

2 Click the **Organize** button

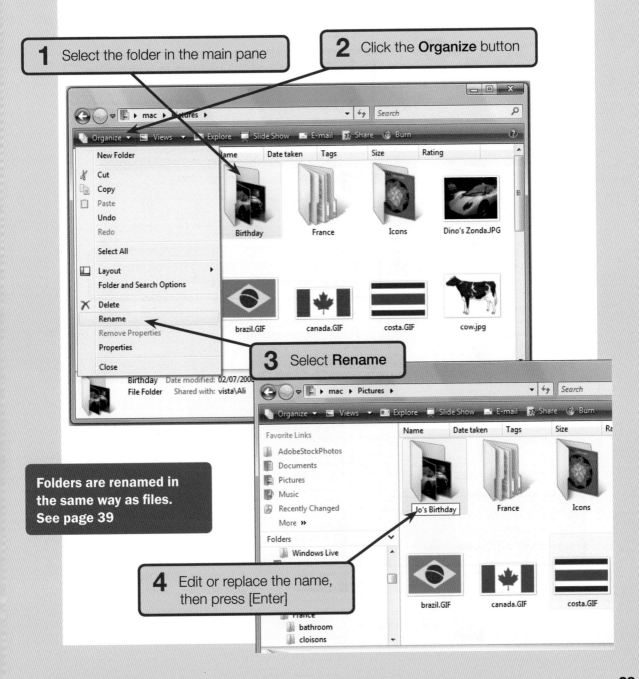

3 Select **Rename**

Folders are renamed in the same way as files. See page 39

4 Edit or replace the name, then press [Enter]

Sorting the display

Files can be sorted into order of any of the headings in the main pane. These relate to the properties of files. They are at the top of the columns in Details view, but the headings are always present, and can always be used for sorting.

The arrow shows you which way it is sorted: Up = A to Z, or first to last

1 Click once on the heading to sort the files into **ascending** order of that property

2 Click twice on a heading to sort them into **descending** order of the property

When sorting by date or size, the Details view will show you how old or how big the files are.

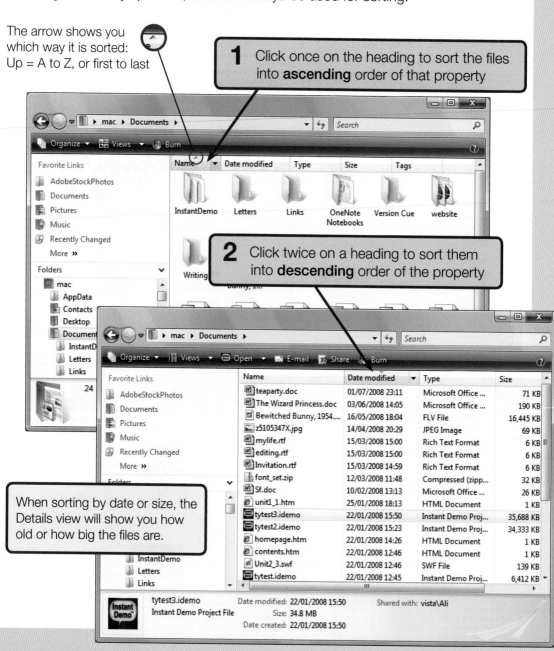

Changing the headings

If you look at the the headings in different folders, you will notice that they vary.
Name is always there, but in picture folders you will see **Date taken**, **Rating** and
Tags (amongst others); in music folders you will see **Artist** and **Album**. These are
the default settings, but any file properties can be used for headings and you can
change them at any time.

1 Right-click on any of the headings

2 Click on a property to turn its display on or off

3 The most common properties are listed. If you want one that isn't in the list, click **More...**

4 Click to add (or remove) properties from the headings

5 Click **OK** when you have finished

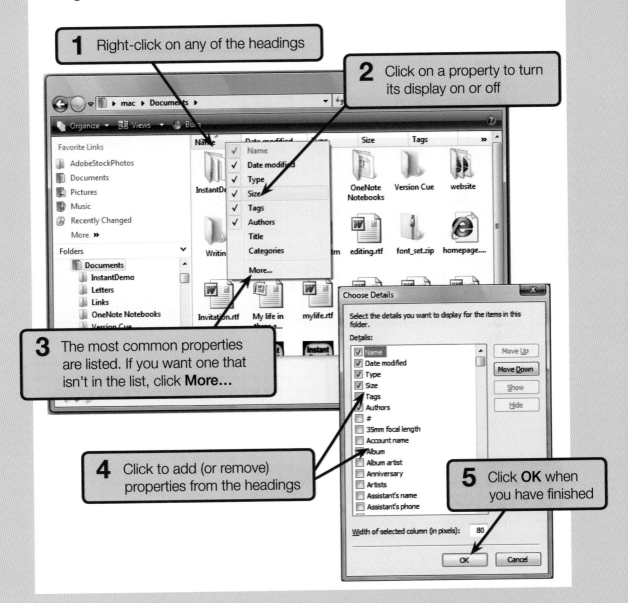

Grouping files

Files can be displayed on groups, based on any of the headings. This can be very useful if you have a lot of files in a folder and want to locate those of a certain type, or that were created at a particular date, or have other properties in common.

1 Point to the heading that you want to use for grouping

2 Click on its arrow to drop down the menu

3 Click the **Group** button

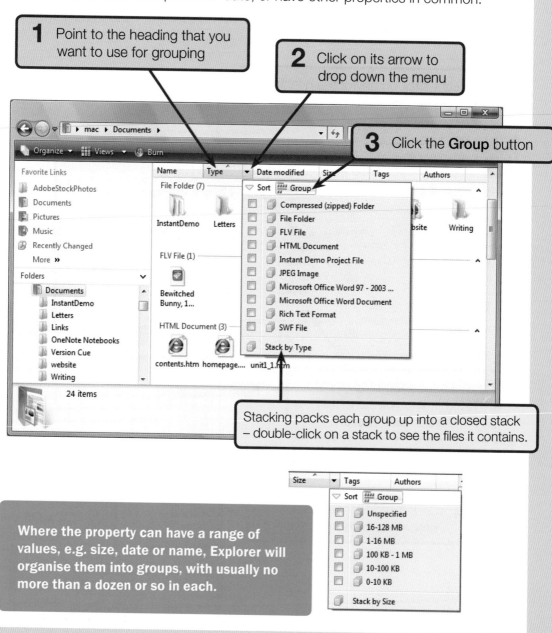

Stacking packs each group up into a closed stack – double-click on a stack to see the files it contains.

Where the property can have a range of values, e.g. size, date or name, Explorer will organise them into groups, with usually no more than a dozen or so in each.

Filtering files

Those categories and ranges that are used for grouping files can also be used for filtering them. You can select which of the groups to display.

When files are filtered out, they disappear from the display, but are not deleted. Clear the filters and they reappear.

1 Point to the heading that you want to use for filtering

2 Click on its arrow to drop down the menu

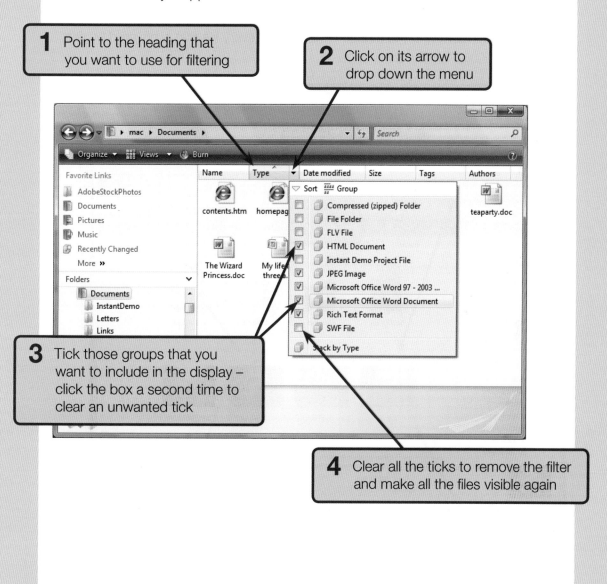

3 Tick those groups that you want to include in the display – click the box a second time to clear an unwanted tick

4 Clear all the ticks to remove the filter and make all the files visible again

Selecting files

Selecting adjacent files

It's simple to select files when they are next to each other, or form a solid block that may spread over several rows and columns. There are two techniques:

- Select the first file, hold down [Shift] and select the last one in the set.
- Drag over them with the mouse – this selects every file that is covered by part of the highlight rectangle

> Try sorting or grouping the display first, to bring the files next to each other.

1 Click on the first file

2 Hold down the [Shift] key

3 Click on the last file

| Name | Date taken | Tags | Size | Rating |

bathroom   cloisons   LaReole   miramont

2004_0910Image...   2004_0912Image...   churchview.JPG   DSCF0003.JPG

3 items selected   Date taken: 09/09/2004 09:30 - 12/0...   Dimensions: 1600 x 1200
Tags: Add a tag   Size: 1.05 MB
Rating: ☆ ☆ ☆ ☆ ☆

1 Click on or near the first file

2 Drag to create a rectangle that covers all the files you want

Selecting scattered files

If you cannot get the files into one convenient block, it doesn't matter. It's simple enough to select files scattered through a folder. All you have to do is know about the [Ctrl] key.

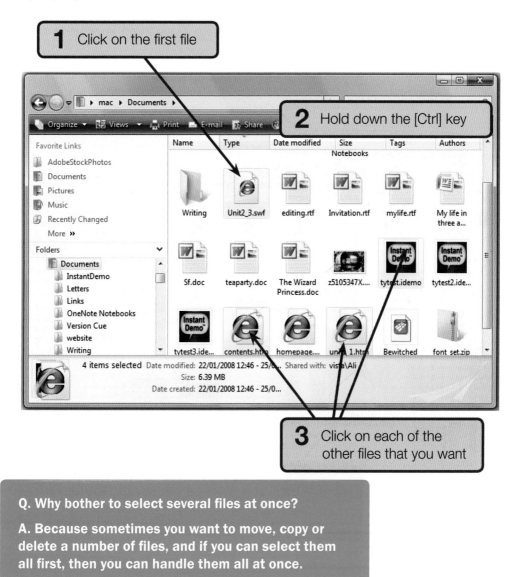

1 Click on the first file

2 Hold down the [Ctrl] key

3 Click on each of the other files that you want

Q. Why bother to select several files at once?

A. Because sometimes you want to move, copy or delete a number of files, and if you can select them all first, then you can handle them all at once.

Moving and copying files

Files can be moved and copied in almost exactly the same way – you just drag them from their original folder and drop them into the target folder.

- If you drag and drop files between folders **on the same disk**, you **move** them
- If the folders are **on different disks or drives**, e.g. CD or memory stick, drag and drop **copies** them.

You can move files one at a time, or select a set and move them all at once.

1 Open the folder containing the files you want to move

2 Arrange the Folder list so you can see the target folder

3 Select the files

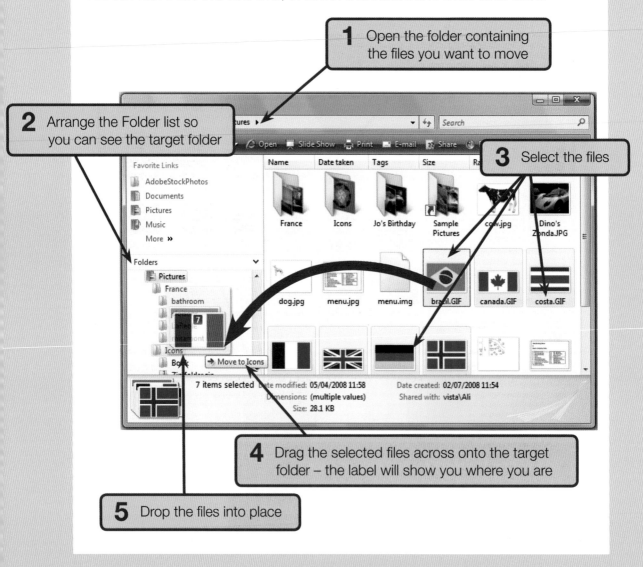

4 Drag the selected files across onto the target folder – the label will show you where you are

5 Drop the files into place

Copying between drives or moving within a drive

You can reverse the normal drag and drop effect:

● If you hold down the [Ctrl] key when you drag and drop, you change the effect, so that files are moved between drives or copied within them.

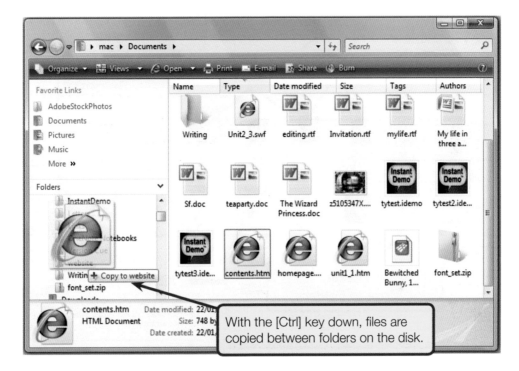

With the [Ctrl] key down, files are copied between folders on the disk.

If you hold the right button down while you drag and drop, when you release it you will see a short menu. You can then:

● Copy the file(s) to the target folder

● Move them

● Create a shortcut to the file – use this to put a link to a file on your Desktop for instant access to it.

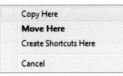

Copying and moving using menu commands

Drag and drop can go wrong if your mouse control isn't that great, so here's another way to move and copy files.

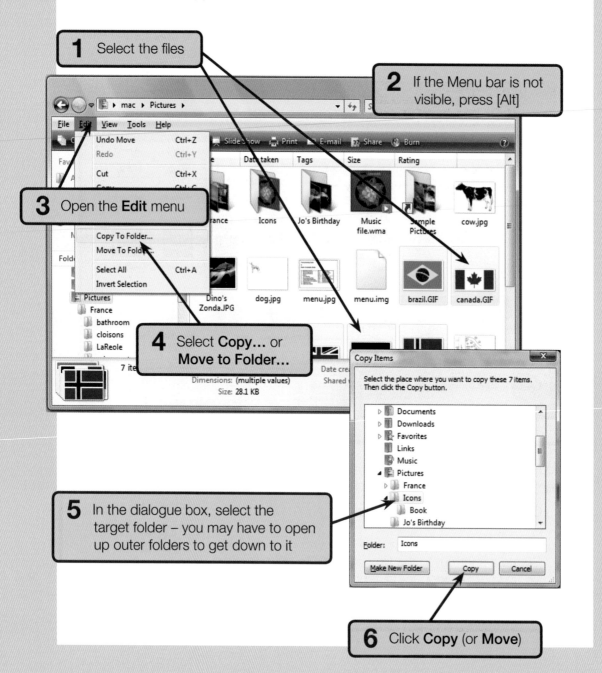

1 Select the files

2 If the Menu bar is not visible, press [Alt]

3 Open the **Edit** menu

4 Select **Copy...** or **Move to Folder...**

5 In the dialogue box, select the target folder – you may have to open up outer folders to get down to it

6 Click **Copy** (or **Move**)

Renaming files

You can easily rename files – this is just as well if you are into digital photography, because the files normally come in with names generated by the camera software. These need replacing with ones that mean something to you.

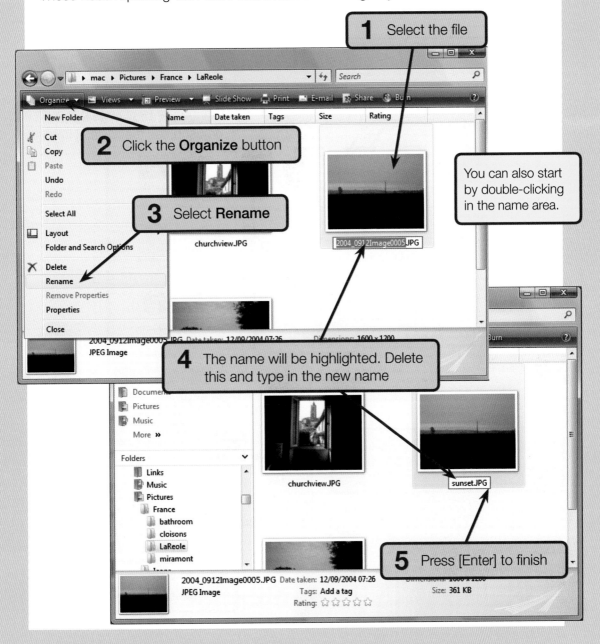

1 Select the file

2 Click the **Organize** button

You can also start by double-clicking in the name area.

3 Select **Rename**

4 The name will be highlighted. Delete this and type in the new name

5 Press [Enter] to finish

Deleting files

A file can be the result of hours or even weeks of hard work, so you do not want to delete it by mistake. Windows Vista makes sure that this can't happen. When you delete a file, it is not actually erased. Instead it is taken from its folder and placed in the Recycle Bin, from which it can easily be recovered.

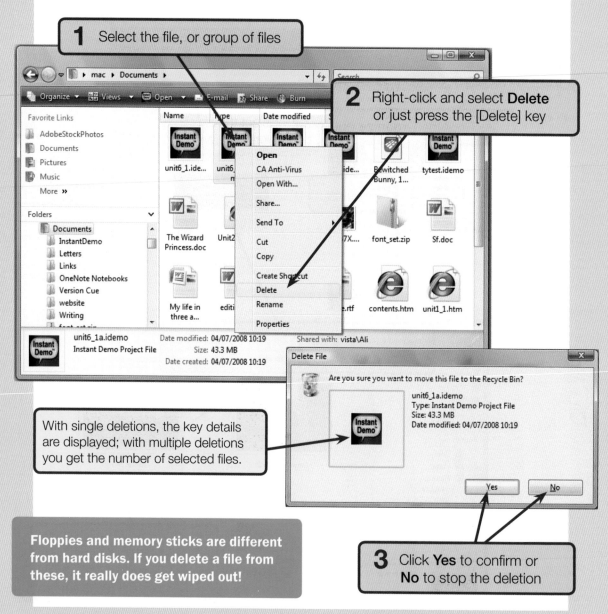

1 Select the file, or group of files

2 Right-click and select **Delete** or just press the [Delete] key

With single deletions, the key details are displayed; with multiple deletions you get the number of selected files.

Floppies and memory sticks are different from hard disks. If you delete a file from these, it really does get wiped out!

3 Click **Yes** to confirm or **No** to stop the deletion

The Recycle Bin

Restoring files

This is great, especially for those of us given to making instant decisions that we later regret. Until you empty the Bin, any 'deleted' files and folders can be restored – and if the folder that they were stored in has been deleted, that is re-created first, so things go back into their proper place.

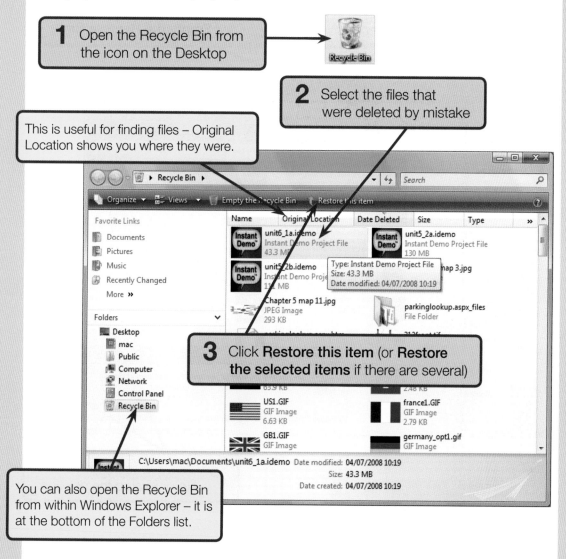

1 Open the Recycle Bin from the icon on the Desktop

2 Select the files that were deleted by mistake

This is useful for finding files – Original Location shows you where they were.

3 Click **Restore this item** (or **Restore the selected items** if there are several)

You can also open the Recycle Bin from within Windows Explorer – it is at the bottom of the Folders list.

Emptying the bin

Files sent to the Recycle Bin stay in it until you delete them from there. You can do this for individual files, by selecting and deleting them in the usual way. You can also empty the whole bin at once – and that's often the best way to clear it out.

1 Check that there is nothing that you want, and restore any files if necessary

2 Click **Empty the Recycle Bin**

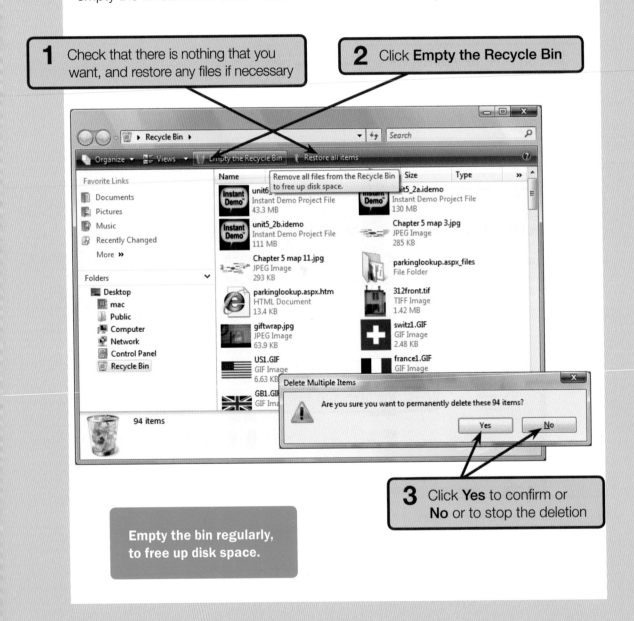

3 Click **Yes** to confirm or **No** or to stop the deletion

Empty the bin regularly, to free up disk space.

Tags

Tags provide a more flexible way of organising files – they can be very handy for classifying digital photos – but they can help in any situation where a file could fit into several categories.

Not all types of files can take tags. You can add them to Word documents and JPGs (the digital photo format) but not to text files, BMP images or web pages.

1 Select the file

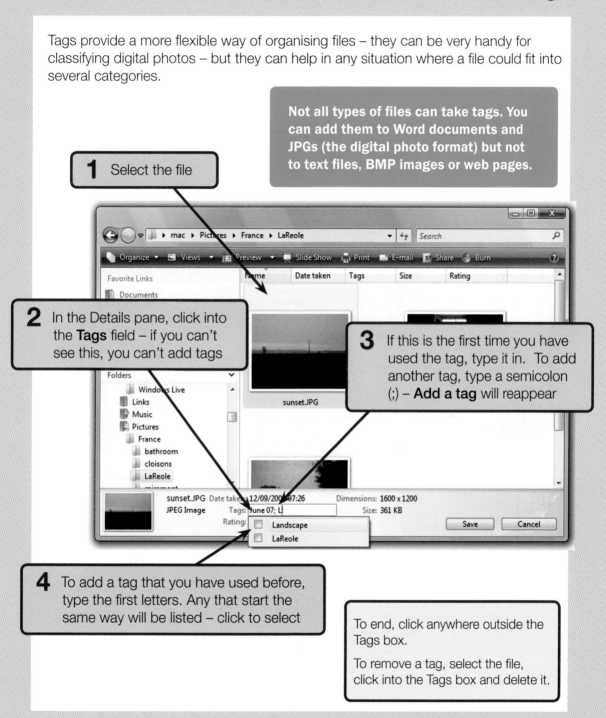

2 In the Details pane, click into the **Tags** field – if you can't see this, you can't add tags

3 If this is the first time you have used the tag, type it in. To add another tag, type a semicolon (;) – **Add a tag** will reappear

4 To add a tag that you have used before, type the first letters. Any that start the same way will be listed – click to select

To end, click anywhere outside the Tags box.

To remove a tag, select the file, click into the Tags box and delete it.

Searching

If you organise your folders properly, and always store files in the right places, you'll never need the Search facility – but if you are like me, you will be glad of it! It will find matches not only in the names of files, but also in their tags, keywords, authors and other properties, and in their text.

2 Click in the Search box and start to type the name or a significant word in its properties or contents – the more you type, the more the results will be filtered

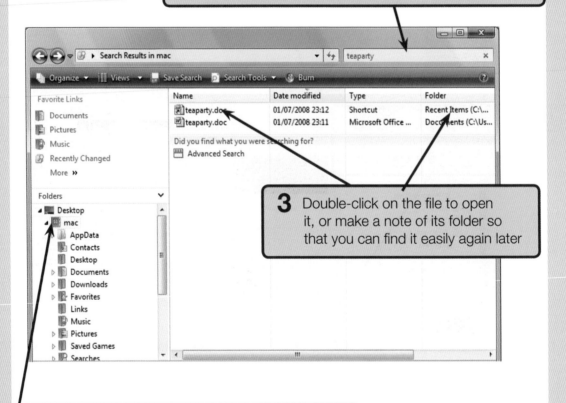

3 Double-click on the file to open it, or make a note of its folder so that you can find it easily again later

1 In the Folders or Favorites lists in Explorer, select the highest level folder that the missing file could be in – the search routine will go through all its subfolders

Advanced search

If the simple search doesn't find the file, click the Advanced Search link at the bottom of the results. The Search panel will open above the toolbar and you can specify other details of the missing file. Set any or all of the options shown here.

Select the highest-level folder or the disk drive. Set this to **Everywhere** if you haven't a clue where it might be.

Type part or all of the filename, tags or title.

Select the type of file.

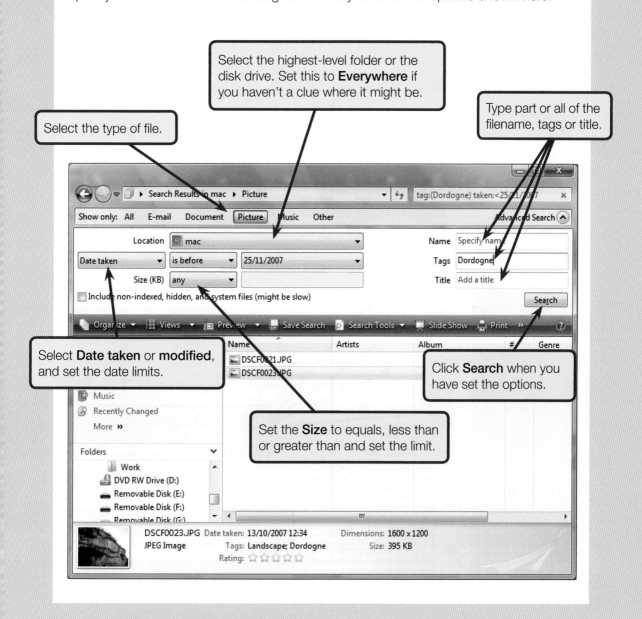

Select **Date taken** or **modified**, and set the date limits.

Click **Search** when you have set the options.

Set the **Size** to equals, less than or greater than and set the limit.

Personalising the Desktop

You can personalise many aspects of your Vista PC, including the colour scheme, background, mouse pointers and the sounds it makes to alert you to events. You can change any or all of the settings whenever and as often as you like.

If the PC has several users, then they can all personalise their own Desktops to suit themselves.

1 Right-click anywhere on the Desktop and select **Personalize** from the menu

View	▶
Sort By	▶
Refresh	
Paste	
Paste Shortcut	
Undo Delete	Ctrl+Z
New	▶
Personalize	

2 The Personalize window will open

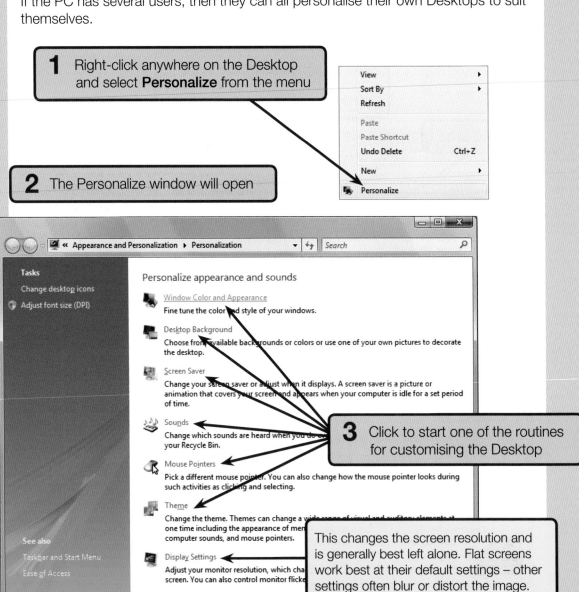

« Appearance and Personalization ▶ Personalization   Search

Tasks

Change desktop icons

Adjust font size (DPI)

Personalize appearance and sounds

Window Color and Appearance
Fine tune the color and style of your windows.

Desktop Background
Choose from available backgrounds or colors or use one of your own pictures to decorate the desktop.

Screen Saver
Change your screen saver or adjust when it displays. A screen saver is a picture or animation that covers your screen and appears when your computer is idle for a set period of time.

Sounds
Change which sounds are heard when you do your Recycle Bin.

Mouse Pointers
Pick a different mouse pointer. You can also change how the mouse pointer looks during such activities as clicking and selecting.

Theme
Change the theme. Themes can change a wide range of visual and auditory elements at one time including the appearance of menus, computer sounds, and mouse pointers.

Display Settings
Adjust your monitor resolution, which cha screen. You can also control monitor flicke

See also

Taskbar and Start Menu

Ease of Access

3 Click to start one of the routines for customising the Desktop

This changes the screen resolution and is generally best left alone. Flat screens work best at their default settings – other settings often blur or distort the image.

Colours and appearance

Use this panel to set the style, colour and fonts for the Desktop and standard Windows elements in all applications – the window frames, menus, dialogue boxes, etc. The initial display is concerned with colour and transparency. There are seven preset colours, but you can also mix your own.

1 In the Personalize window, select **Window Color and Appearance**

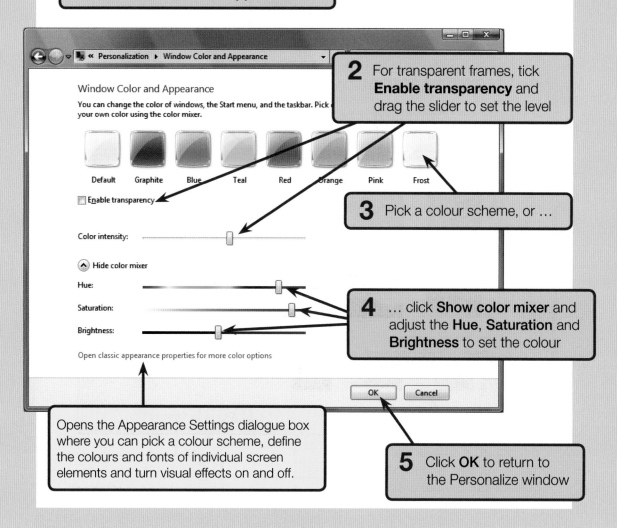

2 For transparent frames, tick **Enable transparency** and drag the slider to set the level

3 Pick a colour scheme, or ...

4 ... click **Show color mixer** and adjust the **Hue**, **Saturation** and **Brightness** to set the colour

Opens the Appearance Settings dialogue box where you can pick a colour scheme, define the colours and fonts of individual screen elements and turn visual effects on and off.

5 Click **OK** to return to the Personalize window

The background

The background can be a plain colour, a single picture or a small image 'tiled' to fill the whole screen. Windows Vista has a selection of small and large images, but any picture in JPG, GIF or BMP file format can be used.

1 Open the Personalize window and click the **Desktop Background** link

2 Drop down the **Location** list to select a folder

Browse will let you reach any folder in your system.

3 Scroll through – if you click on a picture it will be applied so you can see how it looks

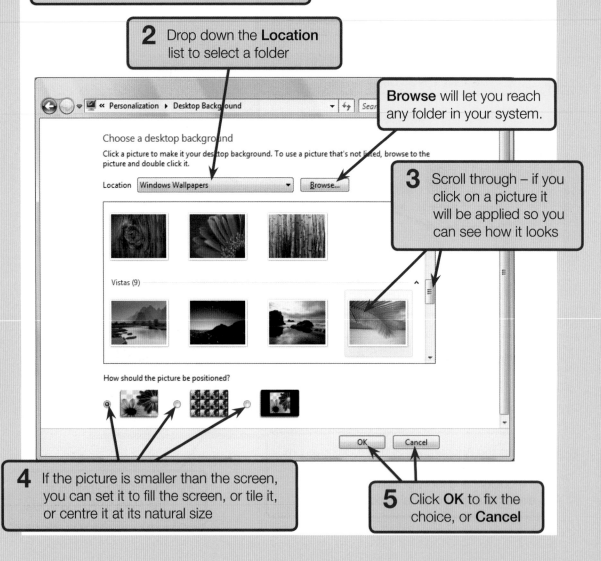

4 If the picture is smaller than the screen, you can set it to fill the screen, or tile it, or centre it at its natural size

5 Click **OK** to fix the choice, or **Cancel**

A screen saver is a moving image that takes over the screen if the computer is left unattended for a while. On older monitors this prevented a static image from burning a permanent ghost image into the screen. Newer monitors do not suffer from this, and most now have an energy saving feature that turns them off when they are not in use. If your monitor has this, the screen saver will only be visible briefly, if at all.

A screen saver can be set to revert to the logon screen, or to run a password entry routine, before the screen is restored. This can be useful if you do not want passers-by to read your screen while you are away from your desk.

1 In the Personalize window, select **Screen Saver**

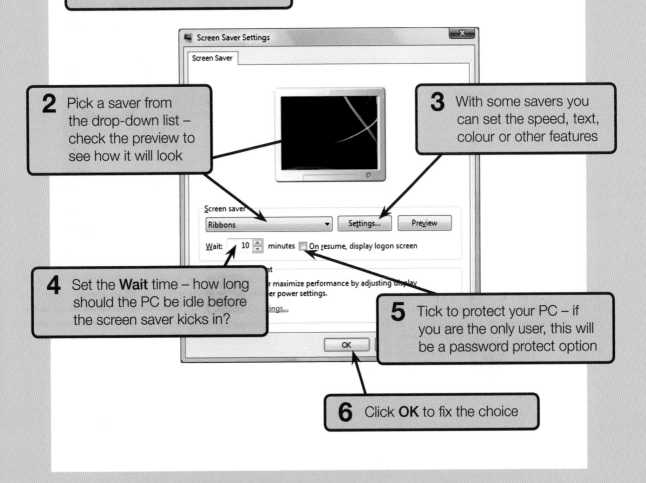

2 Pick a saver from the drop-down list – check the preview to see how it will look

3 With some savers you can set the speed, text, colour or other features

4 Set the **Wait** time – how long should the PC be idle before the screen saver kicks in?

5 Tick to protect your PC – if you are the only user, this will be a password protect option

6 Click **OK** to fix the choice

Gadgets

Gadgets are mini-applications that you can add to your Desktop. Some link to the Web to bring you the latest news headlines, stock reports or weather forecasts, some are handy utilities, others are just for fun. Have a play with them all.

The gadgets are normally shown in the Sidebar, which sits on the right of the Desktop. If this is not visible, click the Sidebar icon in the Notification area.

There are around a dozen gadgets in the Vista package, and more available online. These can be added at any time – and removed again if you don't use them.

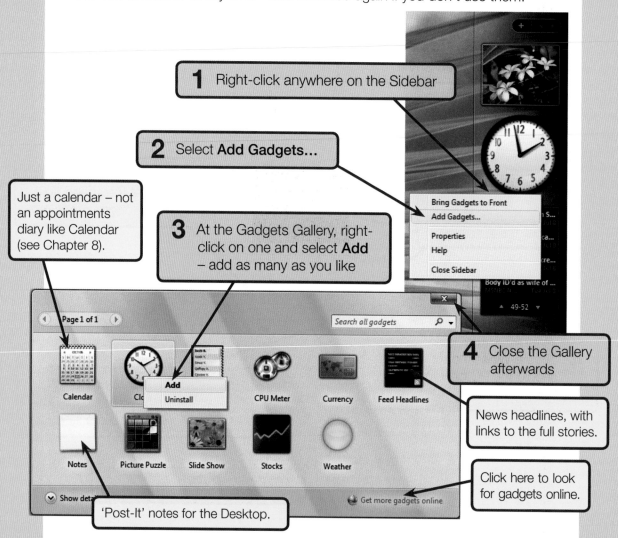

1 Right-click anywhere on the Sidebar

2 Select **Add Gadgets...**

Just a calendar – not an appointments diary like Calendar (see Chapter 8).

3 At the Gadgets Gallery, right-click on one and select **Add** – add as many as you like

Bring Gadgets to Front
Add Gadgets...
Properties
Help
Close Sidebar

4 Close the Gallery afterwards

News headlines, with links to the full stories.

Page 1 of 1   Search all gadgets

Calendar   Clock   CPU Meter   Currency   Feed Headlines

Add
Uninstall

Notes   Picture Puzzle   Slide Show   Stocks   Weather

Click here to look for gadgets online.

Show details   Get more gadgets online

'Post-It' notes for the Desktop.

Customising gadgets

Gadgets can be customised in different ways, depending upon what they are, but the approach is the same. They all have a mini-toolbar which appears when you point to the top right. It has three parts: a Close button, an Options button and a Handle which is used for moving it.

For example, here's how to customise the Clock. You can change the face, name and the time zone. (You can have several clocks, each set to a different time zone, in which case the name could identify the location.)

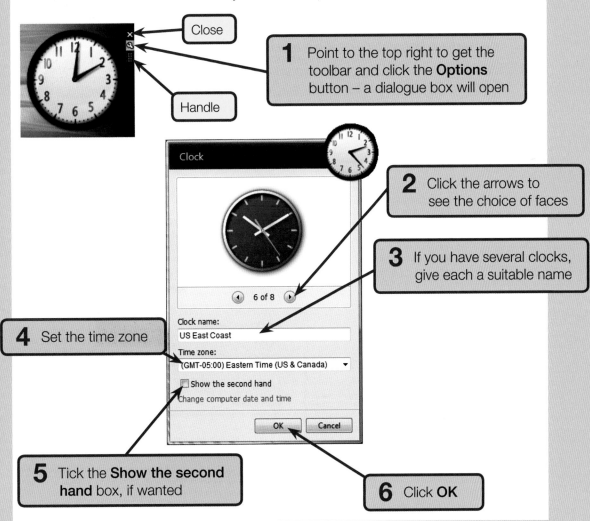

Close

Handle

1 Point to the top right to get the toolbar and click the **Options** button – a dialogue box will open

Clock

6 of 8

2 Click the arrows to see the choice of faces

3 If you have several clocks, give each a suitable name

Clock name:
US East Coast

Time zone:
(GMT-05:00) Eastern Time (US & Canada)

Show the second hand
Change computer date and time

OK   Cancel

4 Set the time zone

5 Tick the **Show the second hand** box, if wanted

6 Click **OK**

Gadget controls

These apply to all gadgets. Right-click on a gadget to display its menu of controls.

- **Add Gadgets**, opens the Gadget Gallery so that you can choose more to add to your Sidebar (see p. 50).

- **Options** opens the dialogue box where you can customise the gadget.

- **Close Gadget** removes the gadget from the screen.

- **Detach from Sidebar** – when a gadget is detached, it can be dragged to anywhere on screen. Some gadgets become larger when detached – Calendar shows the month and the day, Slide Show, Feed Headlines and other information displays become twice the size.

- **Move** – selects the gadget so that you can move it within the Sidebar. To move it, drag on the handle. But notice that you can drag on the handle without using Move, and also that you can drag it off the Sidebar, detaching it, if you like.

- **Opacity** – the gadgets can be distracting, especially if you have dragged them onto the main part of the screen and have set them to be always in front. If you reduce their opacity, making them more transparent, they are less eye-catching. When you point to one, it becomes solid once more.

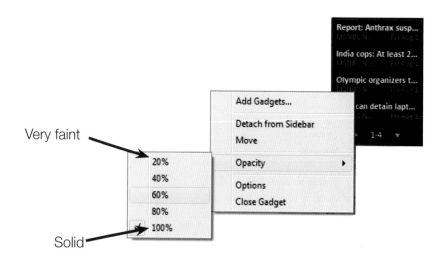

Keeping gadgets in sight

The trouble with the Sidebar is that if you run a program in a full screen window – and that is often the best way to run them – the Sidebar gets covered up, and that means all those handy gadgets are also covered up. If you want to keep any of them in view all the time, no matter what windows are on screen, here's how to do it.

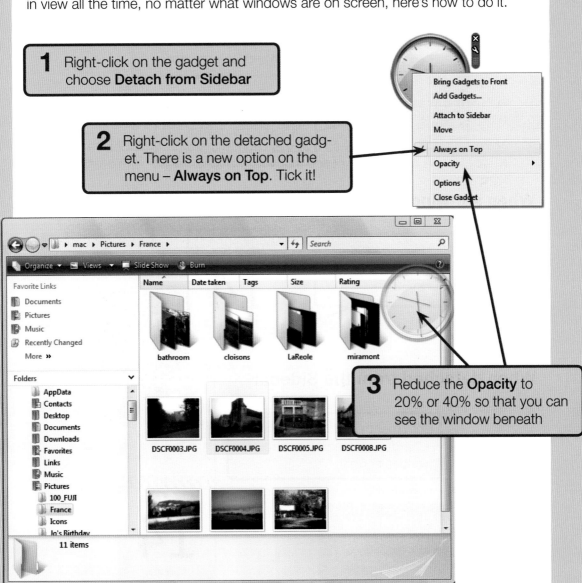

1 Right-click on the gadget and choose **Detach from Sidebar**

2 Right-click on the detached gadget. There is a new option on the menu – **Always on Top**. Tick it!

Bring Gadgets to Front
Add Gadgets...

Attach to Sidebar
Move

Always on Top
Opacity ▶

Options
Close Gadget

3 Reduce the **Opacity** to 20% or 40% so that you can see the window beneath

The Calendar

This is a handy, but limited gadget. It can show the day's date or the whole month. You can switch between the views, and you can show different days or months, but that is end of its options.

When showing a month

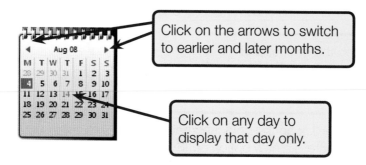

Click on the arrows to switch to earlier and later months.

Click on any day to display that day only.

When showing a day

If the current date is not showing, the bottom left corner will be turned up. Click on this to display today's date.

Click anywhere else to switch to month mode.

When detached from the Sidebar

Both month and day are shown – the day and month controls work as normal.

Vista also has a fully-fledged Calendar application – we'll look at this in Chapter 8.

Feed headlines

Feeds are links to articles in web pages, sent by sites to your PC (normally through the browser). They are typically news stories, opinion articles, weather reports or stock market updates. The Feed Headlines gadget is another way to receive these. Initially it is linked to three MSN sites, which send out news and tips for working with Microsoft products. It can be quite handy for keeping abreast of the latest news.

Here's how to read the feed stories, and to change the feed sources.

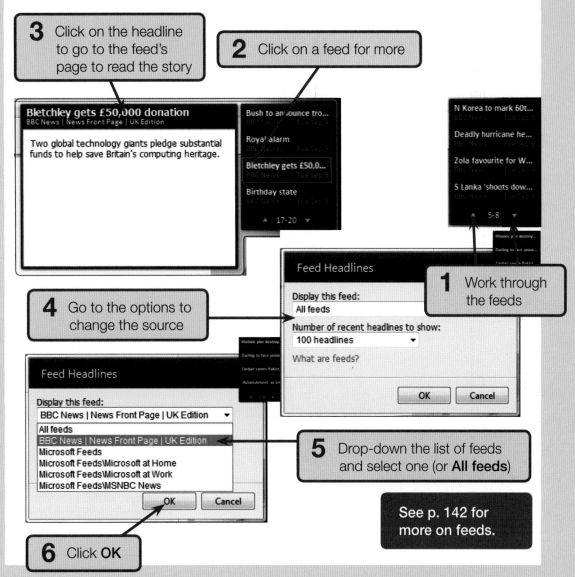

3 Click on the headline to go to the feed's page to read the story

2 Click on a feed for more

1 Work through the feeds

4 Go to the options to change the source

5 Drop-down the list of feeds and select one (or **All feeds**)

6 Click **OK**

See p. 142 for more on feeds.

Bletchley gets £50,000 donation
BBC News | News Front Page | UK Edition

Two global technology giants pledge substantial funds to help save Britain's computing heritage.

Bush to announce tro...
BBC News   Tue Sep 9

Royal alarm
BBC News   Tue Sep 9

Bletchley gets £50,0...
BBC News   Tue Sep 9

Birthday state
BBC News   Tue Sep 9

17-20

N Korea to mark 60t...
BBC News   Tue Sep 9

Deadly hurricane he...
BBC News   Tue Sep 9

Zola favourite for W...
BBC News   Tue Sep 9

S Lanka 'shoots dow...
BBC News   Tue Sep 9

5-8

Feed Headlines

Display this feed:
All feeds

Number of recent headlines to show:
100 headlines

What are feeds?

OK   Cancel

Feed Headlines

Display this feed:
BBC News | News Front Page | UK Edition

All feeds
BBC News | News Front Page | UK Edition
Microsoft Feeds
Microsoft Feeds\Microsoft at Home
Microsoft Feeds\Microsoft at Work
Microsoft Feeds\MSNBC News

OK   Cancel

2 Working with documents

For the screenshots here I have used the Home and Student edition of Word. The only real difference between this and the professional editions is its name in the title bar.

This chapter covers:

- Word processing, using Word 2007
- The Word screen, the Ribbon and the Office button menu
- How to edit text
- Saving and opening files
- Formatting text using the mini toolbar, the Ribbon and dialogue boxes
- Different views and Print Preview
- Page layout and printing
- Styles and lists
- The spell checker
- Images in Word documents
- How to use templates

The Word screen

The main part of the screen is the working area, where you type your text and insert graphics and other objects to create your documents. The tools and controls are in the frame all around this area.

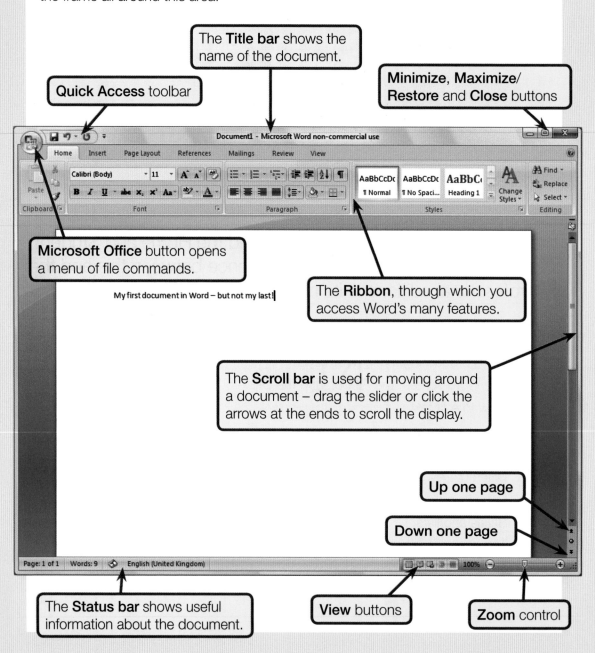

The **Title bar** shows the name of the document.

Quick Access toolbar

Minimize, **Maximize/ Restore** and **Close** buttons

Microsoft Office button opens a menu of file commands.

The **Ribbon**, through which you access Word's many features.

My first document in Word – but not my last!

The **Scroll bar** is used for moving around a document – drag the slider or click the arrows at the ends to scroll the display.

Up one page

Down one page

The **Status bar** shows useful information about the document.

View buttons

Zoom control

The Ribbon

The Ribbon holds the tools that you use to create and format documents. The tools are arranged in groups, on tabs. To bring a tab to the front, click on its name.

The **Home** tab tools are the ones that you use most.

The **Insert** tab tools are for adding pictures, tables and other objects.

The **Page Layout** tab tools control the size and layout of pages, and of the text and objects on them.

The **References** tab tools are for serious writers – footnotes, tables of contents, indexes and the like.

The **Mailings** tab tools are for 'mail merges' – adding names and addresses to standard letters.

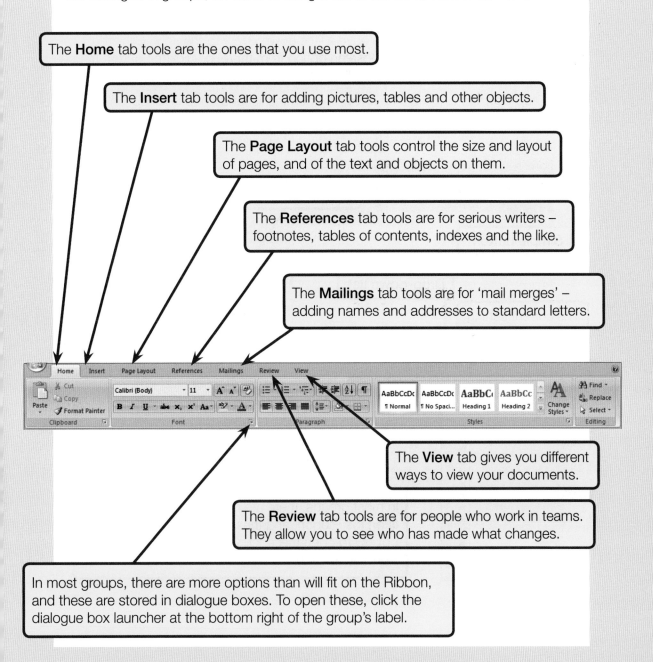

The **View** tab gives you different ways to view your documents.

The **Review** tab tools are for people who work in teams. They allow you to see who has made what changes.

In most groups, there are more options than will fit on the Ribbon, and these are stored in dialogue boxes. To open these, click the dialogue box launcher at the bottom right of the group's label.

Using the Ribbon tools

There are three sorts of tools on the Ribbon:

- Simple buttons – just click to run the command or set the format. A lot of these are 'toggle switchs' – they turn options on or off.

- Buttons with options – these have a little down arrow to the right. Click the arrow to open a list, and choose an option from there, or click the button to use the current default (which is normally the one you chose last time).

- Drop-down lists – click the arrow to open the list and choose an option.

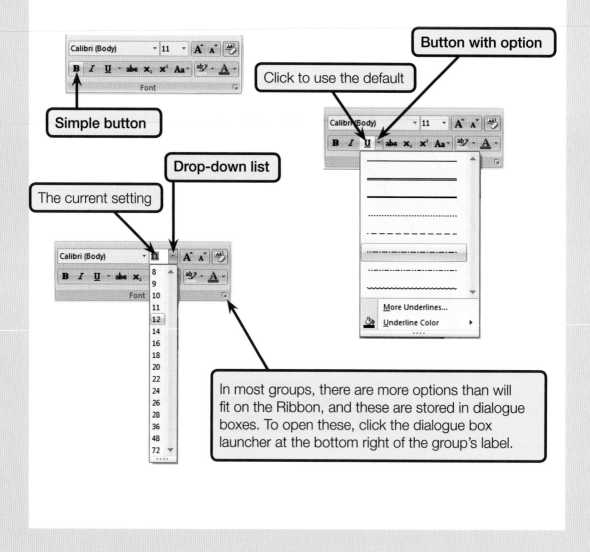

Button with option

Click to use the default

Simple button

Drop-down list

The current setting

In most groups, there are more options than will fit on the Ribbon, and these are stored in dialogue boxes. To open these, click the dialogue box launcher at the bottom right of the group's label.

Keyboard control

You can use the keyboard instead of the mouse to access the commands on the Ribbon. This can be handy when you are typing.

Keyboard control revolves around the [Alt] key – the one to the left of the Space bar.

Notice the numbers by the Quick Access icons – press the number key to run a command.

1 Press [Alt] and letters appear on the Ribbon by the tab names

2 Type a letter, and that tab will come to the front

3 Each icon will have one or two letters or numbers nearby

4 Type the characters to use the tool

The letters at the bottom right of a group launch its dialogue box.

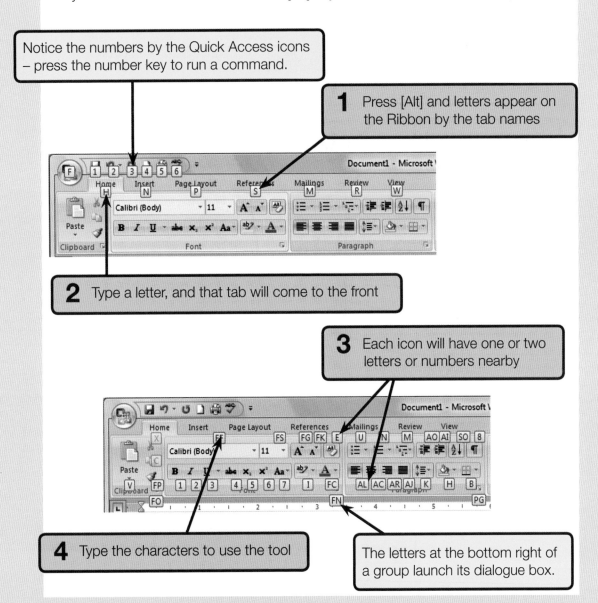

The Microsoft Office button

There is a menu that opens from the Microsoft Office button. This holds commands which relate to the whole document – New, Open, Save, Print and the like. Some of these are simple one-job commands; others have options.

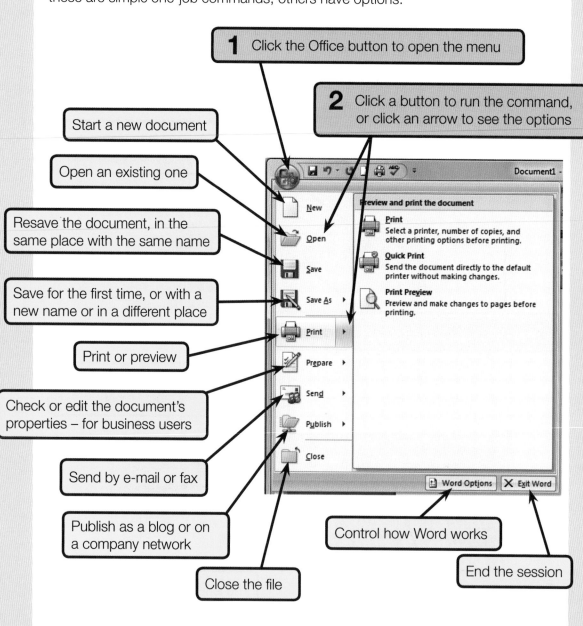

1 Click the Office button to open the menu

2 Click a button to run the command, or click an arrow to see the options

Start a new document

Open an existing one

Resave the document, in the same place with the same name

Save for the first time, or with a new name or in a different place

Print or preview

Check or edit the document's properties – for business users

Send by e-mail or fax

Publish as a blog or on a company network

Close the file

Control how Word works

End the session

The Quick Access toolbar

The Quick Access toolbar gives you one-click access to commands. This can be very useful for those that you use often. At first, it will only have icons for Save, Undo and Redo, but you can add more – or remove these if you don't want them there.

Here's how to customise the Quick Access toolbar.

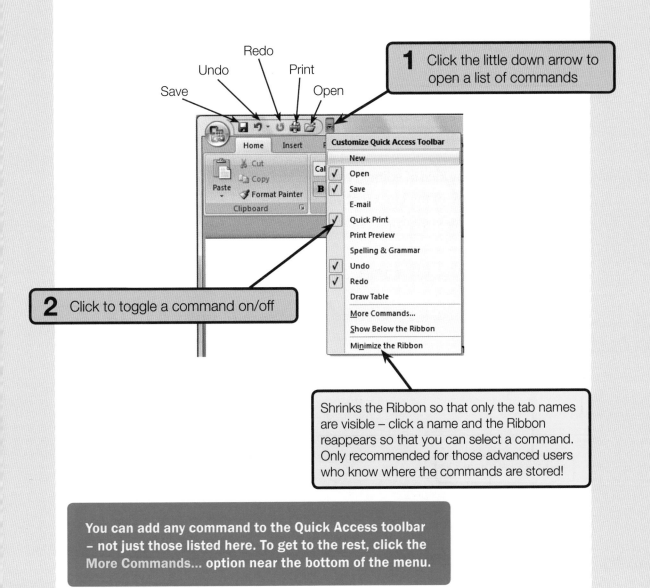

Redo

Undo   Print

Save   Open

1 Click the little down arrow to open a list of commands

2 Click to toggle a command on/off

Shrinks the Ribbon so that only the tab names are visible – click a name and the Ribbon reappears so that you can select a command. Only recommended for those advanced users who know where the commands are stored!

You can add any command to the Quick Access toolbar – not just those listed here. To get to the rest, click the More Commands... option near the bottom of the menu.

Editing text

When you start typing on a blank page, the text will first appear at the top left corner and gradually fill down. In an existing document, text is placed at the insertion point – the flashing line. If this is not where you want to type, click to move the insertion point to the right place.

Selecting text

Before you can do any kind of editing, you must first select the text. How you select depends upon the size of the block that you want.

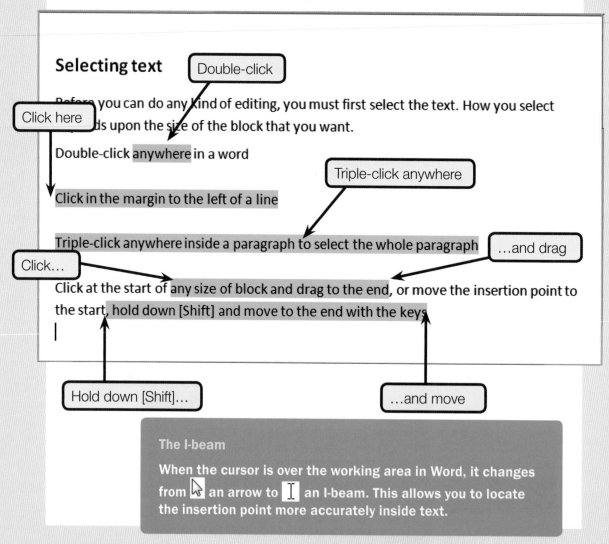

Selecting text

Double-click

Before you can do any kind of editing, you must first select the text. How you select depends upon the size of the block that you want.

Click here

Double-click anywhere in a word

Triple-click anywhere

Click in the margin to the left of a line

Triple-click anywhere inside a paragraph to select the whole paragraph

...and drag

Click...

Click at the start of any size of block and drag to the end, or move the insertion point to the start, hold down [Shift] and move to the end with the keys

Hold down [Shift]...

...and move

The I-beam

When the cursor is over the working area in Word, it changes from an arrow to an I-beam. This allows you to locate the insertion point more accurately inside text.

The editing keys

To move around the text using the keys:

- [Arrows] – one character left or right, one line up or down
- [Ctrl] + [Left] or [Right] – one word left or right
- [PgUp] – move one screenful up
- [PgDn] – move one screenful down
- [Home] – jump to the start of the line
- [Ctrl] + [Home] jump to the start of the text
- [End] – jump to the end of the line
- [Ctrl] +[End] – jump to the end of the text

To erase mistakes:

- Use [Backspace] to erase the character(s) that you have just typed
- Click the insertion point into the text and erase to right with [Delete] or to the left with [Backspace]
- Select the text and press either key.

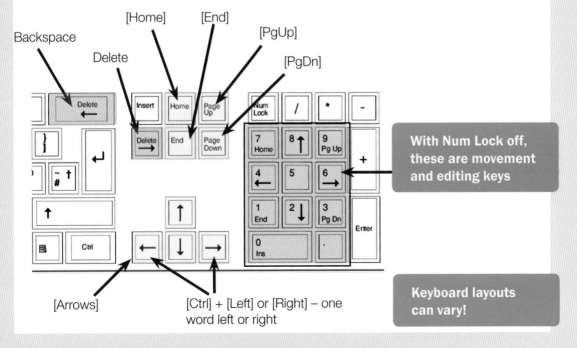

With Num Lock off, these are movement and editing keys

Keyboard layouts can vary!

Undoing mistakes

In the old days, you were lucky if your software let you undo a mistake. With Word, you can undo a whole series of actions. This gives you freedom to experiment. You can do major editing or reformatting, and if at the end you prefer things how they were, you can undo your way back to it. This is managed through the Undo button.

● Click the **Undo** button to undo the last thing you did, or

● Open the Undo list to undo a whole series of actions.

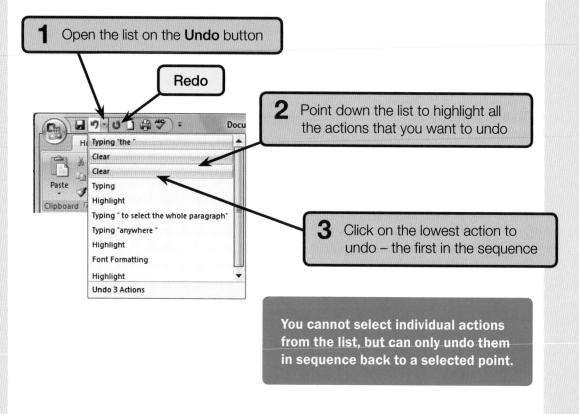

1 Open the list on the **Undo** button

Redo

2 Point down the list to highlight all the actions that you want to undo

3 Click on the lowest action to undo – the first in the sequence

You cannot select individual actions from the list, but can only undo them in sequence back to a selected point.

Redo

This is the undo-undo button! If you undid too much, use this to put it back again. Use it for the last action, or a whole sequence, exactly as with Undo.

Practice time!

Use what you have learnt so far to type out what you have learnt so far. This should include:

- How to start typing
- How to delete unwanted text, using [Backspace] and [Delete]
- How to move around the document with the keys
- How to select text with the mouse
- How to select text with the keys.

If you want to go back up in your document and add something into a line, or add a new line between two existing ones, use the mouse or keys to move the insertion point and just start typing.

The wonders of wordwrap

If you have ever used a typewriter, you will know that when you reach the end of a line, you have to use the carriage return to move the roller back over and turn it up ready for the next line. Word-processing is not like that!

When you get to the right-hand side of the page, keep on typing, do not press [Enter]. Word will automatically take the next word round to the start of the line below. This is wordwrap. Because each paragraph is a continuous piece of text, if you edit it, or change its text size, the words will shuffle round so that each line still uses the full width of the page.

Only press [Enter] when you reach the end of a paragraph. (And a paragraph may be a single line if you are typing an address, or shopping list, or poem.)

Wordwrap is one of the many reasons why people threw their typewriters in the skip when word-processing was invented.

Saving your work

Anything that you type will be lost when you exit from Word – unless you save it as a file on the disk. Saving is quick and simple. You only have to decide two things:

- Where to save it – and the simple solution is to put it in your Documents folder
- What to call it – Word will suggest the first few words of the document (normally its title) as the file name. If you don't like this, change it.

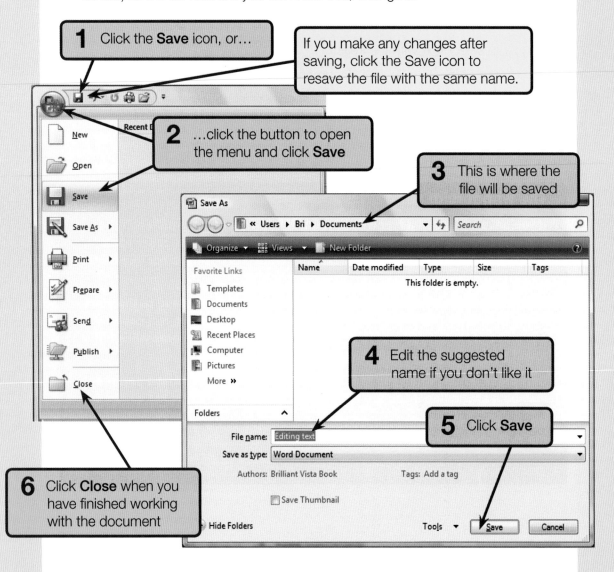

1 Click the **Save** icon, or...

If you make any changes after saving, click the Save icon to resave the file with the same name.

2 ...click the button to open the menu and click **Save**

3 This is where the file will be saved

4 Edit the suggested name if you don't like it

5 Click **Save**

6 Click **Close** when you have finished working with the document

Starting a new document

When you start Word, it offers you a blank page on which to create a document. But what if you have written and saved one document, and are now ready to start another? Here's how to start a new document.

1 Open the Microsoft Office button menu and select **New**

2 Select **Blank document**

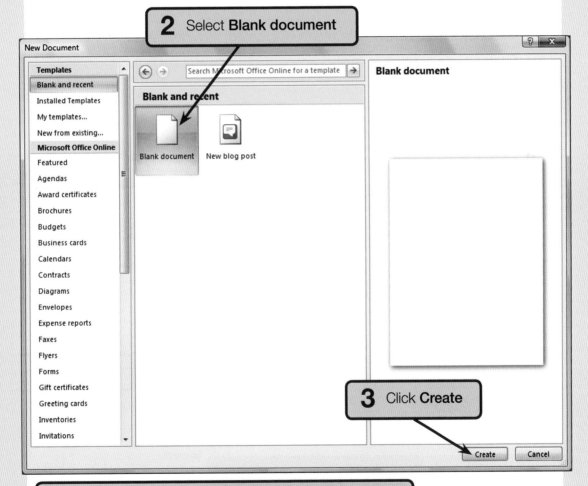

3 Click **Create**

4 A new blank document will be created for you. If you have another document open already, then the new one will be opened in its own Word window

Cut and Paste

When you are word processing, you should never have to write anything twice. If you need to use the same text again, you can copy it. If text is in the wrong place, you can move it. Every Windows application has the commands Cut, Copy and Paste, which use the Clipboard to move and copy text and other objects.

In Word 2007, the commands are in the Clipboard group on the Ribbon. You will also find them on the context menu that opens when you right-click on an object.

- **Copy** copies the selected text, picture, or other object into the Clipboard
- **Cut** copies the selected data into the Clipboard, then deletes the original
- **Paste** copies the data from the Clipboard into a new place in the application, or into a different application – as long as this can handle data in that format.

To copy

1   Select the block of text

2   Click **Copy**

3   Place the cursor where you want the text and click

4   Click **Paste**.

To move

1   Select the block of text.

2   Click **Cut**.

3   Place the cursor where you want the text and click

4   Click **Paste**.

Paste

Cut

Copy

Format Painter – see p. 81

Cut and paste tools

The **Clipboard** is a special part of memory, which can be used for storing any kind of data – text, images, tables and even whole files. It can be used not just for copying or moving data within and between applications.

Drag and drop

If you want to move or copy some text within the same page, and if you can control the mouse accurately, the drag and drop technique is quick and efficient.

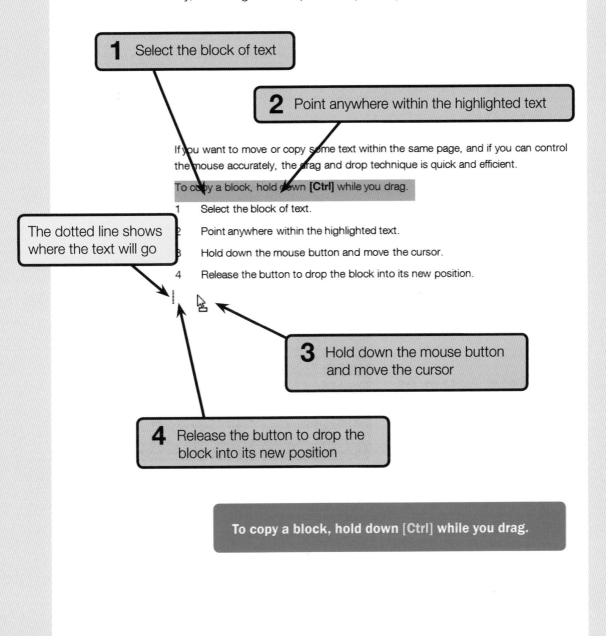

1 Select the block of text

2 Point anywhere within the highlighted text

If you want to move or copy some text within the same page, and if you can control the mouse accurately, the drag and drop technique is quick and efficient.

To copy a block, hold down **[Ctrl]** while you drag.

1   Select the block of text.

2   Point anywhere within the highlighted text.

3   Hold down the mouse button and move the cursor.

4   Release the button to drop the block into its new position.

The dotted line shows where the text will go

3 Hold down the mouse button and move the cursor

4 Release the button to drop the block into its new position

To copy a block, hold down [Ctrl] while you drag.

Formatting

In Word, you can **format** (change the look of) text at two levels:

● **Paragraph** formats set things like the amount of space between lines, and the way the text meets the edges of a page. They can only be applied to whole paragraphs

● **Font** formats can be applied to any amount of text, a single character, a word, part or all of one or more paragraphs, or the entire text. Font formats include things like the font (see below), size or colour of text, or making it **bold**, *italics* or <u>underlined</u>.

And you can apply formatting in two ways:

● Set the format then type. Whenever you type, Word applies whatever formats are in place at that time, so if you know how you want (most of) your text to look, it is a good idea to set the formats at the start

● Type first and format later.

What is a font?

Word uses 'font' to apply to many aspects of the look of characters, but strictly speaking, the font is just the design of the typeface. Some sample fonts:

Times New Roman

Arial

Blackoak

Gautami

French Script

Verdana

The important thing to note about fonts is that they vary in size. These samples are all supposed to be the same size (12 points) but some look much bigger than others. So, when formatting text, always set the font first, then set its size.

Fancy fonts are good for greetings cards, title pages and other special effects. For normal work, use a simpler, more readable font like Times New Roman.

Fonts and font sizes

The font (design) and the font size are set from drop-down lists. In both cases, the basic approach is: click the arrow to drop down the list, and click on an option to select it. There are a few tricks worth noting:

For the **Font**, which is in a very long list:

● Pick from the Recently Used Fonts set – you wouldn't normally use more than two or three different fonts in a document, or

● Type the first letter of the font (if you know its name) to jump down the list.

For the **Font size**:

● If you want a size which is not in the list, type it into the box at the top.

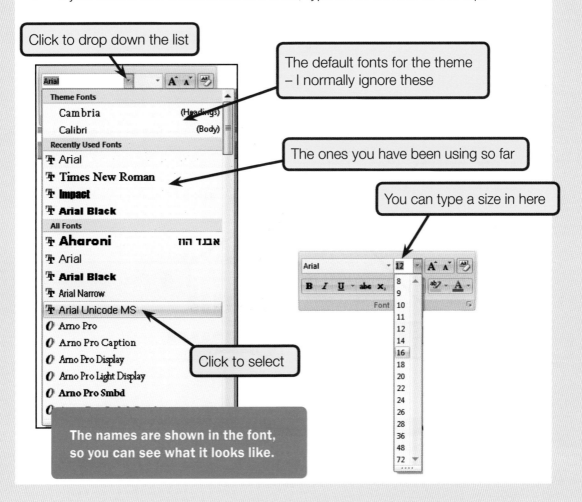

Click to drop down the list

The default fonts for the theme – I normally ignore these

The ones you have been using so far

You can type a size in here

Click to select

The names are shown in the font, so you can see what it looks like.

Formatting with the mini toolbar

This is the simplest way to handle formatting most of the time. At first, this has a standard set of core controls but it adapts to you. Word notes which formatting tools you use most often and adds them to the toolbar. So, while they all start out the same, they gradually adapt to their users. Here's what mine looks like now.

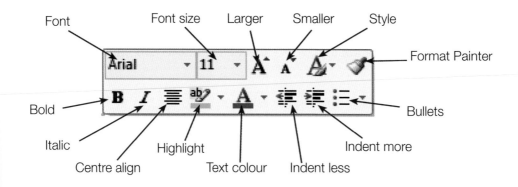

1 Select some text and the toolbar will appear as a ghost image

2 Point to it, and the image firms up

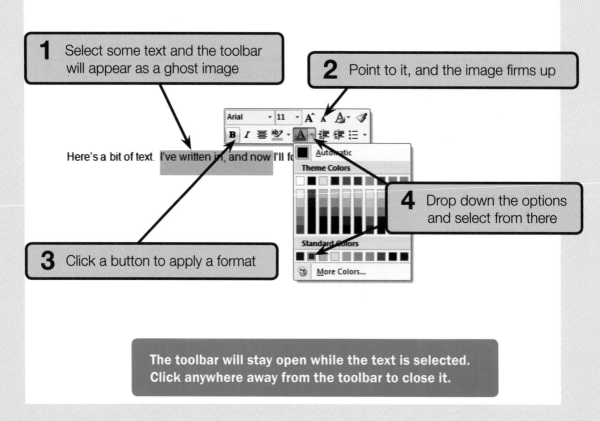

4 Drop down the options and select from there

3 Click a button to apply a format

The toolbar will stay open while the text is selected. Click anywhere away from the toolbar to close it.

The Font group

If you want the less-used format options, or to set up formatting before you type, use the Font group on the Ribbon. This has all the tools that you will find on the mini toolbar, plus the extra commands:

- **Clear Format** restores text to its default settings
- The **Underline** draws a single line under the selected text or you can set double, dotted, dashed or other styles from the drop-down list
- **Strikethrough** puts a line through text, ~~like this~~, and I have never found a use for it – until just now
- **Subscript** and **superscript** are for writing about maths and chemistry
- **Change case** switches text between UPPER and LOWER. The tOGGLE cASE option is for when you type with the Caps Lock on by mistake.

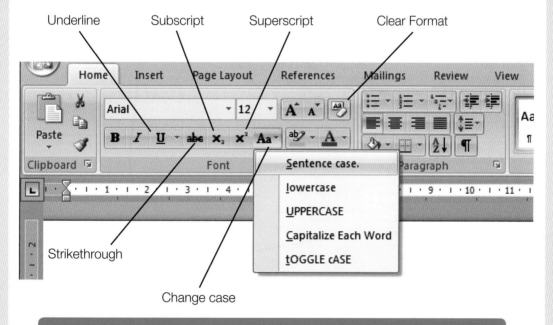

Underline　　Subscript　　Superscript　　Clear Format

Strikethrough

Change case

When you use the Font group for formatting, Live Preview is active. As you point to options in the font, size, colour or underline lists, the current option will be applied to the selected text so that you can see exactly how it will look. If you like it, click the option to select it.

The Font dialogue box

If you want to set several font options at once – perhaps to make a heading larger, bold and in a different font – or you want to set one of the more unusual options, you can do it through the Font dialogue box.

1 Select the text to be formatted, then click the dialogue box launcher on the **Font** group

The **Character Spacing** options set the spacing between letters, and raise or lower them. They are not often used.

2 Set the font, style, size and/or other options

Even more underline options!

Useful for emphasis or titles

Useful for titles, posters, greetings cards, etc.

Not as good as Live Preview, but better than nothing

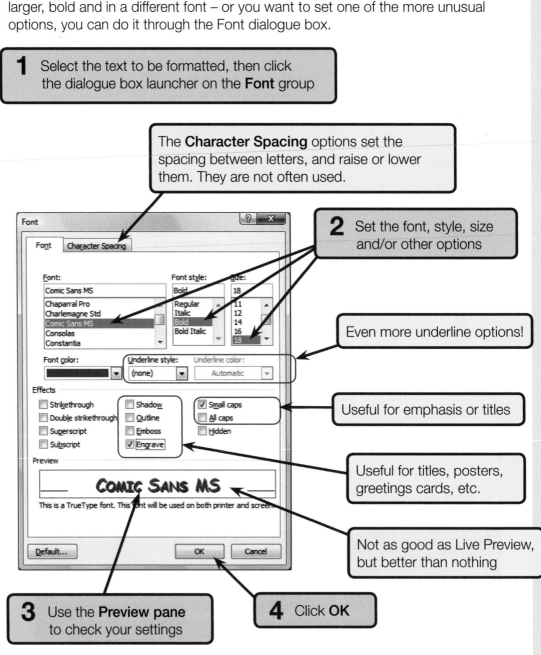

3 Use the **Preview pane** to check your settings

4 Click **OK**

Alignment

Alignment controls how text lines up with the left and right margins. Set the option before you start typing, or apply it to selected paragraphs. A paragraph is selected if the insertion point is in it, or if any part of it is selected.

● To set alignment, use the icons on the mini toolbar or in the **Paragraph** group.

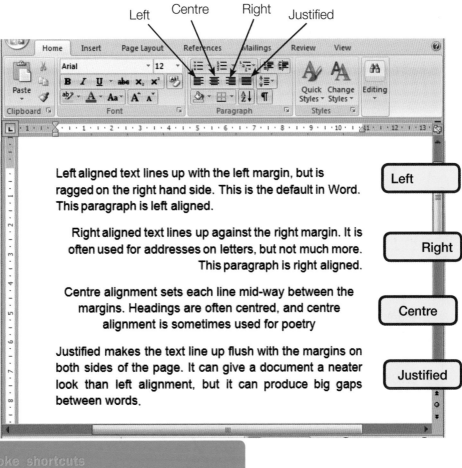

Line spacing

Like alignment, these options can only be applied to whole paragraphs.

● Text is normally set with the spacing at 1.15, leaving a slim gap between the bottom of one line and the top of the next

● If you want to squeeze a couple more lines on a page, drop the spacing to 1.0

● Double spacing is typically used where people want room between the lines for handwritten notes on the printed copy – to mark up errors or to add comments

● Spacing can also be set to 1.15, 1.5, 2.5 or 3.0 – or to any other value through the Paragraph dialogue box.

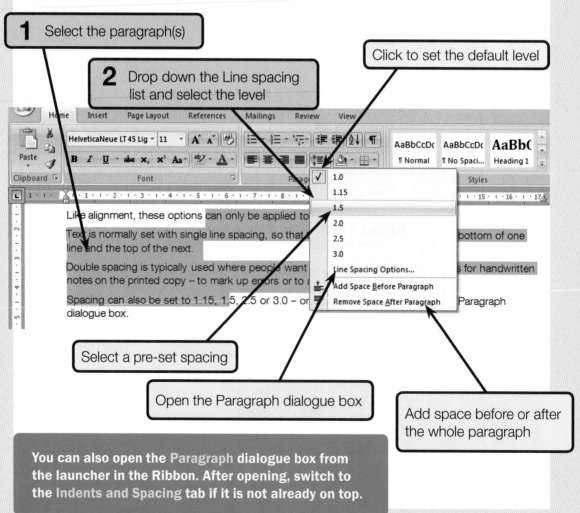

1 Select the paragraph(s)

2 Drop down the Line spacing list and select the level

Click to set the default level

Select a pre-set spacing

Open the Paragraph dialogue box

Add space before or after the whole paragraph

You can also open the Paragraph dialogue box from the launcher in the Ribbon. After opening, switch to the Indents and Spacing tab if it is not already on top.

The Paragraph dialogue box

This can be used for fine-tuning the line spacing, but most people only use it to set the indents and for setting the spacing before and after paragraphs.

Spacing before and after paragraphs is normally set in points (pt). 12 pt is the height of a line of normal text, so 6pt is a half-line space.

The values in these fields can be set either by typing them in, or by clicking the little arrows and scrolling through the range of pre-set values.

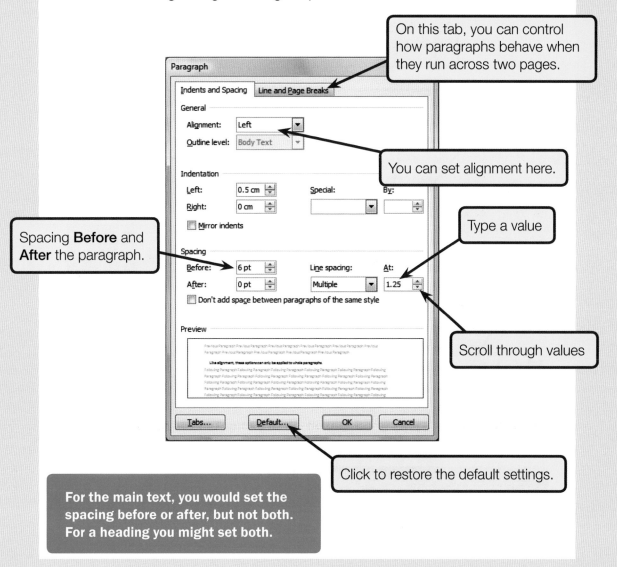

On this tab, you can control how paragraphs behave when they run across two pages.

You can set alignment here.

Type a value

Spacing **Before** and **After** the paragraph.

Scroll through values

Click to restore the default settings.

For the main text, you would set the spacing before or after, but not both. For a heading you might set both.

Coloured text

Most of us now have colour printers, so we should make use of this in our word processing. Put some colour into your text. There are three ways to add colour:

- Colour the font
- Put a highlight colour behind some words
- Add a border or shaded background to the text.

Font colour and highlights are handled with the Font tools.

1 Select the text to colour, or highlight

2 Click a button to use the current highlight or font colour

3 Click the arrow to open the palette, then select a colour

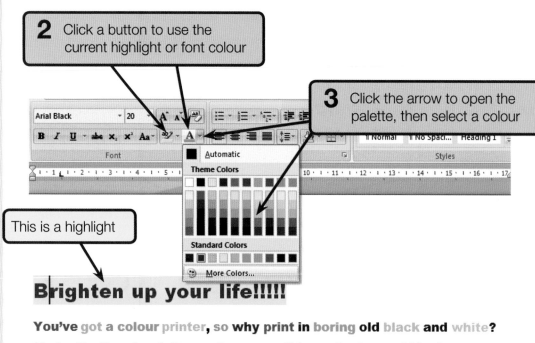

This is a highlight

Brighten up your life!!!!!

You've got a colour printer, so why print in boring old black and white? (Actually, there's a jolly good reason – it is easier to read black on white!)

The Highlight palette is much the same as the Font colour one but a bit simpler.

Format Painter

If you have applied several formats – setting the font, size, colour and making it bold, for example – to a piece of text, and you want to use exactly the same formats on another piece, the Format Painter will save you time. It can copy formatting from one piece of text to another.

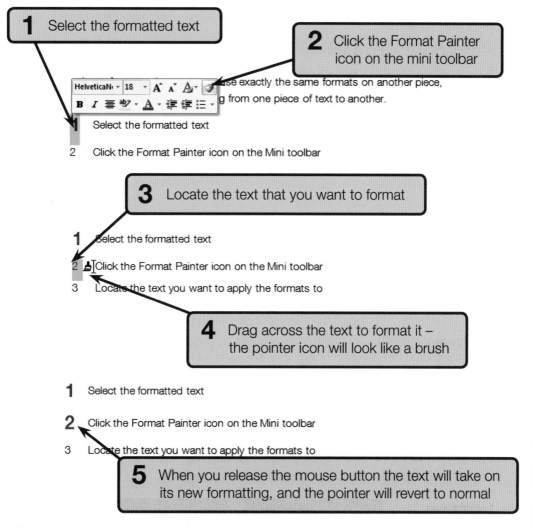

1 Select the formatted text

2 Click the Format Painter icon on the mini toolbar

3 Locate the text that you want to format

4 Drag across the text to format it – the pointer icon will look like a brush

5 When you release the mouse button the text will take on its new formatting, and the pointer will revert to normal

To apply the same formatting to more than one block of text, double-click on the Format Painter icon at Step 2. This will lock it on. When you have finished, click the icon again to revert to the normal pointer.

Practice!

Time to put your newly acquired knowledge of formatting into use. Write a letter – and if there is no letter that actually needs writing, make one up. You could write to the council to complain about the state of the roads or the opening hours at the library; or to Aunt Ethel (who hasn't had a letter from you since Christmas 1983); or to the publishers of this book to tell them about the speiling error on page 82.

Whatever you write, use:

● Alignment, e.g. in the address and date

● Font and size, making the heading different from the rest of the text

● Bold or italics, for emphasis in the letter

● Colour, in the heading, or for extra emphasis in the text.

Dunroaming
Acacia Avenue
Tinbridge Wails

30th February 2009

The Roads Officer
Wails Valley Council
Town Hall Square
Tinbridge Wails

Dear Sir or Madam,

Re: The High Street

I am writing to you to complain about the state of the pavements in the High Street.

Those of us who have the misfortune to have to walk down the High Street regularly cannot fail to have noticed the increasing number of broken slabs, the steady deterioration of the surfaces, the growing encrustations of discarded chewing gum, and the accumulation of litter. Not only is the unsuspecting pedestrian in danger of being tripped up by the cracks *(and outside no 32, to give just one extreme example, there is a crack big enough to lose a walking stick in)*, but there is nowhere safe to land without getting filthy.

Yours in disgust

> **Remember to save the letter when you have done.
> And it will need printing – we'll get on to that shortly.**

Opening a document

Opening files is pretty much the reverse of saving them.

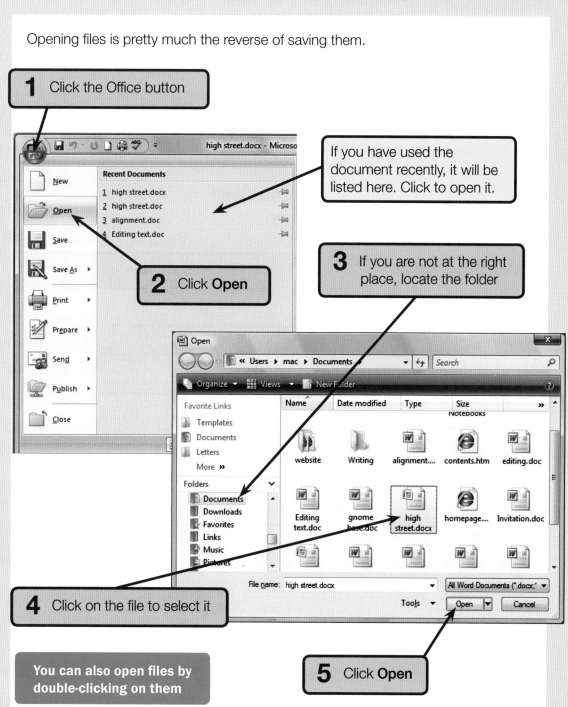

1 Click the Office button

If you have used the document recently, it will be listed here. Click to open it.

2 Click **Open**

3 If you are not at the right place, locate the folder

4 Click on the file to select it

5 Click **Open**

You can also open files by double-clicking on them

Views

Word 2007 offers you five ways to look at a document.

- **Print Layout** shows the page as it would look when printed. This is the best view for most work.

- **Full Screen Reading** hides most of the controls to leave more space for reading the document.

- **Web Layout** is for when you are using Word to create web pages.

- **Outline** shows the structure of a document, as shown by its headings. We'll come back to this when we look at Styles (see p. 90).

- **Draft** just shows your text, ignoring margins and layout on the page.

To change views

1 Open the **View** tab on the Ribbon

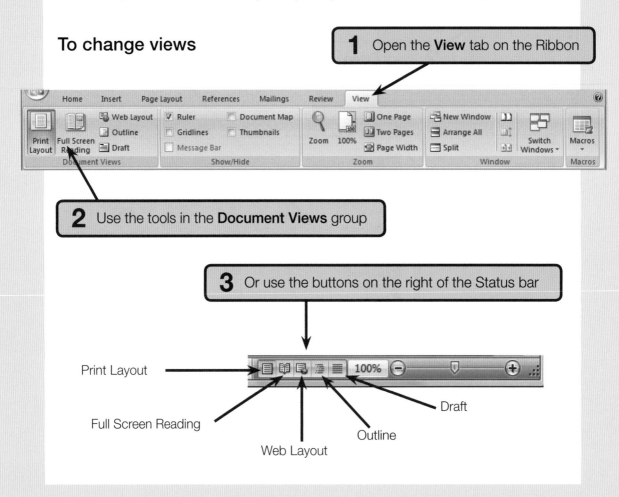

2 Use the tools in the **Document Views** group

3 Or use the buttons on the right of the Status bar

Print Layout

Full Screen Reading

Web Layout

Outline

Draft

Zoom

This controls how large the document appears on screen.

Zoom out to get a better view of complete pages and check the layout. Looking at the whole of this letter, I can see that there's too much space at the bottom – I'll space things out more at the top.

Zoom in to check the details – the more I look at the letter heading, the less I like the font.

To change the Zoom level

1 Use the slider on the far right of the Status bar.

Or

2 Select the **View** tab on the Ribbon and use its **Zoom** tools.

Zoom out   Zoom in

Opens a dialogue box with variable levels of zoom.

Print preview

The Print Layout view gives a good idea of how the document will look when printed. For a simple letter, this is good enough, but where there are inserted graphics or where presentation is really important, it is always a good idea to check the appearance with Print Preview, before printing.

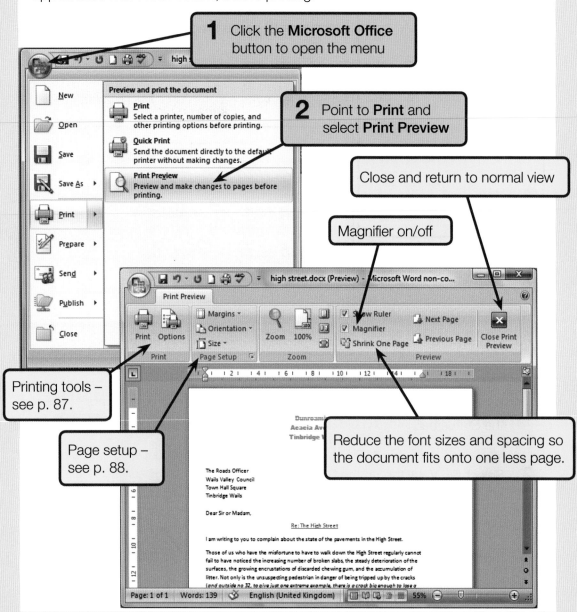

1 Click the **Microsoft Office** button to open the menu

2 Point to **Print** and select **Print Preview**

Close and return to normal view

Magnifier on/off

Printing tools – see p. 87.

Page setup – see p. 88.

Reduce the font sizes and spacing so the document fits onto one less page.

Print

To print one copy of the whole document, on the default printer, click the Print icon in the Quick Access toolbar (if it is there), or use the Quick Print option in the Microsoft Office menu. For a more controlled print you can use the Print dialogue box.

1 Click the **Print** button in **Print Preview** or use the **Print** option on the button menu to open the Print dialogue box

2 If there are several printers, pick the one to use

Print

Printer
Name: Brother HL-2030
Status: Idle
Type: Brother HL-2030
Where: LPT1:
Comment:

Properties
Find Printer...
Print to file

3 How many copies?

Page range
All
Current page   Selection
Pages: 2-4

Type page numbers and/or page ranges separated by commas counting from the start of the document or the section. For example, type 1, 3, 5–12 or p1s1, p1s2, p1s3–p8s3

Copies
Number of copies: 1

Collate

Print what: Document
Print: All pages in range

Zoom
Pages per sheet: 1 page
No Scaling

OK   Cancel

4 Set the **Page range**: **All**, or the **Current page**, or selected **Pages** – give the numbers separated by commas, e.g. 1,3,4 or 2–5,8

5 If **Collate** is on, you don't have to sort the pages into sets at the end

6 Click **OK**

Page layout

The Page Layout tab has a range of tools for controlling the layout of text. The most important ones are in the Page Setup group, and you should certainly know about these three: Orientation, Size and Margins.

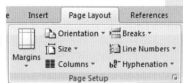

Orientation

This refers to which way round the paper is used. Portrait (upright) is the default, but notices, certificates and brochures, for example, may work better in Landscape, so that they are laid out across the width of the paper.

Size

The standard UK paper size is A4. Printers may initially be set up for (US) Letter size, so it is always worth checking this at the start. You may sometimes want to change the size for printing envelopes.

Margins

The margins are the white space between the edges of the text area and the edges of the paper. You can set these individually yourself, though one or other of the presets will probably do the job most of the time.

Different jobs need different margins. If your document has wide tables or big graphics, setting narrow margins may help them to fit better. If you are printing a short letter on a piece of A4 paper, there will be a lot of blank space and wide margins will help to balance that out more evenly.

Click a preset to apply it.

Mirrored margins are for use when the document is to be bound or stapled. They give extra space on the inside edge of the paper to allow for the fastening.

Use **Custom Margins...** if the none of the presets will do the job.

	Orientation ▾	Breaks ▾
Margins	Size ▾	Line Numbers ▾
	Columns ▾	Hyphenation ▾

	Last Custom Setting	
	Top: 1.27 cm	Bottom: 1.27 cm
	Left: 1.27 cm	Right: 3.64 cm
	Normal	
	Top: 2.54 cm	Bottom: 2.54 cm
	Left: 2.54 cm	Right: 2.54 cm
	Narrow	
	Top: 1.27 cm	Bottom: 1.27 cm
	Left: 1.27 cm	Right: 1.27 cm
	Moderate	
	Top: 2.54 cm	Bottom: 2.54 cm
	Left: 1.91 cm	Right: 1.91 cm
	Wide	
	Top: 2.54 cm	Bottom: 2.54 cm
	Left: 5.08 cm	Right: 5.08 cm
	Mirrored	
	Top: 2.54 cm	Bottom: 2.54 cm
	Inside: 3.18 cm	Outside: 2.54 cm

Custom Margins...

Page setup

The Page Setup dialogue box can be opened from the launcher in the Page Setup group, and also from the Page Setup tool in the Print Preview window. The margins, orientation, size and other aspects of layout can be set here. The Page Layout tools are generally easier to use, but there are two situations when you would use Page Setup:

- You need to set non-standard margins
- You are in Print Preview and want to change the paper size or the orientation before you print.

Change the paper size on this tab.

Headers and footers and other more advanced options are set here.

Set individual margins

Orientation

Check the Preview

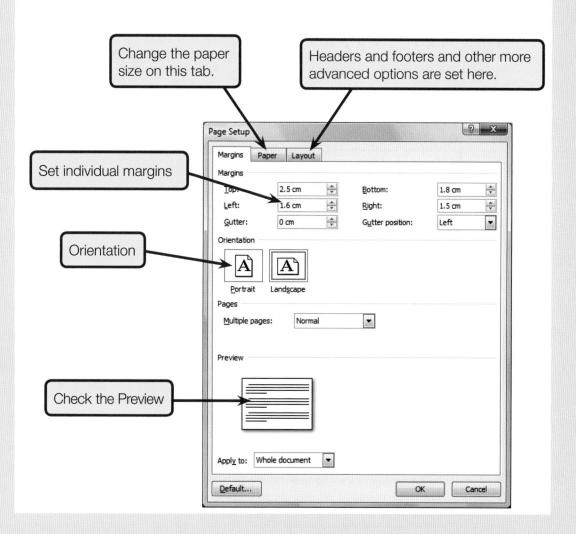

Styles

Styles are ready-made sets of formats. There are styles for different levels of headings, for captions, for emphasis, references and more. There are two big advantages to using styles, rather than formatting 'by hand':

● A style applies a bunch of formats in one stroke, setting the font, size, colour, spacing and more

● After a document has been 'styled', you can redefine the styles and change the look of it all, very quickly.

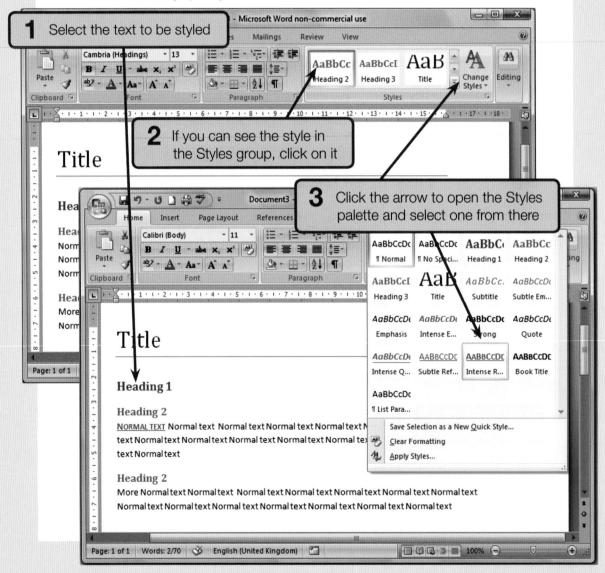

1 Select the text to be styled

2 If you can see the style in the Styles group, click on it

3 Click the arrow to open the Styles palette and select one from there

Style sets

Word has a dozen sets of styles, and you can switch from one set to another, after applying them. You can also apply a different set of colours and/or of fonts to the styled document.

Try it next time you write an essay, report or story that uses different levels of headings. Use the styles to define the headings, and then redefine the style set.

1 Apply styles to your text

2 Click **Change Styles**

3 Point to **Style Set**

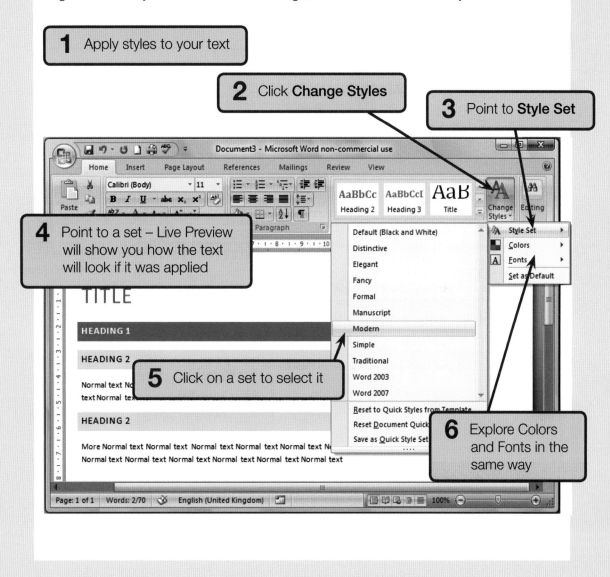

4 Point to a set – Live Preview will show you how the text will look if it was applied

5 Click on a set to select it

6 Explore Colors and Fonts in the same way

Modifying styles

Styles have their limitations. For a start, they only use the fonts that are supplied with Windows and Microsoft Office. If you have other fonts, they will not be used – but there is nothing to stop you from using them. Here are two ways to modify a style: by updating the style, or by using the Modify Style dialogue box.

1 Select an example of text to which a style, e.g. Heading 2, has been applied

2 Reformat it as required

3 Click the Styles dialogue box launcher

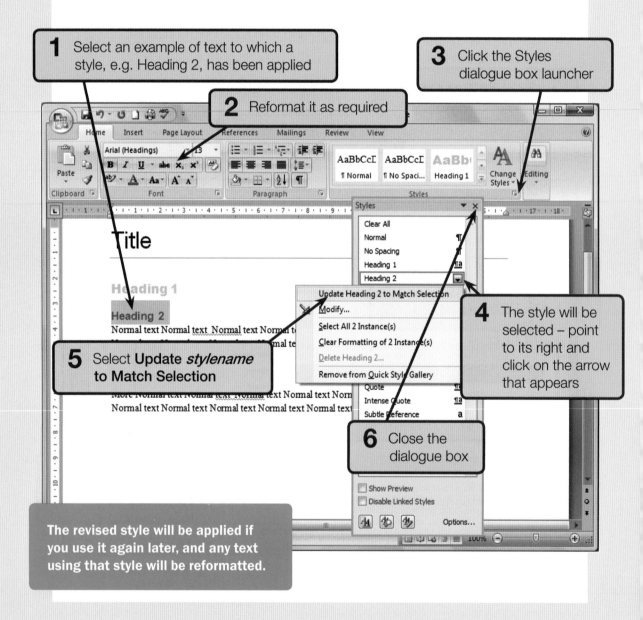

4 The style will be selected – point to its right and click on the arrow that appears

5 Select **Update *stylename* to Match Selection**

6 Close the dialogue box

The revised style will be applied if you use it again later, and any text using that style will be reformatted.

The Modify style dialogue box

This is for people who know exactly what they want! Here you can define all aspects of the style – all the Font and Paragraph options, plus tab settings, borders and shades, and far more.

● To get here, open the Styles dialogue box, select a style and click **Modify**

● The more commonly used formatting options are present in the box. To reach the others, click the **Format** button at the bottom, then select a set.

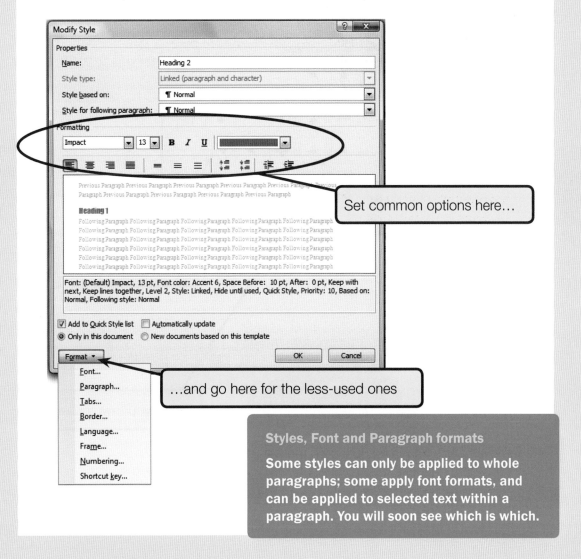

Set common options here...

...and go here for the less-used ones

Styles, Font and Paragraph formats

Some styles can only be applied to whole paragraphs; some apply font formats, and can be applied to selected text within a paragraph. You will soon see which is which.

Bulleted lists

If you have a list of items, it will stand out more if you add bullets or numbers. There are several predefined styles for each, and you can define your own easily enough.

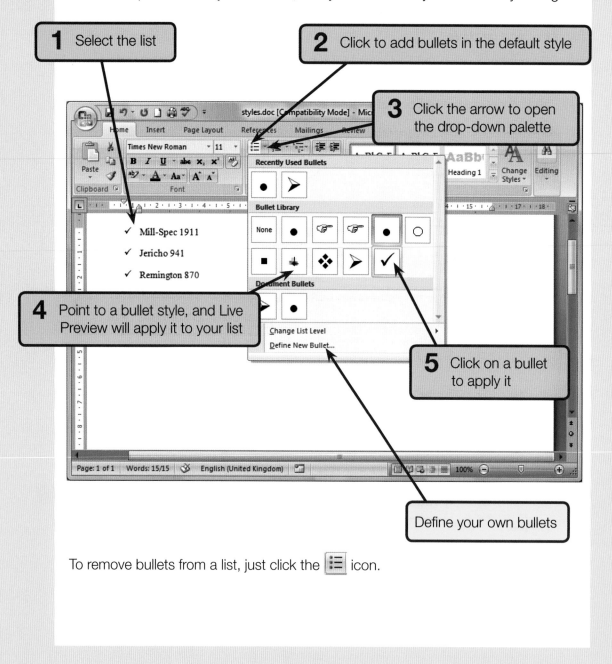

1 Select the list

2 Click to add bullets in the default style

3 Click the arrow to open the drop-down palette

4 Point to a bullet style, and Live Preview will apply it to your list

5 Click on a bullet to apply it

Define your own bullets

To remove bullets from a list, just click the ⊞ icon.

Custom bullets

If you do not like any of the bullets, define your own.

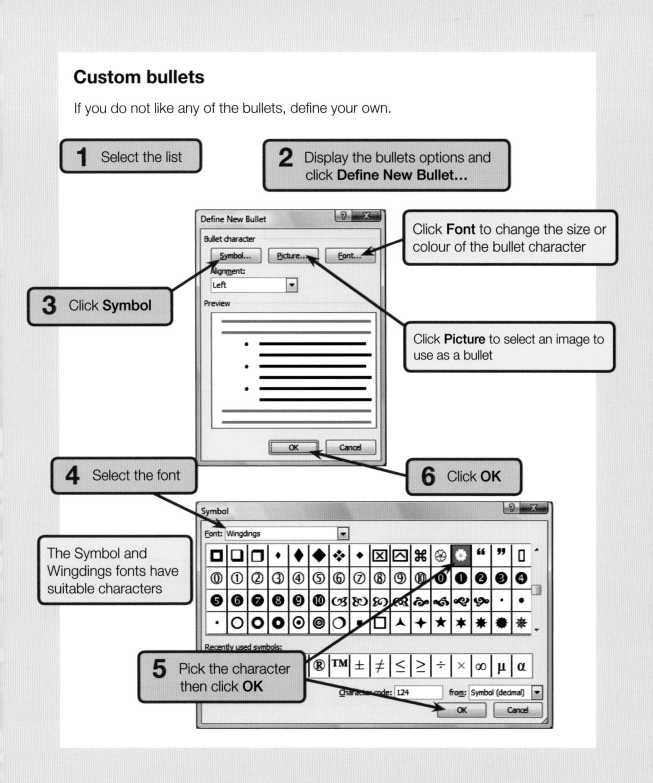

1 Select the list

2 Display the bullets options and click **Define New Bullet...**

Click **Font** to change the size or colour of the bullet character

3 Click **Symbol**

Click **Picture** to select an image to use as a bullet

4 Select the font

6 Click **OK**

The Symbol and Wingdings fonts have suitable characters

5 Pick the character then click **OK**

Multiple lists

If you want a list within a list, that's easily done.

1 Type your text, as one continuous list

2 Apply a bullet style to the whole lot

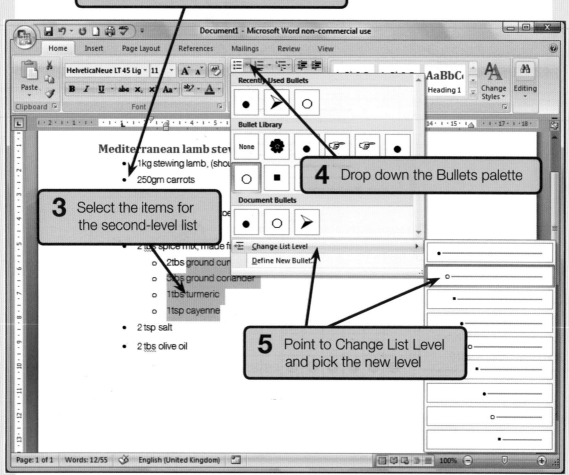

3 Select the items for the second-level list

4 Drop down the Bullets palette

5 Point to Change List Level and pick the new level

Numbered lists

Numbers are set (and cleared) in the same way as bullets. You can have normal numbers, Roman numerals or letters, in upper or lower case.

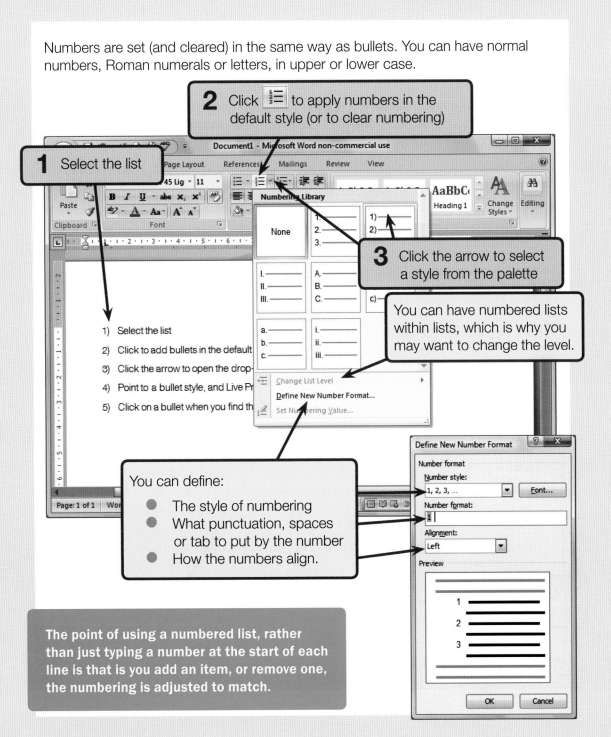

2 Click ⊞ to apply numbers in the default style (or to clear numbering)

1 Select the list

3 Click the arrow to select a style from the palette

You can have numbered lists within lists, which is why you may want to change the level.

You can define:
- The style of numbering
- What punctuation, spaces or tab to put by the number
- How the numbers align.

The point of using a numbered list, rather than just typing a number at the start of each line is that is you add an item, or remove one, the numbering is adjusted to match.

The spell checker

The spelling and grammar checker normally works alongside you, checking your text as you type. If it spots any errors, it underlines them – spelling mistakes in red, and grammatical errors in green.

It will tell you that some things are spelled wrongly when they aren't. The dictionary is very comprehensive, but it doesn't have every place name or technical term and doesn't recognise many slang or foreign words.

The grammar checker applies fairly strict rules, so if you are writing poetry, or plays, or brief notes, expect lots of green underlines.

You can set it to ignore the grammar when checking the spelling, and even the spelling check is optional or can be run when you want it.

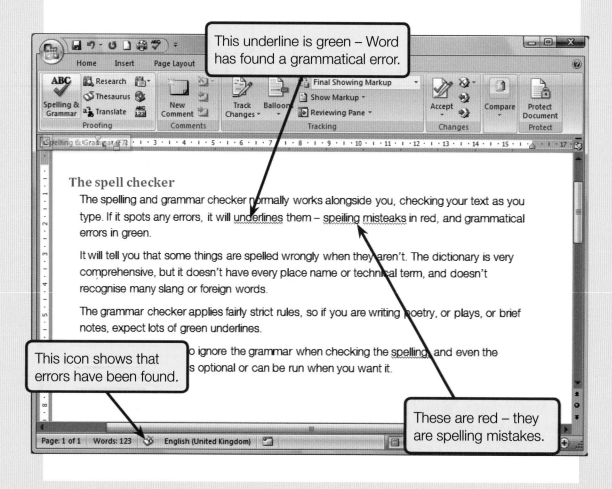

This underline is green – Word has found a grammatical error.

This icon shows that errors have been found.

These are red – they are spelling mistakes.

Checking as you type

You can deal with errors, one by one, as they are found by the checker. This can be the simplest way to deal with them – especially if you don't make many mistakes.

Spelling mistakes

1 Right-click on the underlined word to open the context menu

2 There will normally be several suggestions at the top of the list. If one of these is what you meant to type, click on it and it will replace the error

3 If the word is correct, but one that Word doesn't know, you have three choices:

- **Ignore** it this time
- **Ignore all** uses of the word in the document
- **Add it to the dictionary**, so that it is recognised whenever you use it in future in any document.

Grammatical mistakes

1 Right-click on the underlined word or phrase

2 If there is a suggestion at the top of the menu, and if that is correct, then click on it to accept it

3 If you meant it the way you wrote it, click **Ignore Once**

4 If you want to know why it is complaining about your grammar, the **About This Sentence** button will explain.

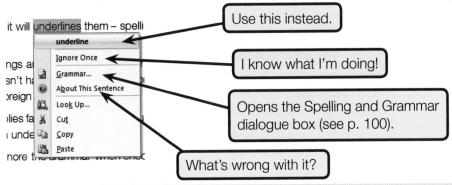

Use this instead.

I know what I'm doing!

Opens the Spelling and Grammar dialogue box (see p. 100).

What's wrong with it?

Running a check

Rather than breaking the flow to correct errors, you may prefer to finish your typing and then go back and sort them out all at once. And if you are going to do that, it is simpler to use the **Spelling and Grammar** dialogue box, than to right-click on them one by one.

- Click the **Spelling and Grammar** icon on the Status bar
- Or click the button on the **Review** tab on the Ribbon.

The checker will work through the document, stopping at each error in turn, and offering you several options. As in the one-off menu, you can:

- Ignore the error (once or every time)
- Add it to the dictionary
- Change it to the suggested word (once or every time).

But you can do more here.

- You can edit the fragment of text in the dialogue box, then click the **Change** button to copy the editing into the document
- If you make the same mistake regularly (I often type 'hte' for 'the') select the correct word and click **AutoCorrect**. It will be automatically corrected in future.

After you have dealt with the error, the checker will move on to the next, until it reaches the end. Click **Close** if you want to stop the check early.

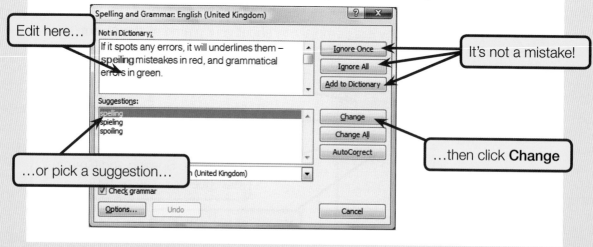

The grammar check

As with the spelling, you have the same options here as in the context menu, but with a couple of extra features:

● There's a brief description of the error at the top of the box, which can be enough to tell you what the problem is – or why Word thinks there's a problem, though you know there isn't

● The **Ignore Rule** option will ignore any later 'errors' of the same type – use this if your writing style is looser than the checker likes

● The **Options...** button opens the relevant part of the **Word Options** dialogue box where you can specify what you want it to check, and how

● You can turn off the grammar check completely.

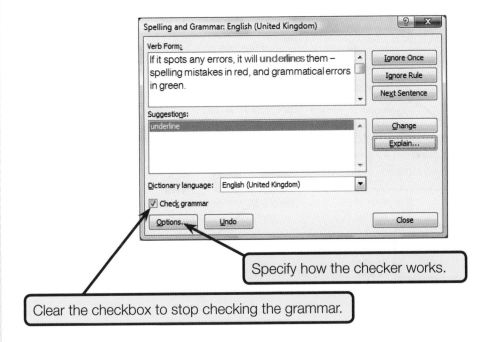

Specify how the checker works.

Clear the checkbox to stop checking the grammar.

Inserting images

Photos and other files

In Word you can insert two types of images into documents:

- **Pictures** includes any image files that you have on the PC, e.g. photos or art-work created in Paint

- **Clip art** refers to the cartoons, drawings, photos and other images supplied by Microsoft (and others) with Word and online.

Here's how to insert a picture.

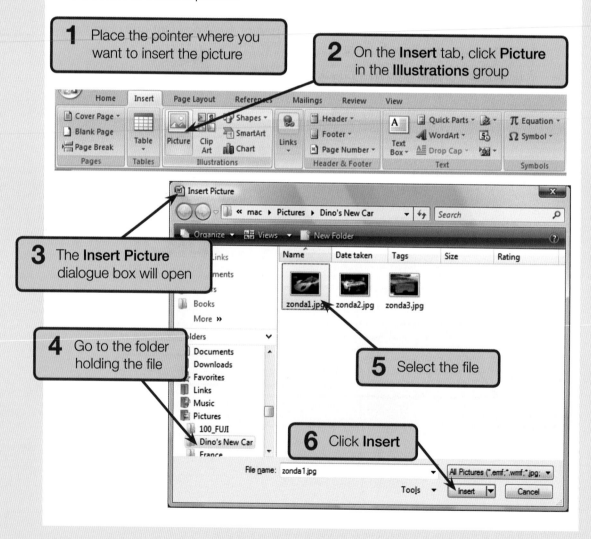

1 Place the pointer where you want to insert the picture

2 On the **Insert** tab, click **Picture** in the **Illustrations** group

3 The **Insert Picture** dialogue box will open

4 Go to the folder holding the file

5 Select the file

6 Click **Insert**

Clip art

The only real difference between clip art and other pictures is where it comes from. Clip art comes from clip art collections. A small collection is supplied with Microsoft Office, but a much larger one is available at Office Online. You may be asked if you want to include the online collection in the search, though that option may already be turned on. This gives you lots more choice, but takes longer.

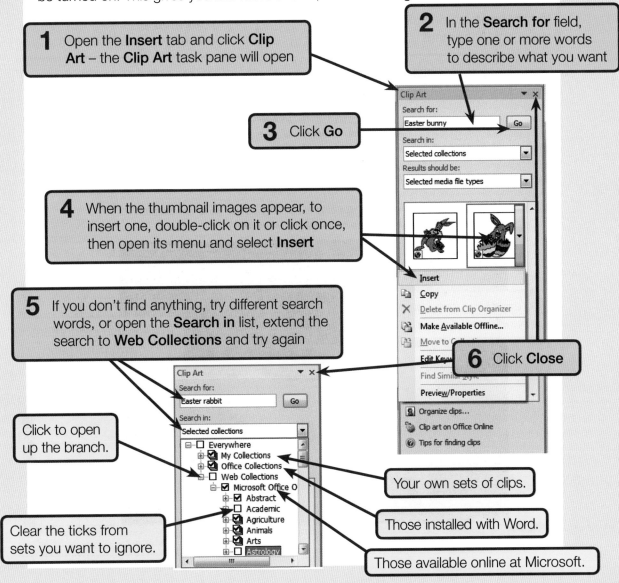

1 Open the **Insert** tab and click **Clip Art** – the **Clip Art** task pane will open

2 In the **Search for** field, type one or more words to describe what you want

3 Click **Go**

4 When the thumbnail images appear, to insert one, double-click on it or click once, then open its menu and select **Insert**

5 If you don't find anything, try different search words, or open the **Search in** list, extend the search to **Web Collections** and try again

6 Click **Close**

Click to open up the branch.

Clear the ticks from sets you want to ignore.

Your own sets of clips.

Those installed with Word.

Those available online at Microsoft.

Working with images

After inserting a picture or clip art, you can adjust its size and position, change its brightness, the contrast or the shades of colour, and add a border or other effects. The tools are on the **Format** tab of the Ribbon. This should come to the front automatically when a picture is selected.

To centre the image, select it, then go to the **Home** tab and click the **Centre** tool in the **Alignment** group, or...

Click the **Position** tool and select a **Text Wrapping** option – this controls how the image fits with the text.

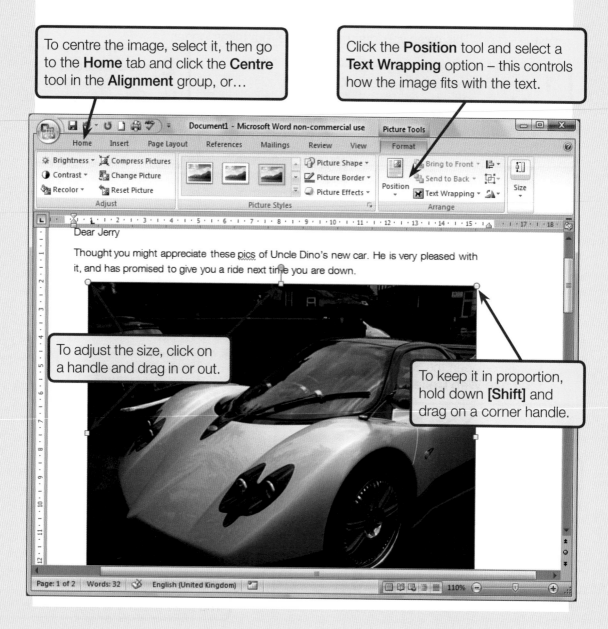

To adjust the size, click on a handle and drag in or out.

To keep it in proportion, hold down **[Shift]** and drag on a corner handle.

Brightness, contrast and colours

One of the great things about working with images on a computer is that you can easily adjust the colours and tones in different ways. The Brightness and Contrast tools are in the **Adjust** group and are used in the same way.

1 Click the button to drop down the options – you can adjust the levels up or down by 40%

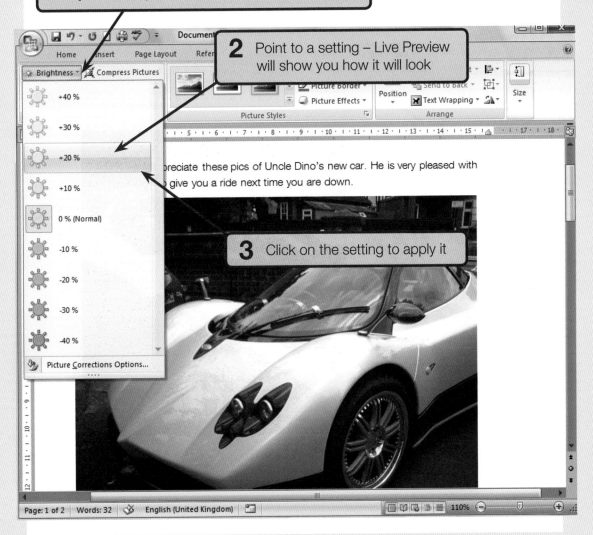

2 Point to a setting – Live Preview will show you how it will look

3 Click on the setting to apply it

Recolor

Recolor is for special effects. It changes the overall colour scheme, so your normal colour photo can be turned into black and white (either with the normal range of greyscales or in high contrast, as here), or shades of a colour.

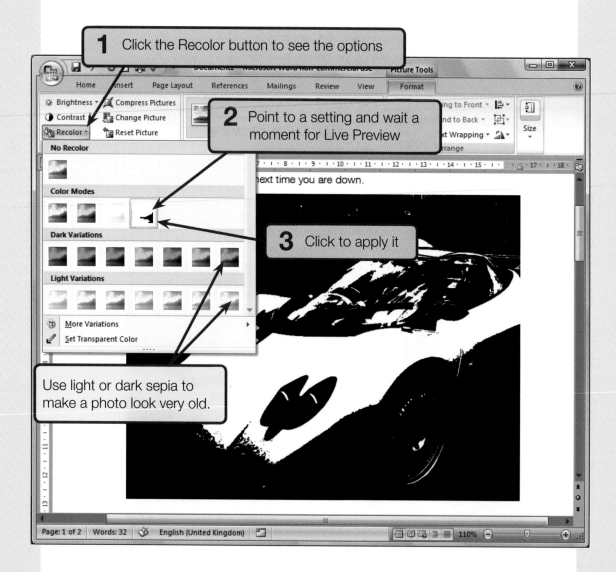

1 Click the Recolor button to see the options

2 Point to a setting and wait a moment for Live Preview

3 Click to apply it

Use light or dark sepia to make a photo look very old.

Using templates

Templates are ready-made designs for documents, with layout, font formatting, colours and sometimes also images, already in place. Once you have replaced the temporary text with your own words, you have a professional-looking brochure, certificate, greetings card, or whatever – there are templates for many different types of documents.

1 Open the Microsoft Office button menu and select **New**

2 At the New Document window, select a template type

3 Click on a thumbnail to see a larger preview

4 When you find one you like, click **Create** (if the template is on your PC) or **Download** if it is at Office Online

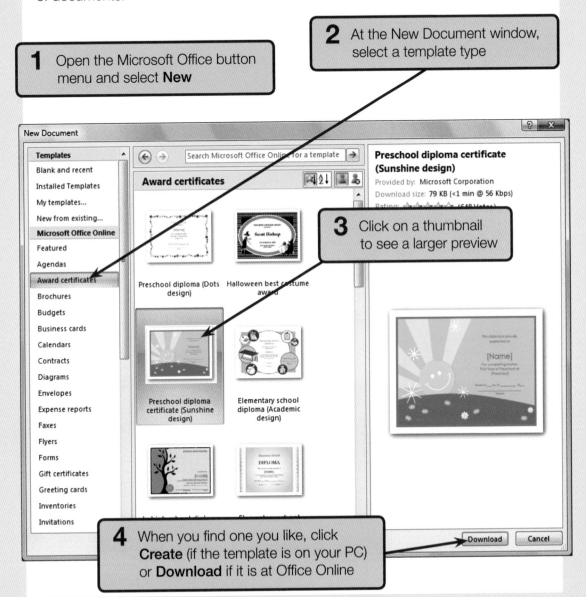

Making an invitation

The templates are good for greetings cards and invitations. Try them, next time you are having a party.

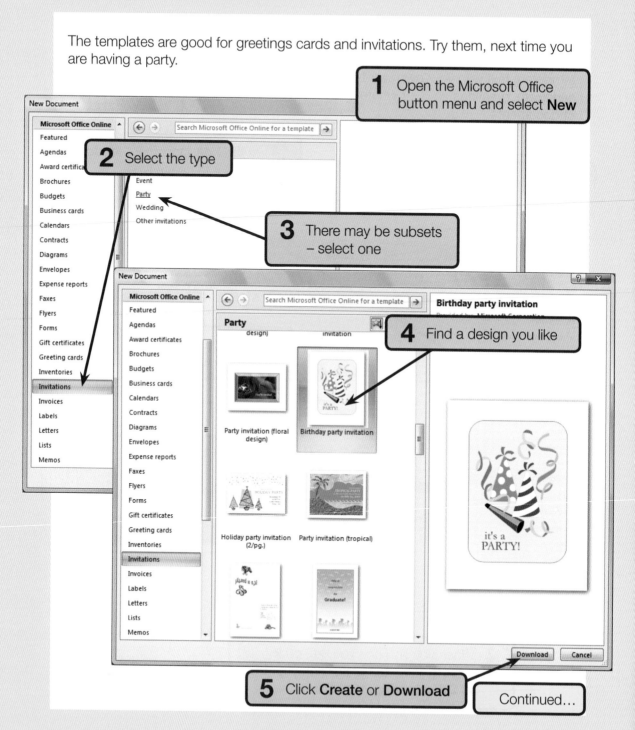

1 Open the Microsoft Office button menu and select **New**

2 Select the type

3 There may be subsets – select one

4 Find a design you like

5 Click **Create** or **Download**

Continued...

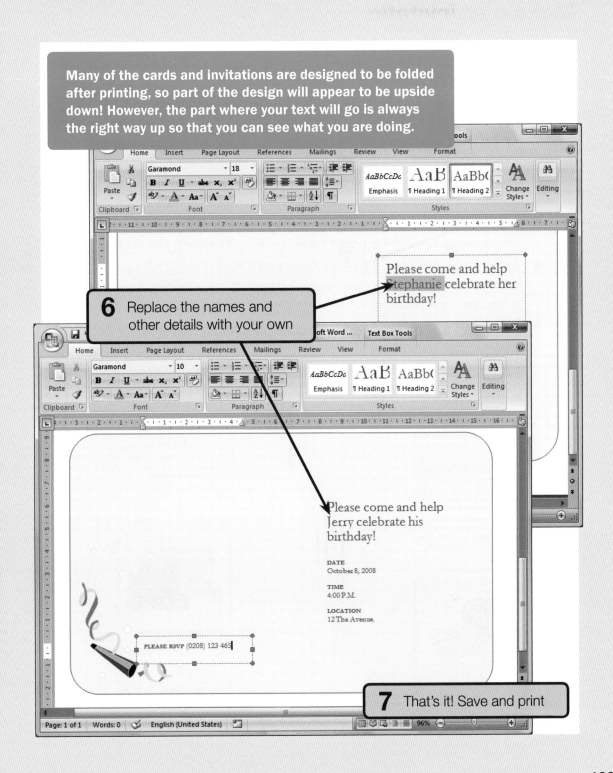

Many of the cards and invitations are designed to be folded after printing, so part of the design will appear to be upside down! However, the part where your text will go is always the right way up so that you can see what you are doing.

6 Replace the names and other details with your own

Please come and help Stephanie celebrate her birthday!

Please come and help Jerry celebrate his birthday!

DATE
October 8, 2008

TIME
4:00 P.M.

LOCATION
12 The Avenue.

PLEASE RSVP (0208) 123 465

7 That's it! Save and print

Make a brochure

In the templates you will find some for brochures, flyers and other two-page documents. Some, like the one here are designed to be folded, others are single sheets – but the important thing is that they must be printed back to back. This can get complicated. Follow these tips for better two-sided printing.

1 For the first pass, use the Print dialogue box to set the Page Range to Page 1, and the Number of copies to a few more than you need, to allow for errors

2 After printing the first side, square up the pile of paper carefully. The more it looks like a fresh pack, the better it will go through the printer

3 Put the paper back into the printer, the right way round. This varies, but you should probably have the printed side upwards. However, just in case…

4 Print a single copy of the second page. Has it been printed on the right side of the paper? Is it the right way round? If not, go back to step 3 and turn the printed pages round to suit.

5 Once you have one page come out correctly, print the required number of copies.

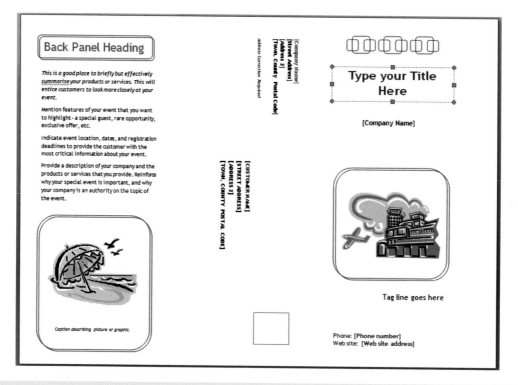

Creating a template

You can create your own templates, and these can be started from scratch or from a Word template. For example, suppose you were running a small business for which you needed invoices. Instead of paying the local printer to produce pre-printed forms, you could set up a template, then start each invoice from that, type in the details and print out copies for the customer and your records.

There's a good choice of invoice designs in Microsoft's templates. Use one of these as the base.

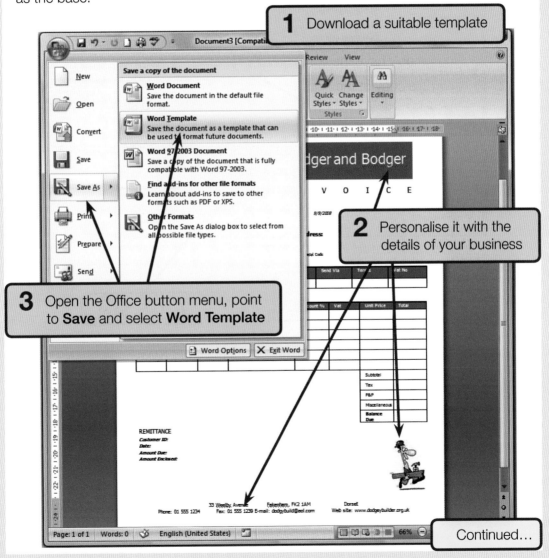

1 Download a suitable template

2 Personalise it with the details of your business

3 Open the Office button menu, point to **Save** and select **Word Template**

Continued...

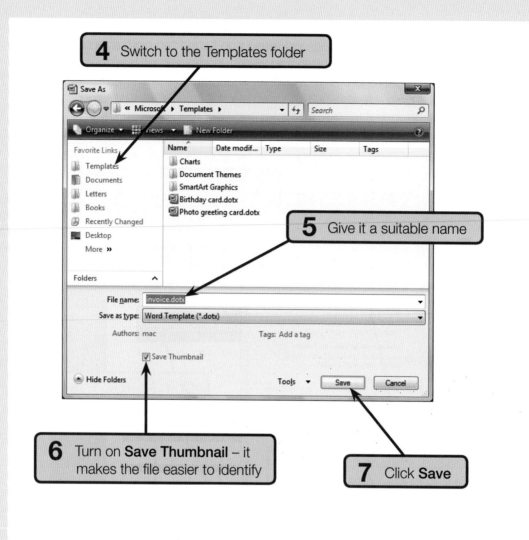

4 Switch to the Templates folder

5 Give it a suitable name

6 Turn on **Save Thumbnail** – it makes the file easier to identify

7 Click **Save**

Next time you need an invoice, open your new template – you will find it in **My Templates**.

3 Exploring the Internet

When you are online, things can go wrong – a site may fail to load in, you may get yourself lost – but it doesn't matter much. It won't break your PC, or the Internet. Have fun, explore, and if you get in a mess, close down Internet Explorer and start it up again – that will sort things out.

This chapter covers:

- The basics of the Internet and the World Wide Web
- How to use Internet Explorer and customise it to suit yourself
- How to browse the Web
- Favorites and the History list
- How to save and print web pages or selected text and images
- How to stay safe online
- Controling cookies and pop-ups
- Add-ons to extend Internet Explorer

The Internet and the Web

Let's start by clearing up a common misconception. The 'Web' and the 'Internet' are not the same thing. Some people use the terms interchangeably, but they shouldn't.

- The Internet is the underlying framework. It consists of the computers, large and small, that store and process information for the Internet; the telephone wire, network cable, microwave links and other connections between them; and the software systems that allow them all to interact.

- The World Wide Web is the most visible and one of the simplest and most popular ways of using the Internet. It consists of – literally – billions of web pages, which can be viewed through browsers, such as Internet Explorer. The pages are constructed using HTML, a coding system that tells browsers how to display text and images, and how to manage links between pages. Clicking on a hypertext link in a page tells the browser to go to the linked page (or some-times to a different type of linked file) – wherever it may be.

E-mail is another simple and very popular use of the Internet, and there are other more specialised Internet activities, which we will touch on later in this book.

Essential jargon

Browser – software application specially designed for accessing and displaying the information in the World Wide Web. This is also true the other way: the web is an information system designed to be viewed on browsers.

E-mail – electronic mail, a system for sending messages and files across the Internet and other networks.

Net – short for Internet. And Internet is short for interlinked networks, which is what it is.

HTML – HyperText Markup Language, a system of instructions that browsers can interpret to display text and images. HTML allows hypertext links to be built into web pages.

Page – or web page, a document displayed on the Web. It may be plain or formatted text; and may hold pictures, sounds and videos.

Web – World Wide Web. Also shortened to WWW or W3.

Internet Explorer

Internet Explorer is supplied as part of Windows Vista, and is a powerful piece of software – easy to use but with all the sophisticated features that you need to get the best out of browsing the World Wide Web. Only the main features are covered here, but that is all you need to get started.

There are several optional elements to the Internet Explorer window, so yours may well not look like this at the moment. Try to identify as many features as you can.

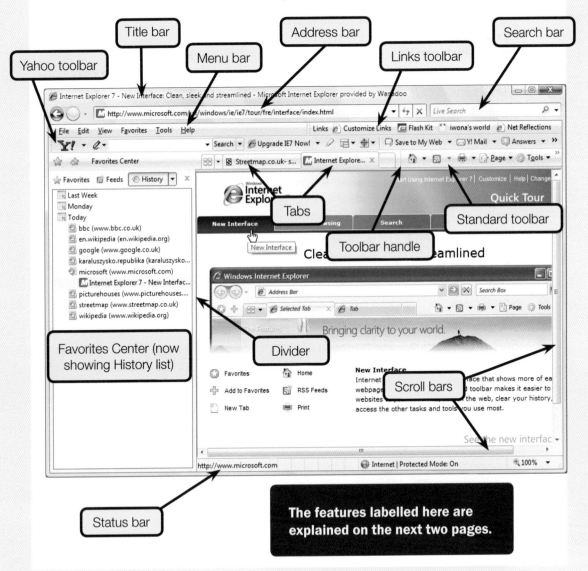

The features labelled here are explained on the next two pages.

The toolbars

- **Title bar** – shows the title of the web page, which is not the same as its URL.
- **Menu bar** – gives you access to the full set of commands.
- **Standard toolbar** – with tools for the most commonly used commands.
- **Address bar** – shows the URL (Uniform Resource Locator, the address and filename) of the page. Addresses can be typed here.
- **Go button** – click after typing an URL in the Address bar.
- **Links toolbar** – links to selected sites. There are predefined links to Microsoft's sites, but you can change these and add your own links.
- **Toolbar handles** – you can drag these to move the toolbars.

Other features

- **Explorer bar** – can be opened when it is needed to display your History (links to the places visited in the last few days) or your Favorites (links to selected pages), or to run a search for information. Clicking on a link in the Explorer bar will display its page in the main window.
- **Divider** – click and drag on this to adjust the width of the Explorer bar. You may need more space when using the Explorer bar for a search.
- **Scroll bars** – will appear on the right and at the bottom if a web page is too deep or too wide to fit into the window.
- **Status bar** – shows the progress of incoming files for a page. When they have all downloaded, you'll see 'Done'. It also shows the address in a link when you point to it.

> I am assuming that you you have a broadband connection already in place, and that it has been set up to link to the Internet automatically when the PC is turned on – that is the normal setting.

The navigation tools

Use these to move between the pages you have already visited during the session.

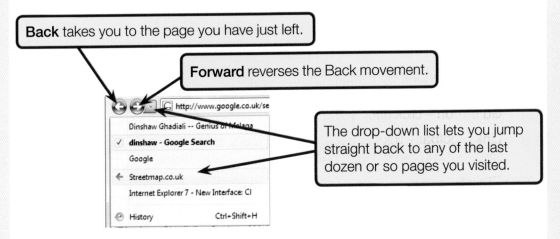

Back takes you to the page you have just left.

Forward reverses the Back movement.

The drop-down list lets you jump straight back to any of the last dozen or so pages you visited.

The standard toolbar

These buttons contain almost all of the controls that you need when you are online.

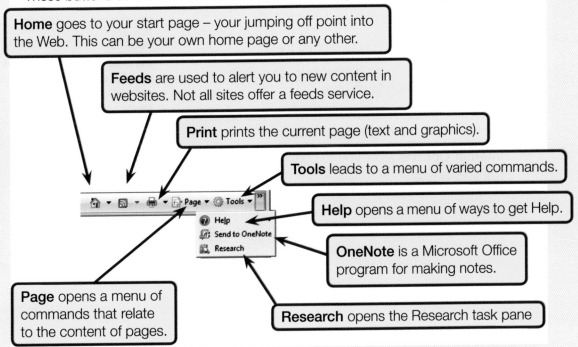

Home goes to your start page – your jumping off point into the Web. This can be your own home page or any other.

Feeds are used to alert you to new content in websites. Not all sites offer a feeds service.

Print prints the current page (text and graphics).

Tools leads to a menu of varied commands.

Help opens a menu of ways to get Help.

OneNote is a Microsoft Office program for making notes.

Page opens a menu of commands that relate to the content of pages.

Research opens the Research task pane

The Page menu

You should know these commands:

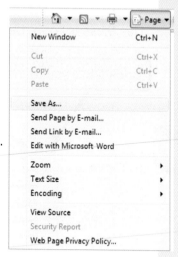

- **Copy** – copies text or images. You can then paste them into a Word document or a graphics application.

- **Save As** – stores a copy of the page.

- **Send Page/Link by E-mail** – connects you to Windows Mail to send someone the page, or a link to it.

- **Zoom** – enlarges the text and graphics.

- **Text size** – enlarges, or reduces, the text size.

The Tools menu

You should know these commands:

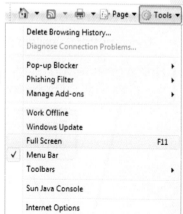

- **Pop-up Blocker** – when you visit some web pages, little windows appear, carrying adverts. Turn the blocker on to stop these windows opening.

- **Phishing Filter** – phishing e-mails are ones that try to con you into giving out banking and other personal details. Turn the filter on to restrict these.

- **Full screen** – removes the toolbars and uses the entire screen to display a page.

- **Toolbars** – leads to a submenu where you can control the display of toolbars and sidebars.

- **Internet Options** allow you to configure Explorer to suit your needs.

Using the Address bar

Typing a URL

The Address bar serves two purposes. As you navigate round the Web, the address of the current page is shown in it, but you can also use the bar to go to places. Type an address into it, and the browser will go to that page.

AutoComplete

Internet Explorer remembers every address that goes into the Address bar. When you start to type an address, it will offer you any that start the same way – if the one you want is there then simply select it from the list.

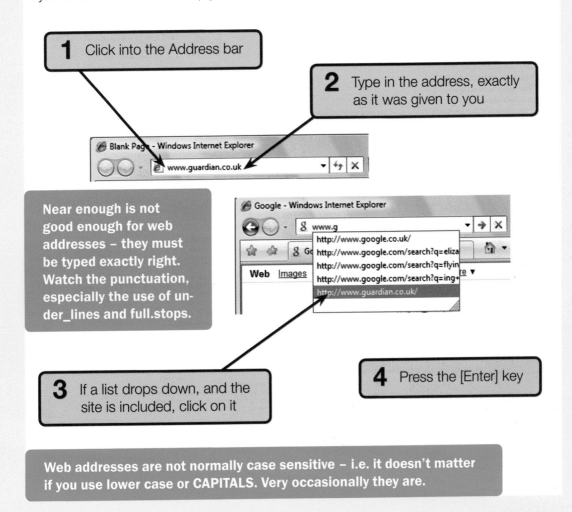

1 Click into the Address bar

2 Type in the address, exactly as it was given to you

Blank Page - Windows Internet Explorer

www.guardian.co.uk

Near enough is not good enough for web addresses – they must be typed exactly right. Watch the punctuation, especially the use of un-der_lines and full.stops.

Google - Windows Internet Explorer

www.g

http://www.google.co.uk/
http://www.google.com/search?q=eliza
http://www.google.com/search?q=flyin
http://www.google.com/search?q=ing+
http://www.guardian.co.uk/

Web   Images

3 If a list drops down, and the site is included, click on it

4 Press the [Enter] key

Web addresses are not normally case sensitive – i.e. it doesn't matter if you use lower case or CAPITALS. Very occasionally they are.

Selecting from the Address list

The addresses that you have typed – but not those generated within sites – are stored in a list that drops down from the Address bar. You can select one from here by simply opening the list.

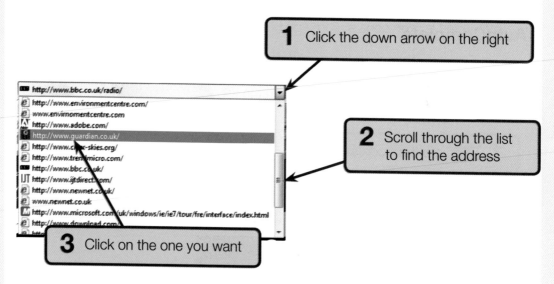

1 Click the down arrow on the right

2 Scroll through the list to find the address

3 Click on the one you want

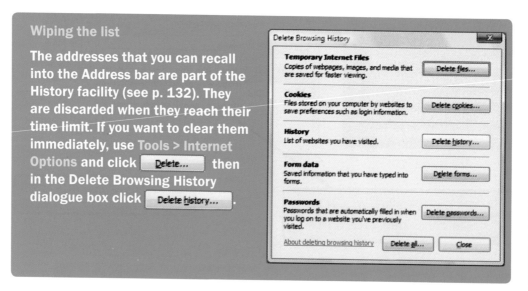

Wiping the list

The addresses that you can recall into the Address bar are part of the History facility (see p. 132). They are discarded when they reach their time limit. If you want to clear them immediately, use Tools > Internet Options and click Delete... then in the Delete Browsing History dialogue box click Delete history... .

Browsing the web

If you want to browse the web, all you need is a good place to start, and one of the best places is a 'Net directory' – a site with sets of organised links to other sites.

One of the best directories is Yahoo! (Actually there are a whole bunch of Yahoos! – the original in the USA, and local Yahoos! in many countries.) What makes Yahoo! so useful is that it is extremely comprehensive, but all the sites listed there have been recommended by someone at some point. Quality control is rare on the web.

If you are having trouble downloading a web page, it may help to start again from scratch. Click **Stop**, then **Refresh**.

1 Type into the Address bar: uk.yahoo.com

Refresh

Stop

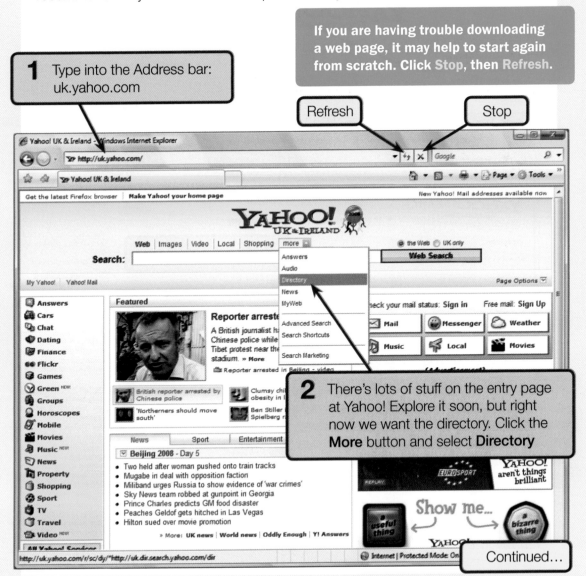

2 There's lots of stuff on the entry page at Yahoo! Explore it soon, but right now we want the directory. Click the **More** button and select **Directory**

Continued...

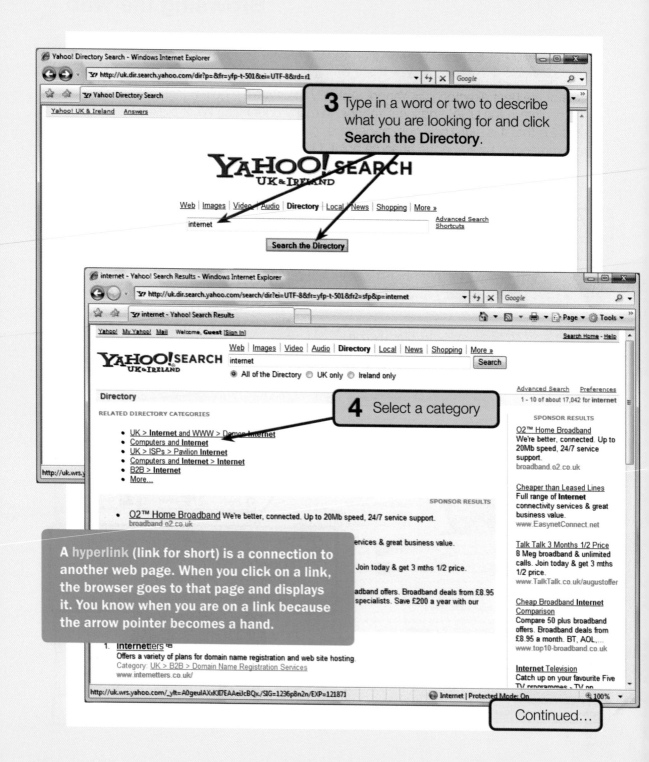

3 Type in a word or two to describe what you are looking for and click **Search the Directory**.

4 Select a category

A hyperlink (link for short) is a connection to another web page. When you click on a link, the browser goes to that page and displays it. You know when you are on a link because the arrow pointer becomes a hand.

Continued...

The Yahoo! directory

The directory is organised as a hierarchy with many levels. At each level there are three sets of links.

- At the top are links to Categories – most will be subdivisions of the current category; those with @ after the name are links to other parts of the hierarchy

- The second set are Sponsored links to firms that have paid to be included

- The third set are the Site listings.

As you work down through the levels, the first set shrinks and the third set grows.

5 Use the category links to get down through two or three levels, to reach a specialised topic of your choice

6 Click on a link to go to the page

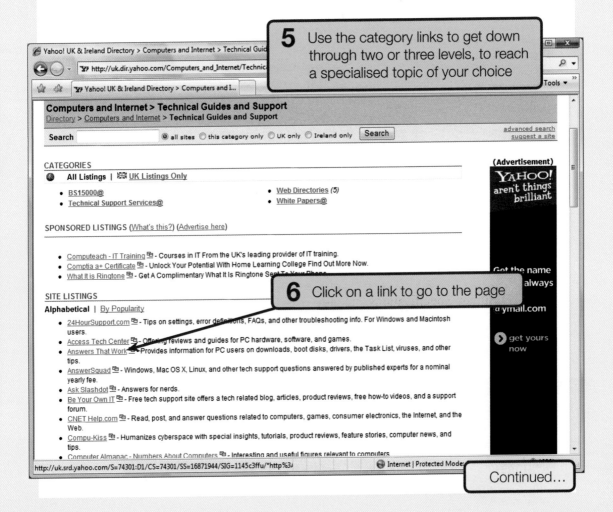

Continued...

There's so much to see on the Web! In fact, there's too much. You can often find links to scores – or even hundreds – of sites on a topic, so you have to learn to be selective or you can waste an awful lot of time online. Dip into a site to get an idea of what it is like, and if this is not really what you are looking for, move on and try elsewhere.

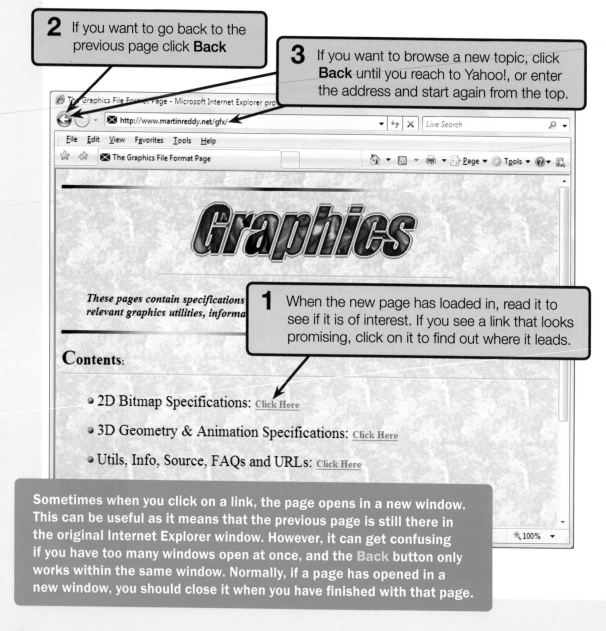

2 If you want to go back to the previous page click **Back**

3 If you want to browse a new topic, click **Back** until you reach to Yahoo!, or enter the address and start again from the top.

http://www.martinreddy.net/gfx/

The Graphics File Format Page

These pages contain specifications relevant graphics utilities, informa

1 When the new page has loaded in, read it to see if it is of interest. If you see a link that looks promising, click on it to find out where it leads.

Contents:

• 2D Bitmap Specifications: Click Here

• 3D Geometry & Animation Specifications: Click Here

• Utils, Info, Source, FAQs and URLs: Click Here

Sometimes when you click on a link, the page opens in a new window. This can be useful as it means that the previous page is still there in the original Internet Explorer window. However, it can get confusing if you have too many windows open at once, and the Back button only works within the same window. Normally, if a page has opened in a new window, you should close it when you have finished with that page.

Searching the Web

Web directories offer one approach to finding material on the web. Search engines offer another, and this is often the best way if you are looking for very specific information. A search engine is a site that has compiled an index to web pages, and which lets you search through the index. There are several dozen search engines, and they compile their indices in different ways and to different levels of completeness, but some of the best know what's on 80% or more of the pages on the web. The most complete and the most effective is Google. It is so well used and loved that searching the Web is now often called 'googling'.

You search by giving one or more words to specify what you are looking for. Try to be specific. If you search for 'football', 'bridge' or 'gardening' you will get millions of links to possible pages.

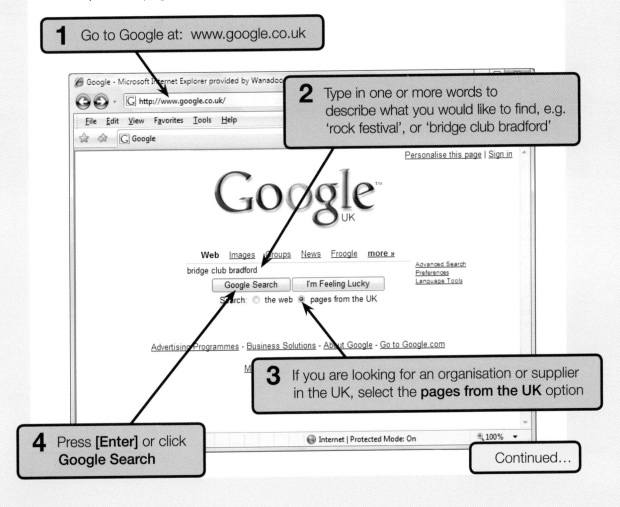

1 Go to Google at: www.google.co.uk

2 Type in one or more words to describe what you would like to find, e.g. 'rock festival', or 'bridge club bradford'

3 If you are looking for an organisation or supplier in the UK, select the **pages from the UK** option

4 Press **[Enter]** or click **Google Search**

Continued...

Google has links to over 8 billion pages in its index! Which is why you have to be as specific as possible when looking for particular information. However, sometimes it pays to be less specific, as this can produce leads that you might never have thought of yourself.

It doesn't matter too much if you get millions of results from a search as the good stuff tends to be listed at the top. (Google has developed some very clever systems for rating pages.)

5 The results show the names and the first couple of lines of details from the matching pages – scroll through to find the ones that look most promising

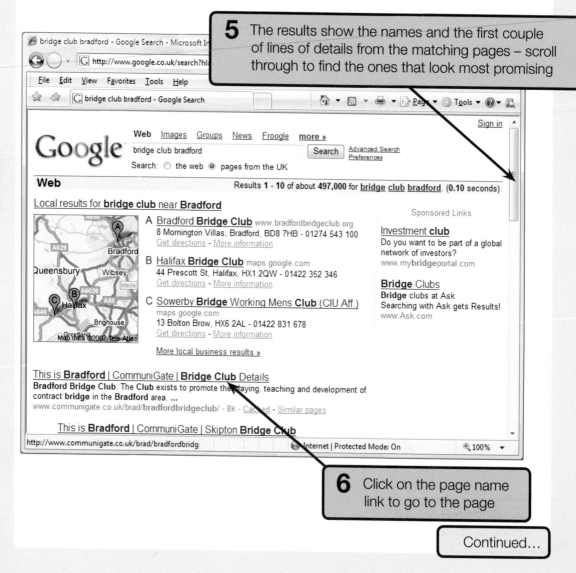

6 Click on the page name link to go to the page

Continued...

7 Click the **Back** button to return to Google if you want to follow up other links

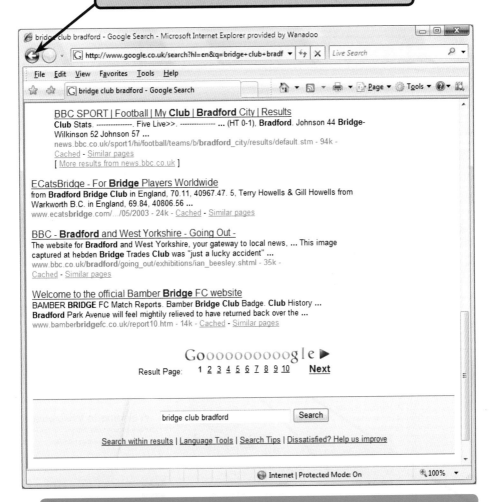

You will find a link to the next page at the bottom of the results listing, but as a general rule, if you don't see anything useful in the first page, subsequent pages are unlikely to be any better. Try a new search, with different words.

The Favorites Center

A favourite is an address stored in an easily managed list. To return to a favourite place you simply click on it in the list. Favourites can be accessed through the Favorites Center or the Favorites menu. We'll use the Center.

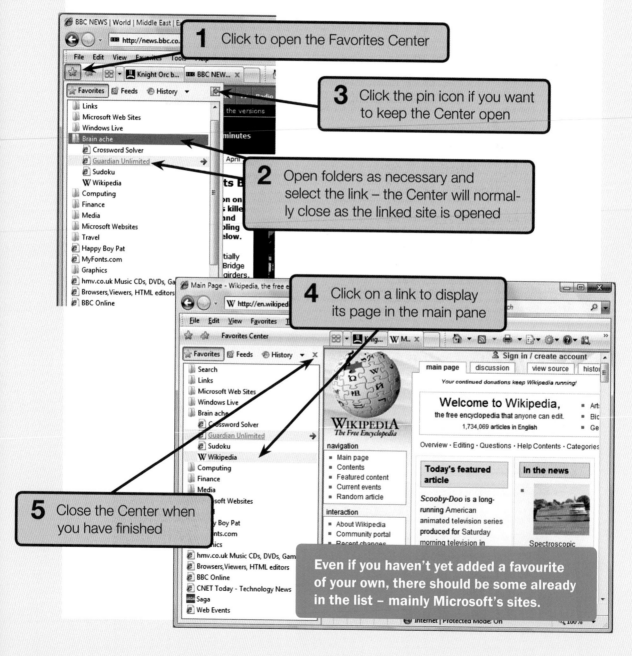

1 Click to open the Favorites Center

3 Click the pin icon if you want to keep the Center open

2 Open folders as necessary and select the link – the Center will normally close as the linked site is opened

4 Click on a link to display its page in the main pane

5 Close the Center when you have finished

Even if you haven't yet added a favourite of your own, there should be some already in the list – mainly Microsoft's sites.

Adding a Favorite

Addresses are a pain to type. One mistake and either you don't get there at all, or you find yourself at a totally unexpected site. (Try www.microsort.com or www. microsort.co.uk sometime.) Favorites are one way of being able to return to a site without having to retype its address.

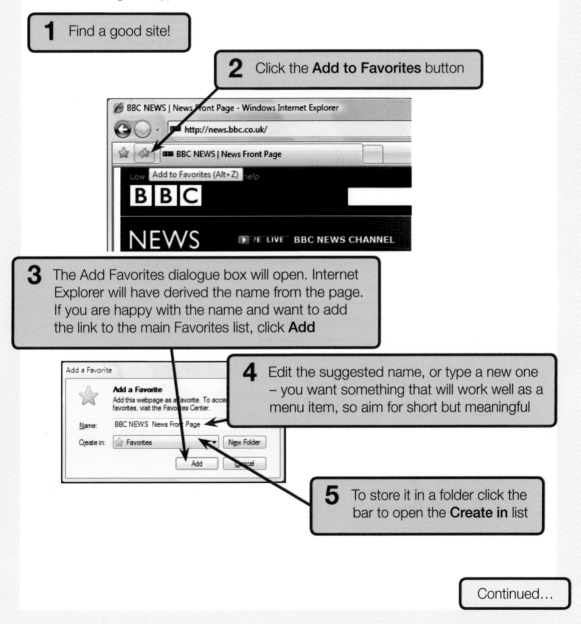

1 Find a good site!

2 Click the **Add to Favorites** button

3 The Add Favorites dialogue box will open. Internet Explorer will have derived the name from the page. If you are happy with the name and want to add the link to the main Favorites list, click **Add**

4 Edit the suggested name, or type a new one – you want something that will work well as a menu item, so aim for short but meaningful

5 To store it in a folder click the bar to open the **Create in** list

Continued...

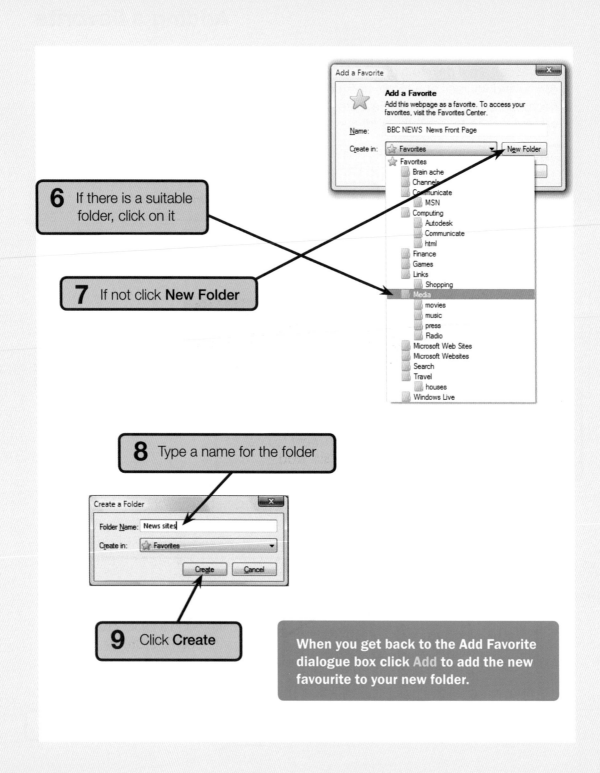

6 If there is a suitable folder, click on it

7 If not click **New Folder**

8 Type a name for the folder

9 Click **Create**

When you get back to the Add Favorite dialogue box click Add to add the new favourite to your new folder.

Organising your favourites

You can store your favourites in one simple list, but this soon gets unwieldy. If there are more than about 20 items, the list takes up too much screen space and it can be hard to find the favourite you want. The solution is to organise your favourites into folders. It's easy to create new folders and to move entries into them.

You can use the Favorites Center for this, but it is best done through the Organize Favorites dialogue box. This can only be opened from the Favorites menu – if the Menu bar is not visible, right-click on any toolbar and turn it on.

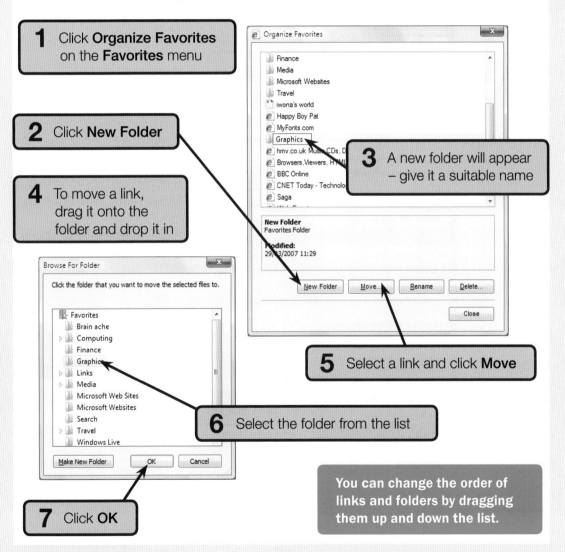

1 Click **Organize Favorites** on the **Favorites** menu

2 Click **New Folder**

4 To move a link, drag it onto the folder and drop it in

3 A new folder will appear – give it a suitable name

5 Select a link and click **Move**

6 Select the folder from the list

7 Click **OK**

You can change the order of links and folders by dragging them up and down the list.

Using History

As you browse, each page is recorded in the History list as an Internet shortcut – i.e. a link to the page. You can view the History list in the Favorites Center, and click on a link there to go to the page.

If you are online at the time, Internet Explorer will connect to the page. If you are off-line, it will display the page if all the necessary files are still available in the Temporary Internet Files folder, otherwise it will ask you to connect.

1 Open the Favorites Center

2 Click on the **History** button in the Center's toolbar

3 Click on the name to open the day and the site folders (if relevant in that view)

4 Click on a link

5 To close a folder, click on its name

6 Close the Favorites Center when you have finished

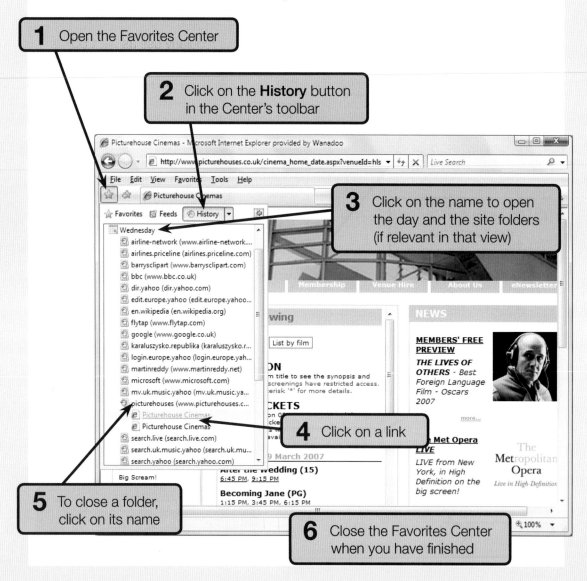

Viewing the History list

The History list can be viewed in four ways:

- **By Date** groups the links into folders by date and then by site. This is useful if you know when you were last there, but not the name of the site – and you may well not know where a page was if you reached it through a hyperlink.

- **By Site** groups the links into folders by site. This is probably the most convenient view most of the time.

- **By Most Visited** lists individual page links in the order that you visit them most. If there are search engines or directories that you regularly use as start points for browsing sessions, they will be up at the top of the list.

- **By Order Visited Today** lists the individual pages in simple time order. Use this view to backtrack past the links that are stored in the drop-down list of the Back button.

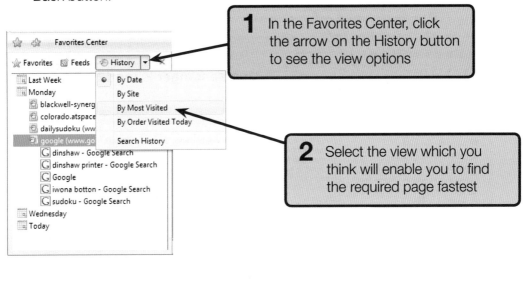

1 In the Favorites Center, click the arrow on the History button to see the view options

2 Select the view which you think will enable you to find the required page fastest

If the History list starts to get clogged up, you can delete sites or pages within sites. Right-click on the site or page and select Delete from the pop-up menu.

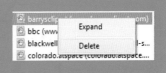

Searching the History list

If you have visited a lot of sites in the last few days, the History list may have so many entries that it is difficult to find a page, whichever view you use. When this happens, a search through the History list may be the answer.

1 Click the arrow on the **History** button in the Favorites Center and select **Search History** from the menu

2 Type a word that will be in the title or text of the page

3 Click **Search Now**

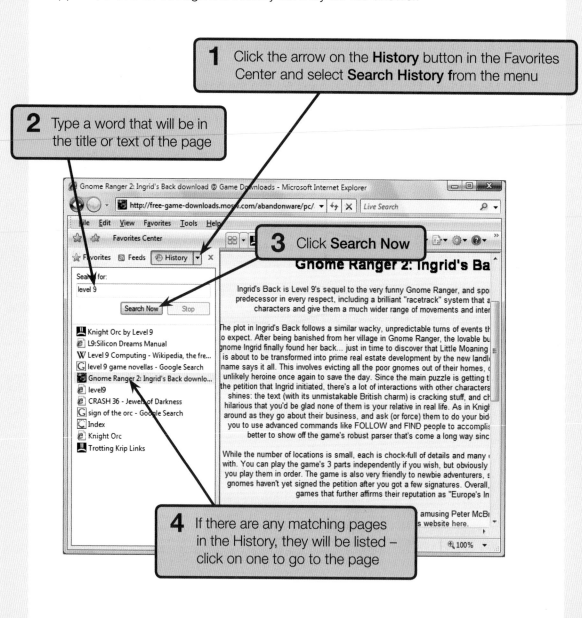

4 If there are any matching pages in the History, they will be listed – click on one to go to the page

Saving a web page

You sometimes find really interesting pages that you would like to have close at hand for future use – on- and offline. Saving a page stores the files on your PC, and if you save it as a web page, complete, all the files, including any images, sounds or videos will be saved.

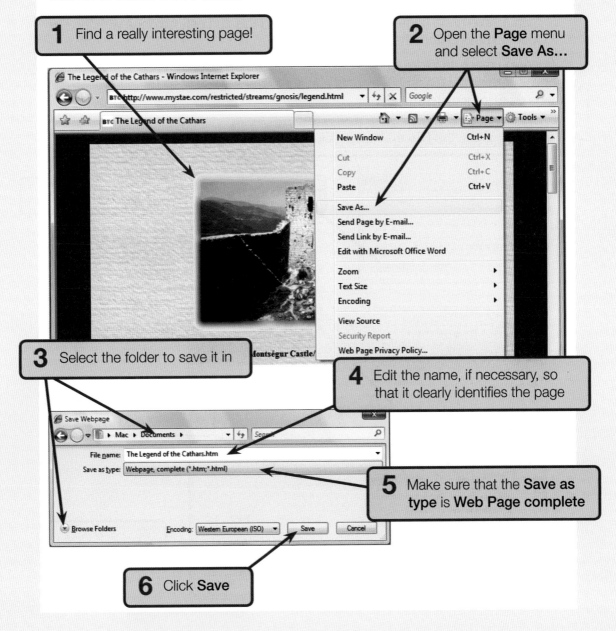

1 Find a really interesting page!

2 Open the **Page** menu and select **Save As...**

3 Select the folder to save it in

4 Edit the name, if necessary, so that it clearly identifies the page

5 Make sure that the **Save as type** is **Web Page complete**

6 Click **Save**

Opening a saved page

> If the Menu bar is not visible, you can bring it up just to select the command. Press [Alt] and it will appear – then disappear again after you have used it.

To read a saved web page you must open it, and this can only be done with the File > Open command from the Menu bar.

When you reach its folder, notice that as well as the page file (marked with an .htm extension), there will normally also be a folder of the same name. The page's images and other files are stored here.

1 Open the **File** menu and select **Open...**

2 At the **Open** dialogue box, click **Browse...**

3 At the dialogue box, locate the folder, where the file is stored

4 Select the file

5 Click **Open**

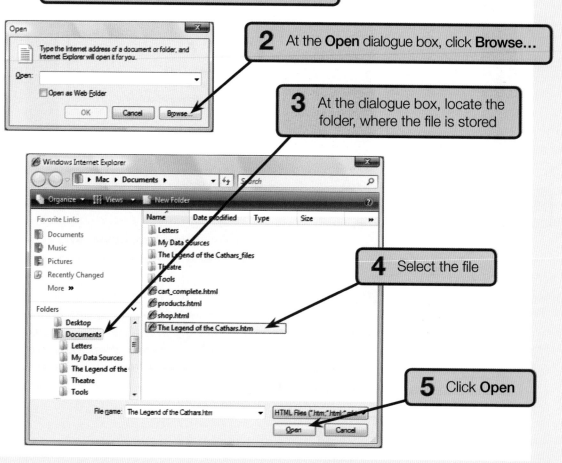

Saving a picture from a web page

If you come across a picture in a web page that you would like to keep for future viewing, it can easily be saved to a disk.

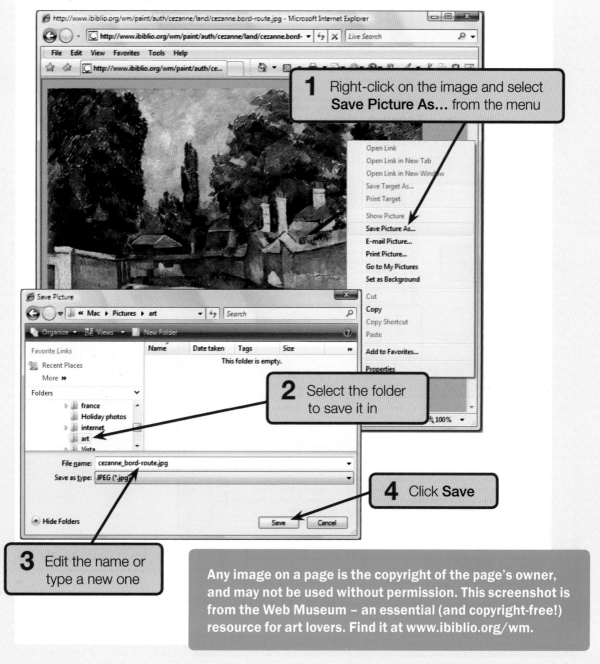

1 Right-click on the image and select **Save Picture As...** from the menu

2 Select the folder to save it in

3 Edit the name or type a new one

4 Click **Save**

Any image on a page is the copyright of the page's owner, and may not be used without permission. This screenshot is from the Web Museum – an essential (and copyright-free!) resource for art lovers. Find it at www.ibiblio.org/wm.

Saving text from a web page

There are two ways to save the text from a web page. You can save the page as a text file, but this may not be very successful. There are several ways of producing web pages, and with some of these, the Save routine will not save the visible text.

A second – and more reliable – method is to copy the text, paste it into a word processing program and save it from there.

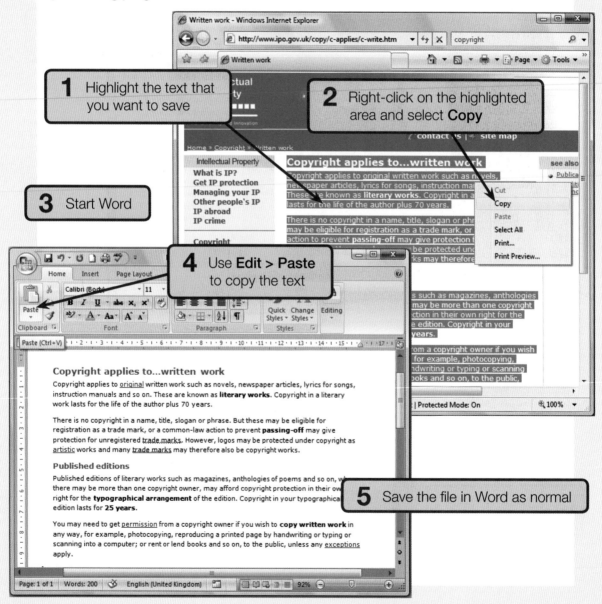

1 Highlight the text that you want to save

2 Right-click on the highlighted area and select **Copy**

3 Start Word

4 Use **Edit > Paste** to copy the text

5 Save the file in Word as normal

Using Print Preview

A sheet of A4 paper and a computer screen are different shapes, and pages can be laid out on the screen in different ways. This means that you can not be sure what a web page will look like when it is printed, or how many sheets it will need – unless you use Print Preview. If the preview looks good, you can print it straight away. If you need to adjust the layout to get a better printout, you can open the Page Setup dialogue box and change the settings.

1 Click the **Print** tool and select **Print Preview...**

4 Close the window to return to the normal display without printing

3 Click to print

Set the size of the text and images when printed

To adjust the page layout, click the **Page Setup** tool

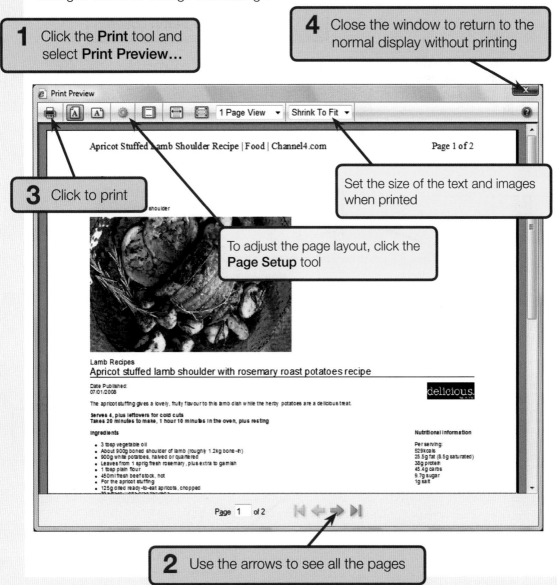

2 Use the arrows to see all the pages

Adjusting the Page Setup

The Page Setup controls how pages fit onto paper. The key features are the orientation, and the margins. The headers and footers can include plain text or details of the web pages – Internet Explorer automatically adds codes to display the page's title, address, page numbers and date. You can move or remove these, or add your own text.

1 If you are in Print Preview, click the **Page Setup** button.

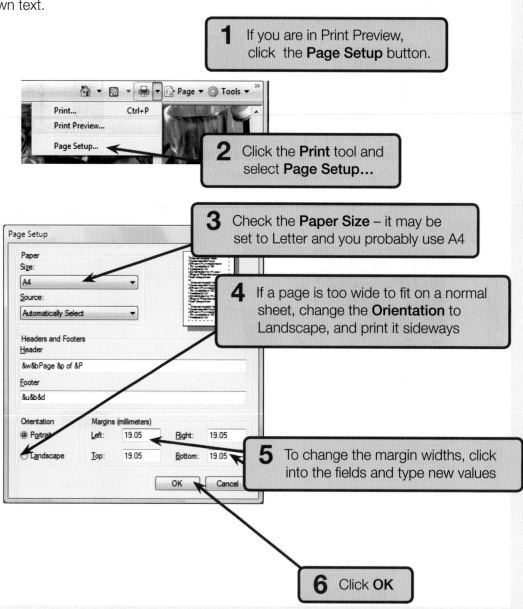

2 Click the **Print** tool and select **Page Setup...**

3 Check the **Paper Size** – it may be set to Letter and you probably use A4

4 If a page is too wide to fit on a normal sheet, change the **Orientation** to Landscape, and print it sideways

5 To change the margin widths, click into the fields and type new values

6 Click **OK**

Printing web pages

If you just want a printed copy of the whole of the current page, you simply click the Print button. Sometimes you need to control the printout – you may only want part of a long page or a section of a framed page, or you may want to print sideways on the paper (landscape orientation), or print several copies. In these cases, you need to go into the Print dialogue box.

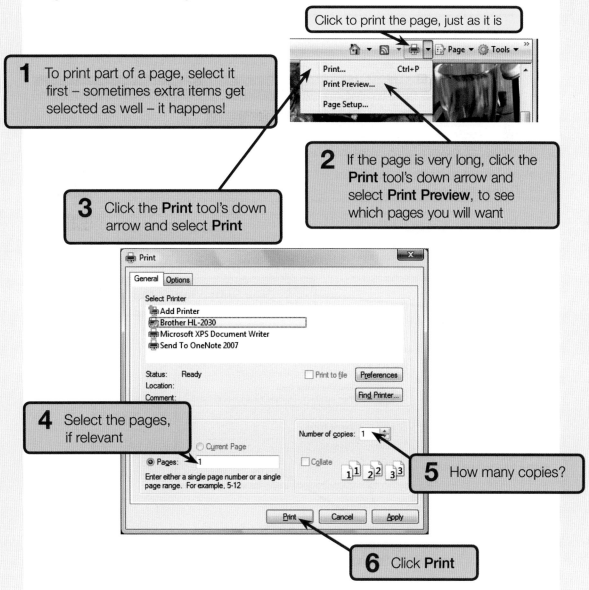

Click to print the page, just as it is

1 To print part of a page, select it first – sometimes extra items get selected as well – it happens!

2 If the page is very long, click the **Print** tool's down arrow and select **Print Preview**, to see which pages you will want

3 Click the **Print** tool's down arrow and select **Print**

4 Select the pages, if relevant

5 How many copies?

6 Click **Print**

Feeds

We met feeds earlier when we were looking at gadgets (see p. 55), but they are mainly intended to be read through the browser. Here's how to get feeds into Internet Explorer.

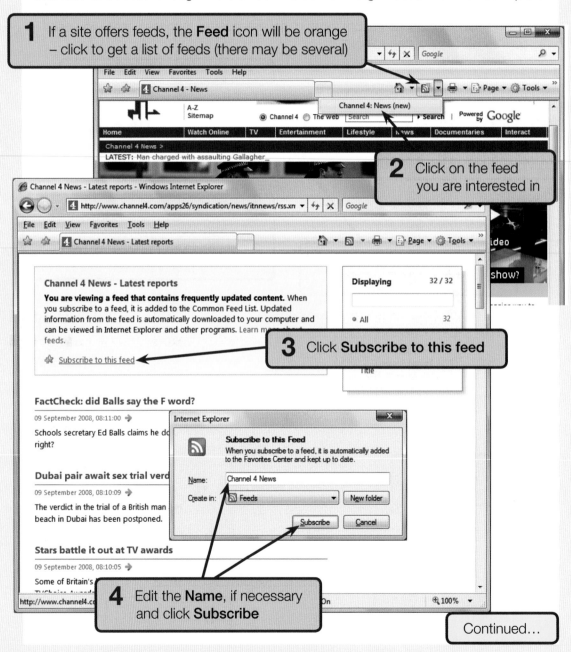

1 If a site offers feeds, the **Feed** icon will be orange – click to get a list of feeds (there may be several)

2 Click on the feed you are interested in

3 Click **Subscribe to this feed**

4 Edit the **Name**, if necessary and click **Subscribe**

Continued...

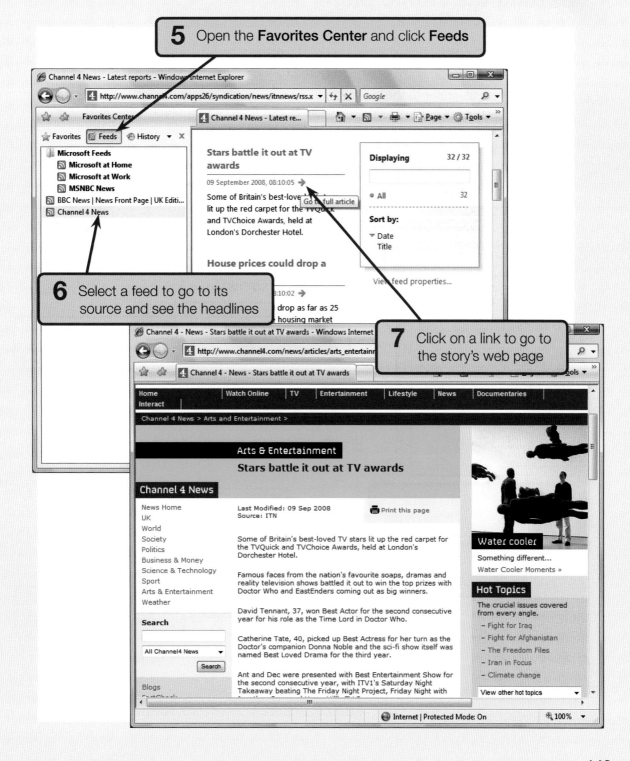

5 Open the **Favorites Center** and click **Feeds**

6 Select a feed to go to its source and see the headlines

7 Click on a link to go to the story's web page

Setting the Home page

There are many ways to customise Internet Explorer, and the first of these is to set your home page.

'Home page' can refer to the top page at a website, but it also means the page that the browser connects to when you first go online. The default home page is at MSN (MicroSoft Network) or at your internet service provider's site. You can change it, any time you like, to any other site, e.g. your favourite search engine, or it can be left blank, if you tend to start at a different site each time you go online.

1 If there is a site that you want to use as your home page, go to it now

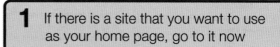

2 Click the **Tools** button and select **Internet Options...**

3 The dialogue box will open with the General tab on top – the Home Page is the first option

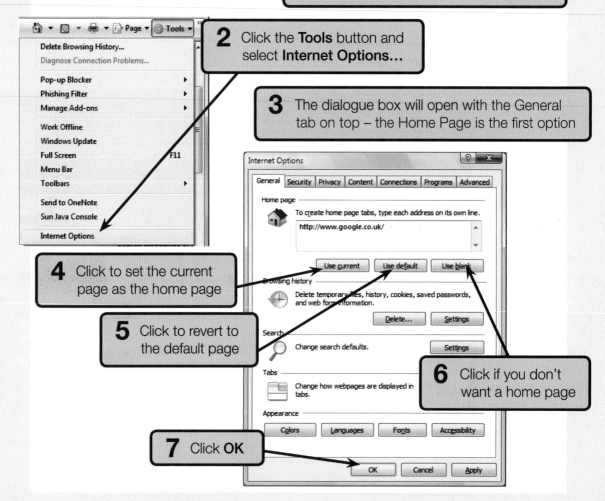

4 Click to set the current page as the home page

5 Click to revert to the default page

6 Click if you don't want a home page

7 Click **OK**

Customising the Command Bar

The contents and appearance of the Command Bar can be altered to suit your needs. You can add or remove tools, set the size of the icons and choose whether to show text labels on all tools, on a selected few, or on none.

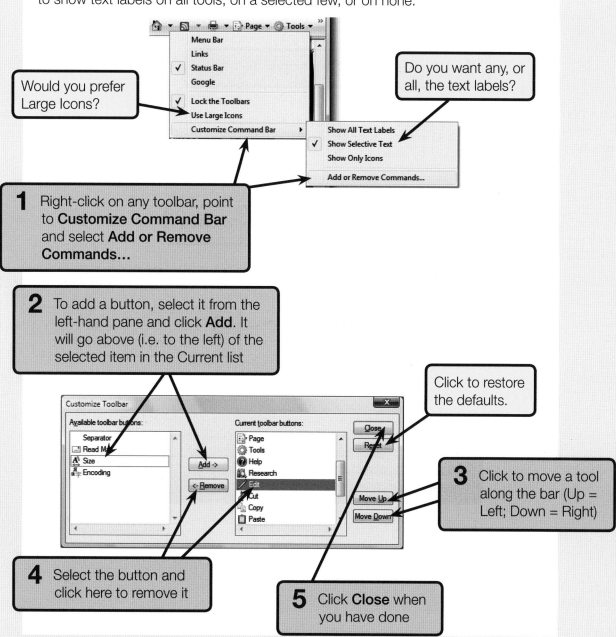

Would you prefer Large Icons?

Do you want any, or all, the text labels?

1 Right-click on any toolbar, point to **Customize Command Bar** and select **Add or Remove Commands...**

2 To add a button, select it from the left-hand pane and click **Add**. It will go above (i.e. to the left) of the selected item in the Current list

Click to restore the defaults.

3 Click to move a tool along the bar (Up = Left; Down = Right)

4 Select the button and click here to remove it

5 Click **Close** when you have done

Setting the text size

The basic size of the text on a web page is set by its creator, but you can make it larger or smaller to suit yourself with the commands on the Page button menu. You may want to increase the text size for one site, but reduce it on another – people have different ideas about what makes a page good to look at and easy to read!

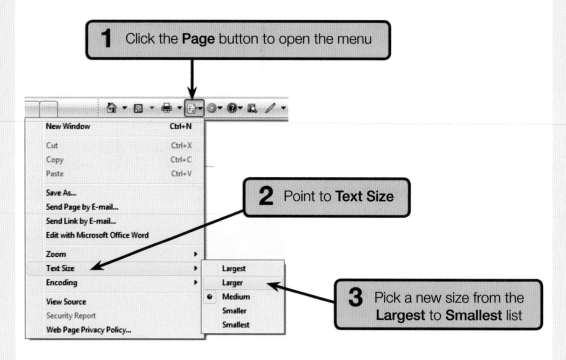

1 Click the **Page** button to open the menu

2 Point to **Text Size**

3 Pick a new size from the **Largest** to **Smallest** list

The size change is applied to the different levels of headings as well as to the main text, with everything being made proportionately larger or smaller.

The Security options

There would be fewer security problems if all web pages were simply displays of text and images, but some are more than this. They can contain active elements, which make pages more interesting, but also let malicious people create problems for others. These elements are small programs written in languages such as Java and ActiveX, and may be essential for the page to work properly – Java is often used to create pop-up menus for navigating around a site, while ActiveX controls are regularly used by online banks and retailers to create secure connections.

The options on the Security tab let you control whether, and when, these programs are allowed to run. If you disable them, you will not be able to use some useful and safe sites. If you allow them to run on any page, one day you may find that a program has got into your PC and erased files, or otherwise messed with the system.

The default levels set different restrictions depending upon whether a page is on the Internet in general, a local intranet, a Trusted site or a Restricted site. For each zone, you can accept the default settings or set your own levels. To start with, check that the default settings are in place.

1 Use **Tools > Internet Options...** to open the dialogue box

2 Switch to the **Security** tab

3 Click on each in turn to check the levels

The **Internet** zone should be set to **Medium-high**

If you have access to an intranet, check that it is set to **Medium-low**

Initially there won't be any **Trusted** or **Restricted** sites.

4 If the levels have been changed, click **Reset all zones to the default level**

5 Click **OK**

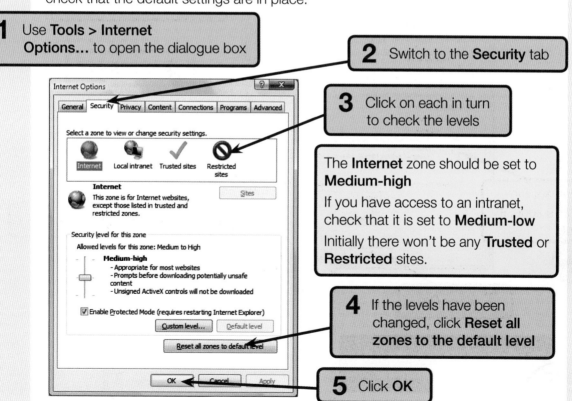

Security zones

The Trusted and Restricted zones are lists of sites. Initially these lists are empty – it's up to you to add sites to them, though you may never feel the need.

A site should be added to the Trusted zone if it has active content that cannot run under the standard Internet zone security level – you will be told if this is the case – and which is owned by an organisation that you trust implicitly, e.g. your bank.

A site should be added to the Restricted zone if you want to be able to go to it, but are not convinced that the standard Internet zone level is sufficiently secure.

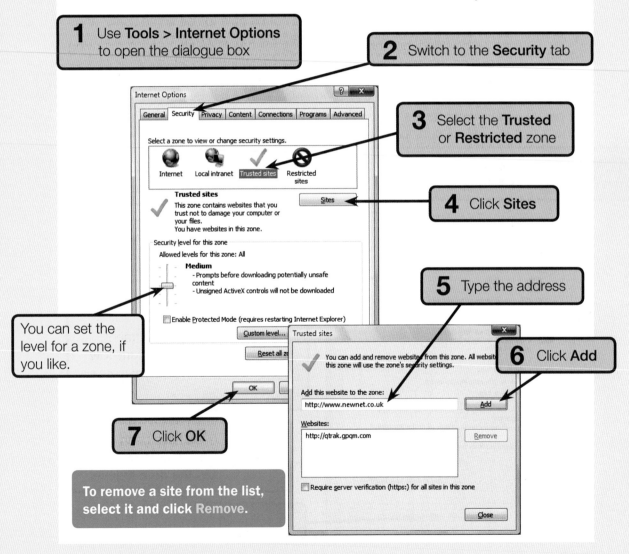

1 Use **Tools > Internet Options** to open the dialogue box

2 Switch to the **Security** tab

3 Select the **Trusted** or **Restricted** zone

4 Click **Sites**

5 Type the address

6 Click **Add**

You can set the level for a zone, if you like.

7 Click **OK**

To remove a site from the list, select it and click Remove.

Controlling cookies

Cookies are small files that a website stores on your computer's hard disk, and which can be read by that site. Some sites use them to offer a 'personalised page' service – one which is tailored to your interests or needs – and here the cookie will hold the options and other details that you set. Some sites use cookies to keep track of their visitors, recording when they visited and which pages they viewed. Some use cookies to build a database of their visitors' activities and preferences, and may sell this information on to other firms.

Internet Explorer offers several levels of protection from cookies, but you can also control them yourself.

- They can be disabled, but this can create problems. It will stop you from having personalised pages, and there are some sites that you cannot use at all if you have disabled cookies.

- You can ask for a prompt before a cookie is set. This way you can choose not to accept cookies from a site, but some irritating sites want to write cookies for every new page – sometimes for every image – that you download.

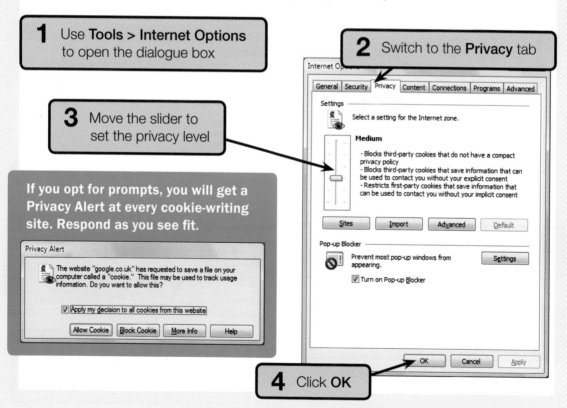

1 Use **Tools > Internet Options** to open the dialogue box

2 Switch to the **Privacy** tab

3 Move the slider to set the privacy level

If you opt for prompts, you will get a Privacy Alert at every cookie-writing site. Respond as you see fit.

4 Click **OK**

Pop-ups

Blocking pop-ups

Pop-ups are windows that open on top of the Internet Explorer display. They usually have no menu bar, toolbar or other controls, and are typically quite small. Pop-ups are often used to carry adverts, and can be irritating, which is why Internet Explorer lets you block them. They are also used to provide extra information or services off the main page – which is why there is a way to allow pop-ups past the block.

1 Use **Tools > Internet Options** to open the dialogue box

2 Switch to the **Privacy** tab

3 Turn on the **Pop-up Blocker**

4 Click **Settings**

5 Tick **Play a sound...** if you want to know when a pop-up is blocked

6 If you might to allow some pop-ups tick **Show Information Bar...**

7 Set the **Filter Level** to High – if this blocks too much, go back and set it to Medium

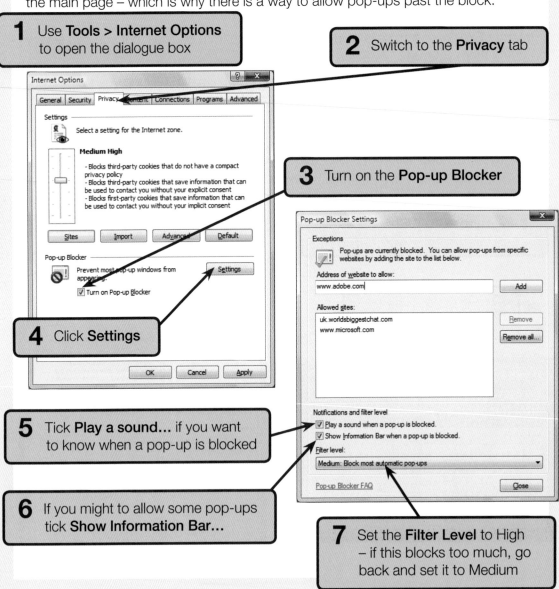

Allowing pop-ups

You may find, especially if the pop-up filter level is set to high, that you cannot use some pages properly – you click on a link and nothing happens (apart from the pop-up blocked sound). If the Information Bar is open, you can allow the pop-ups – either for just the current page or for the site every time you visit. You can also add sites to a list of exceptions so that their pop-ups are always allowed.

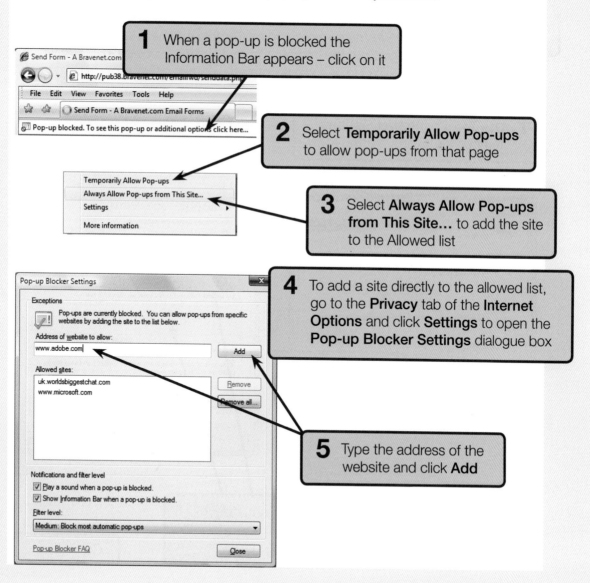

1 When a pop-up is blocked the Information Bar appears – click on it

2 Select **Temporarily Allow Pop-ups** to allow pop-ups from that page

3 Select **Always Allow Pop-ups from This Site...** to add the site to the Allowed list

4 To add a site directly to the allowed list, go to the **Privacy** tab of the **Internet Options** and click **Settings** to open the **Pop-up Blocker Settings** dialogue box

5 Type the address of the website and click **Add**

Content Advisor

Set Content options

If children can access the Internet through your PC, you may want to use Content Advisor to limit the sites that they can visit. This works through a system of ratings, and initially uses those set by RSACi – Recreational Standards Advisory Council (internet), which rate sites on language, nudity, sex and violence. You can set the level for each of these, and only sites within those limits will then be accessible.

There is a problem – the system is voluntary and many perfectly safe sites do not have a RSACi rating. It was never accepted as the sole Internet standard and RSACi has recently been merged into the Internet Content Rating Association (ICRA) which uses a different form of filtering. If a site is unrated, you can either allow free access or control access through a password.

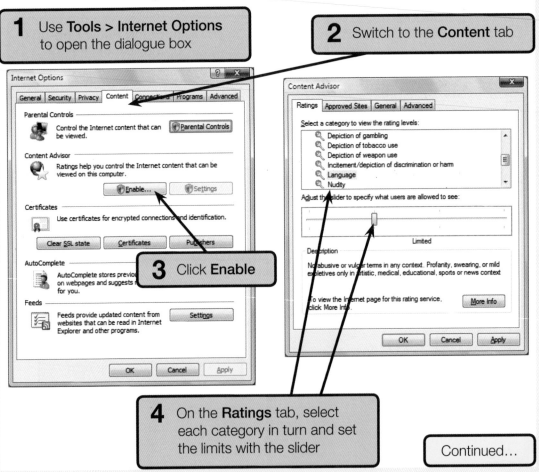

1 Use **Tools > Internet Options** to open the dialogue box

2 Switch to the **Content** tab

3 Click **Enable**

4 On the **Ratings** tab, select each category in turn and set the limits with the slider

Continued...

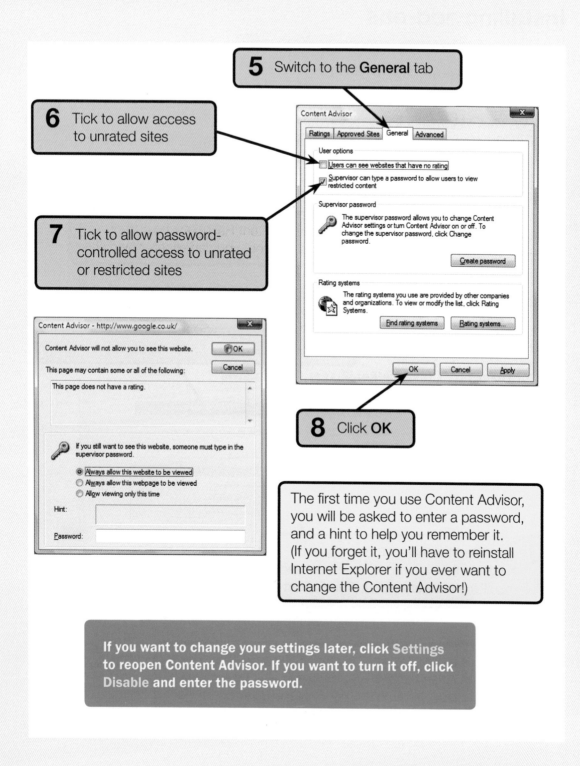

5 Switch to the **General** tab

6 Tick to allow access to unrated sites

7 Tick to allow password-controlled access to unrated or restricted sites

Content Advisor

Ratings | Approved Sites | General | Advanced

User options

☐ Users can see websites that have no rating

☑ Supervisor can type a password to allow users to view restricted content

Supervisor password

The supervisor password allows you to change Content Advisor settings or turn Content Advisor on or off. To change the supervisor password, click Change password.

Create password

Rating systems

The rating systems you use are provided by other companies and organizations. To view or modify the list, click Rating Systems.

Find rating systems | Rating systems...

OK | Cancel | Apply

Content Advisor - http://www.google.co.uk/

Content Advisor will not allow you to see this website.

OK

This page may contain some or all of the following:

Cancel

This page does not have a rating.

If you still want to see this website, someone must type in the supervisor password.

◉ Always allow this website to be viewed
◯ Always allow this webpage to be viewed
◯ Allow viewing only this time

Hint:

Password:

8 Click **OK**

The first time you use Content Advisor, you will be asked to enter a password, and a hint to help you remember it. (If you forget it, you'll have to reinstall Internet Explorer if you ever want to change the Content Advisor!)

If you want to change your settings later, click Settings to reopen Content Advisor. If you want to turn it off, click Disable and enter the password.

Installing add-ons

Browsers can display only formatted text and GIF and JPG graphics; but add-ons extend the range of files that they can handle. These are extensions to the browser, not independent applications. Some are present from the start, others can be downloaded from their manufacturer when they are needed. Whenever you meet a file that needs an add-on, it will normally be accompanied by a link that you can use to get the software. How you download and install the add-on varies, but normally the process is straightforward and there are clear instructions. Here, for example, is what happens when you install RealPlayer.

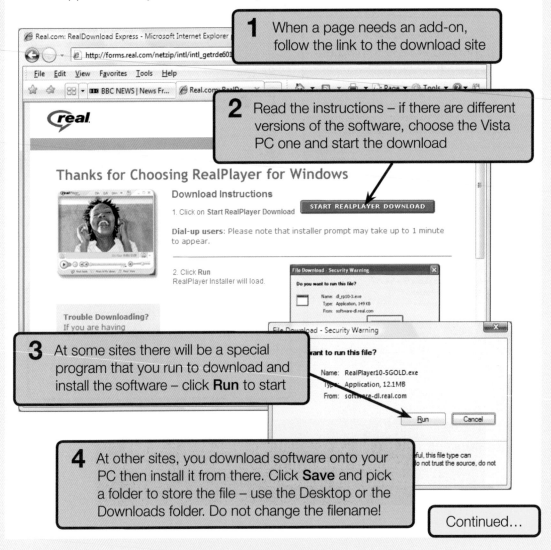

1 When a page needs an add-on, follow the link to the download site

2 Read the instructions – if there are different versions of the software, choose the Vista PC one and start the download

3 At some sites there will be a special program that you run to download and install the software – click **Run** to start

4 At other sites, you download software onto your PC then install it from there. Click **Save** and pick a folder to store the file – use the Desktop or the Downloads folder. Do not change the filename!

Continued…

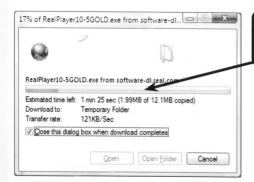

5 Wait while the file downloads – with broadband, this rarely takes long!

6 Installation should start automatically. If it does not, locate the file on the Desktop or in the Download folder and double-click on it to start the installer.

7 You will be asked if to confirm you want to install the software – agree!

8 You may be asked to configure the software to your system. Set the options, leaving at the default any that you do not understand.

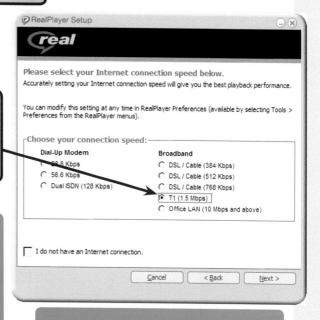

Add-ons are almost always free. Their manufacturers make money by charging for the applications that create the files that the add-ons play, or by selling de-luxe versions with more and better features.

Only install add-ons when they are offered by established sites and which come from trusted sources. They could carry viruses.

Adobe Reader

Adobe Reader is one add-on that you really should have, as it is what you need to view and print PDF documents. People use PDFs for booklets and brochures, for books (this one went to the printer's as a PDF), for paper sculpture kits – in fact, for any document where well-formatted text and images are needed.

1 When you try to open a PDF file on a web page you should find a link to get the Adobe Reader Plug-in – click it

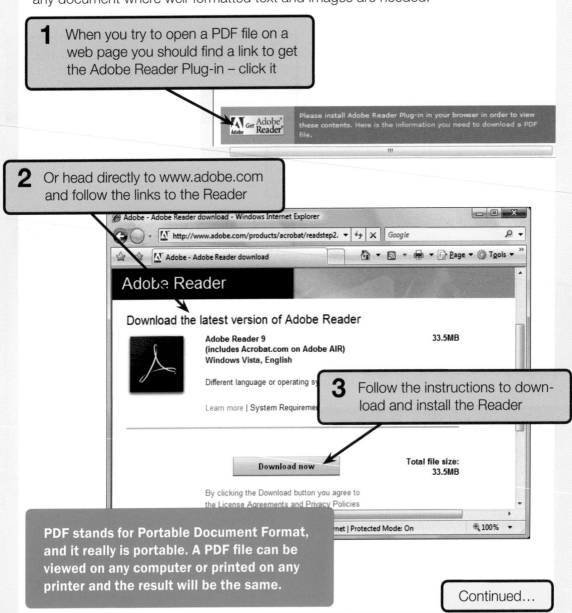

Please install Adobe Reader Plug-in in your browser in order to view these contents. Here is the information you need to download a PDF file.

2 Or head directly to www.adobe.com and follow the links to the Reader

Adobe - Adobe Reader download - Windows Internet Explorer

http://www.adobe.com/products/acrobat/readstep2.

Google

Adobe - Adobe Reader download

Page ▼ Tools ▼

Adobe Reader

Download the latest version of Adobe Reader

Adobe Reader 9
(includes Acrobat.com on Adobe AIR)
Windows Vista, English

33.5MB

Different language or operating s

Learn more | System Requireme

3 Follow the instructions to download and install the Reader

Download now

Total file size:
33.5MB

By clicking the Download button you agree to the License Agreements and Privacy Policies

net | Protected Mode: On

100%

PDF stands for Portable Document Format, and it really is portable. A PDF file can be viewed on any computer or printed on any printer and the result will be the same.

Continued...

4 When you next come across a PDF file,
Reader will start up inside Internet Explorer

Use Reader's toolbar buttons to work with the document

Print

Save a copy

Move through pages

Zoom controls

Show full width of screen

Shrink the page to fit the window

Search the text

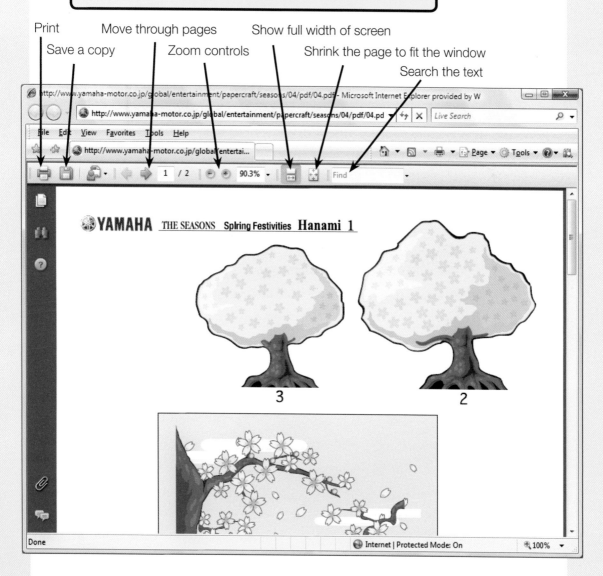

4 Communicating online

I'm assuming that you have an e-mail account already set up, through your Internet service provider. If you haven't yet, then you really do need to!

This chapter covers:

- Windows Mail and e-mail software
- The Mail layout and elements
- How to send and receive e-mail messages
- Formatting and stationery
- How to send and receive images and other files by e-mail
- E-mail addresses and using your Contacts folder
- How to customise Mail to suit your way of working
- The key options and settings

E-mail

The World Wide Web may well be the most glamorous aspect of the Internet and the one that grabs newcomers, but e-mail is the aspect that many people find the most useful in the long run. It is quick, reliable and simple to use.

- E-mail is quick. When you send a message to someone, it will normally reach their mailbox within minutes – and usually within half an hour. However, it will only be read when the recipient collects the mail, and that may be anything from a few minutes later to when they get back from holiday.

- E-mail is reliable. As long as you have the address right, the message is almost certain to get through. And on those rare occasions when it doesn't, you will usually get it back with an 'undeliverable' note attached.

- E-mail is simple to use. You can learn the essential skills in minutes – as you will see very shortly!

How does e-mail work?

When you send an e-mail message, it does not go direct to your recipient, as a phone call does. Instead it will travel through a dozen or more computers before arriving at its destination – in the same way that snail mail passes through several post offices and depots.

- The message goes first to the mail server at your ISP. This will work out which computer to send it to, to help it towards its destination. The server will normally hold the message briefly, while it assembles a handful of messages to send to the next place – in the same way that the Post Office sorts and bags its mail.

- Each mail server along the way will do the same thing, bundling the message with others heading in the same direction. This method gives more efficient internet traffic and at the cost of very little delay – most messages will normally be delivered in less than an hour.

- Your recipients may not read the message within the hour. The delivery is to their mail boxes at their service providers. People only get their e-mail when they go online to collect it. (Though with a broadband account and automated collection it can feel as if it is delivered.)

> **If you understand how e-mail works, you can use it more efficiently and are less likely to get fazed when things don't quite go according to plan!**

File formats

E-mail messages are sent as text files. A plain text message will normally be very short, as it takes only one byte to represent a character – (plus about 10 per cent more for error-checking). A ten-line message, for example, will make a file of around 1 Kb, and that can be transmitted in a fraction of a second. Images, video clips and other files can be sent by e-mail (see p. 241) but they must first be converted into text format. You don't need to worry about how this is done, as Windows Mail does all the conversion automatically. What you do need to know is that conversion increases the size of files by around 50 per cent, so even quite small images can significantly increase the time it takes to send or receive messages.

E-mail jargon

Error-checking – the techniques used to make sure that data sent over the Internet arrives intact. If a block of data is damaged, it is sent again.

ISP (Internet service provider) – the company that supplies your connection to the Internet.

Mail server – computer that stores and handles e-mail.

Plain text – text without any layout or font formatting.

Snail mail – hand-delivered by the postman.

Exploring Windows Mail

Most of the elements of the Windows Mail display are optional, so your screen may well look very different from mine. Try to identify as many of the labelled elements as you can – just don't worry if you can't find some of them.

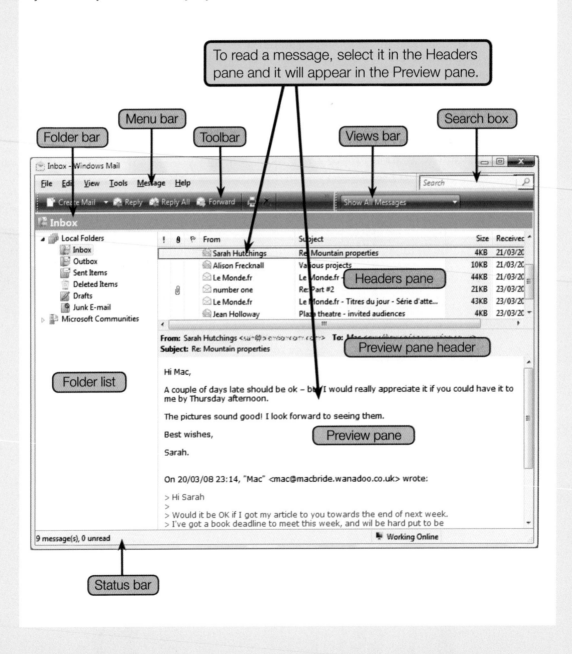

- The **Views bar** lets you switch between displaying all messages and those you have not yet read. The options are also available on the View menu.

- The **Folder bar** shows the name of the current folder.

- The **Folder list** shows your e-mail and news folders. New e-mail folders can be created if needed, and newsgroup folders are created automatically when you subscribe to groups. The contents of the current folder are displayed in the Headers area.

- The **Headers pane** is the only part of the display which is not optional, but even here you can control the layout and which items are displayed.

- The **Preview pane** displays the current message from the Headers area. If this pane is turned off, messages are displayed in a new window. The pane can sit below or beside the Headers – below is usually more convenient.

- The **Preview pane header** repeats the From and Subject details from the Headers area.

- The **Status bar**, as always, helps to keep you informed of what's going on. Amongst other things, it tells you how many messages are in a folder, and shows the addresses behind hyperlinks in e-mails.

Exploring the toolbar

Windows Mail has a lot of commands that most of us will rarely use, and if you don't join the newsgroups (which few people use nowadays), there are some that you will never use at all. In practice, all the commands that you will use regularly can be found on buttons on the toolbar.

- **Create Mail** starts a new message in plain text or with the default formatting, or click the arrow to drop down a list and select your Stationery (see page 171).

- **Reply** starts a new message to the sender of the current message.

- **Reply All** sends a reply to all the people who had copies of the message.

- **Forward** copies the message into the New Message window, ready for you to send it on to another person, adding your own comments if you like.

- **Print** prints the current message, using the default printer settings.

- **Delete** moves the selected message(s) to the Deleted Items folder. Like the Recycle Bin, this allows you to recover items deleted by mistake. They are only properly removed when you delete them from the Deleted Items folder.

- **Send/Receive** sends anything in the Outbox and picks up any new mail. If there's a message in your Outbox that you do not want to send yet, e.g. one with a big attachment that will take a long time to send, click the down arrow and select Receive All from the short menu. If you want to send a message but do not have time to deal with incoming mail, click the arrow and select Send All.

- **Contacts** opens your Contacts folder, to add a new contact, or to manage existing ones.

- **Find** will search through your stored messages, on the basis of the sender, subject, text within the message, date or other factors.

You can change the selection of buttons in the toolbar, and adjust its appearance. See page 183.

Picking up your mail

Unlike snail mail, e-mail does not get delivered directly to you. Instead, it goes into a mailbox at the provider and you must go online to get it. You can set Windows Mail to check for new mail automatically on start-up and/or at regular intervals while you are online, or you can pick up your mail when you feel like it.

New mail is placed into the Inbox folder, and its sender, subject and other details will be listed, in bold, in the Headers area. Select a message to read it.

1 If you are not online already, get connected now

If the message is clearly junk, delete it immediately

2 Click the **Send/Receive** button or click its drop-down arrow and select **Receive All**

3 Wait a moment for the messages to come in

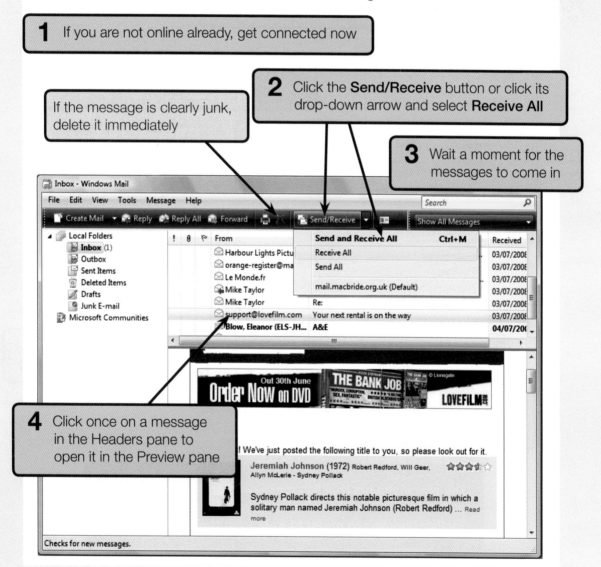

4 Click once on a message in the Headers pane to open it in the Preview pane

Adjusting the layout

There are several ways in which you can customise your display. The first of these is to select the screen elements that you want to include in the layout. This is done in the Window Layout Properties dialogue box. Simply add or clear the ticks to turn elements on and off.

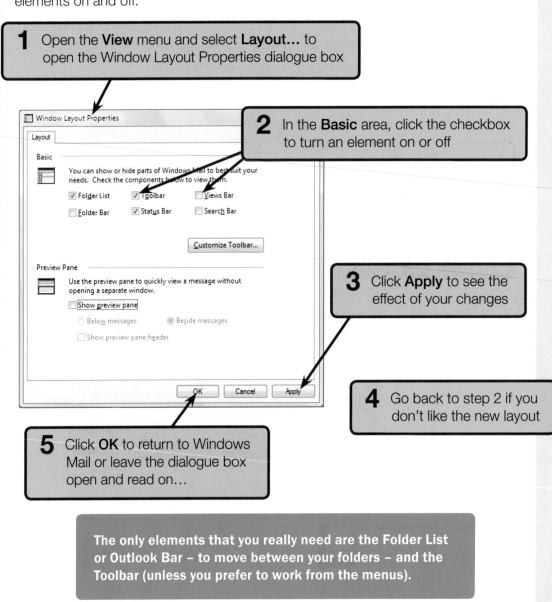

1 Open the **View** menu and select **Layout...** to open the Window Layout Properties dialogue box

2 In the **Basic** area, click the checkbox to turn an element on or off

3 Click **Apply** to see the effect of your changes

4 Go back to step 2 if you don't like the new layout

5 Click **OK** to return to Windows Mail or leave the dialogue box open and read on...

The only elements that you really need are the Folder List or Outlook Bar – to move between your folders – and the Toolbar (unless you prefer to work from the menus).

Controlling the Preview pane

The Preview pane is optional – a message can also be opened into its own window. If the pane is present, it automatically displays whatever message is selected in the Headers pane. This can be useful, but it can cause problems – it all depends on how much spam (junk mail) you get and how good your Internet service provider is at filtering out messages that contain viruses. If spam and viruses are not a worry, then the Preview pane can be used safely. If not, turn the pane off so that you control which messages are opened.

1 Open the Window Layout Properties dialogue box

2 Click the checkbox to turn the Preview pane on or off

If the pane is on…

3 Turn on the preview pane header if you want it – it repeats the From and Subject information from the Headers pane

4 Select where the pane is to go – below is generally better as you can read the whole width of the message without scrolling

5 Click **OK**

Window Layout Properties

Layout

Basic

You can show or hide parts of Windows Mail to best suit your needs. Check the components below to view them.

☑ Folder List ☑ Toolbar ☐ Views Bar
☐ Folder Bar ☑ Status Bar ☐ Search Bar

Customize Toolbar...

Preview Pane

Use the preview pane to quickly view a message without opening a separate window.

☑ Show preview pane

○ Below messages ● Beside messages

☐ Show preview pane header

OK Cancel Apply

Writing a message

Messages are written in the New Message window. The main part of this is the writing area, but in the top part of the window there are several boxes:

- **To:** is the address of the recipient(s).

- **Cc:** (carbon copy) is for the addresses of those people, if any, to whom you want to send copies.

- You can also have **Bcc:** (blind carbon copy) recipients. These people will not be listed, as the To and Cc recipients will be, at the top of the message.

- **Subject**: a few words to describe your message, so that your recipients know what's coming.

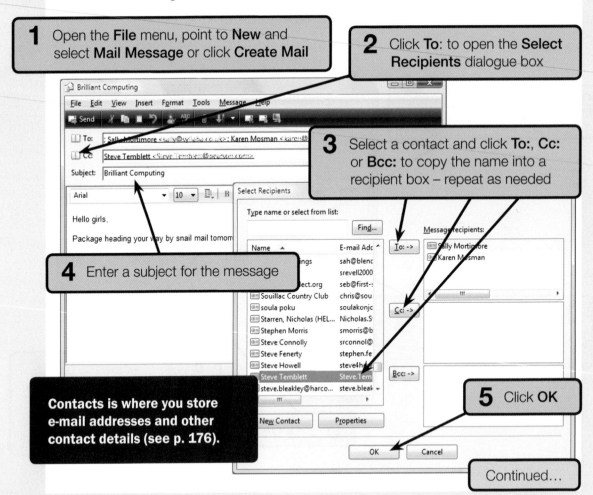

1 Open the **File** menu, point to **New** and select **Mail Message** or click **Create Mail**

2 Click **To:** to open the **Select Recipients** dialogue box

3 Select a contact and click **To:**, **Cc:** or **Bcc:** to copy the name into a recipient box – repeat as needed

4 Enter a subject for the message

Contacts is where you store e-mail addresses and other contact details (see p. 176).

5 Click **OK**

Continued...

Sending

A message can be sent straight after it has been written, or stored in the Outbox to be sent later. If you have a broadband connection, you will normally be online while you are writing the messages, and send them immediately. If you connect through the normal phone line, being online ties up the phone and (probably) costs money. In this case, it would be better to write your messages offline, store them in the Outbox then send all the new ones in one batch.

You can set the options so that either the Send button will send immediately or it will store messages. If you want to handle a message differently, there are Send and Send Later commands.

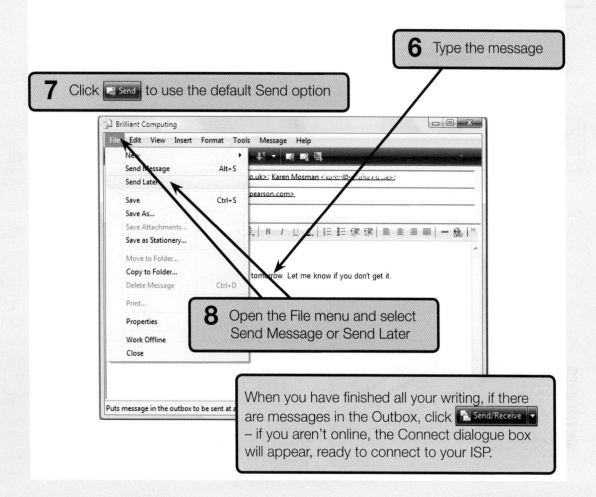

6 Type the message

7 Click ⬛ Send to use the default Send option

8 Open the File menu and select Send Message or Send Later

When you have finished all your writing, if there are messages in the Outbox, click ⬛ Send/Receive ▾ – if you aren't online, the Connect dialogue box will appear, ready to connect to your ISP.

Formatting a message

An e-mail message can have plain or formatted text. Formatting offers the normal range of fonts, size, style, colour and alignment options. You can insert images, or text from other documents, and you can also write hyperlinks into a message, so that your reader can go straight to a web page.

To use formatting, the New Message window must be in Rich Text (HTML) mode – if it is, the Formatting toolbar will be present. If you didn't set HTML as the default in the options (see p. 189), you can switch to it before writing the message.

1 If you can't see the Formatting toolbar, open the **Format** menu and select **Rich Text (HTML)**

2 Select the text to format

3 Use the toolbar buttons

4 Or open the **Format** menu and select **Font**

6 Click **OK**

5 At the **Font** dialogue box, define the font style, size and colour

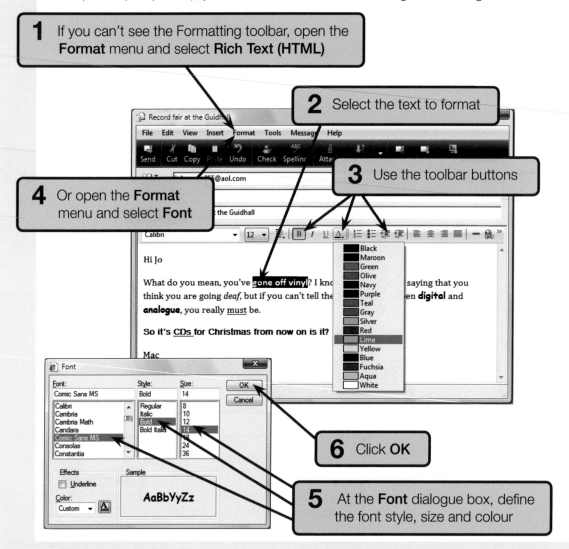

Using stationery

Stationery gives a coordinated text colour and background to a message. You can start a new message using stationery or apply it to an existing message.

Start with stationery

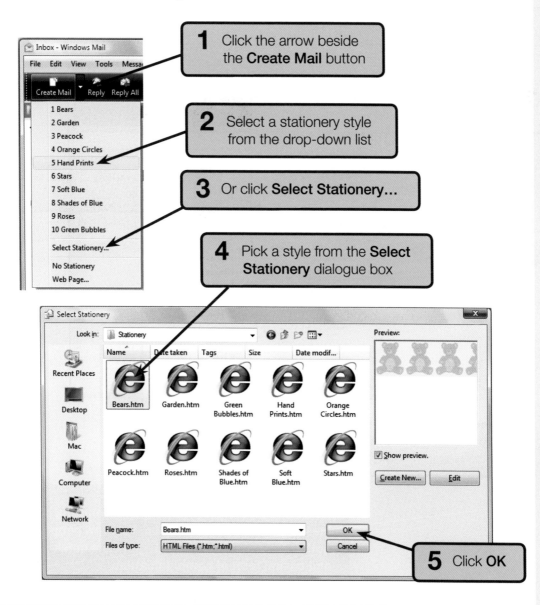

1 Click the arrow beside the **Create Mail** button

2 Select a stationery style from the drop-down list

3 Or click **Select Stationery...**

4 Pick a style from the **Select Stationery** dialogue box

5 Click **OK**

Apply stationery to a message

If you want to use stationery (or to change the style) after you have written the message, that's not a problem.

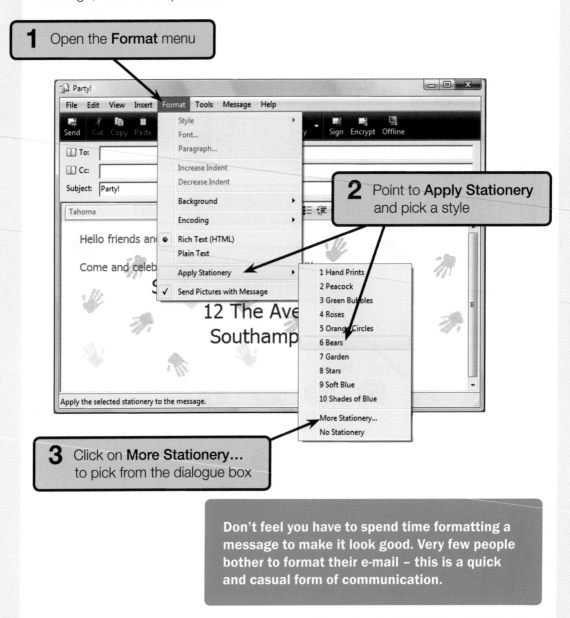

1 Open the **Format** menu

2 Point to **Apply Stationery** and pick a style

3 Click on **More Stationery...** to pick from the dialogue box

> Don't feel you have to spend time formatting a message to make it look good. Very few people bother to format their e-mail – this is a quick and casual form of communication.

Spell-checking a message

Even though e-mail is a casual form of communication, spell-checking is still worthwhile – some mistypes can be causes of great confusion! You can opt for automatic spell-checking, or run the spell-checker when you are ready.

Windows Mail has a good dictionary, but names and some technical terms may be missing. You can add words to your own dictionary so that spell-checker does not treat them as errors the next time around.

1 If automatic spell-checking is turned on, the check will start when you click Send. Otherwise click to start it

2 When the checker meets a word it does not recognise, it will ask you what to do

3 Click **Ignore** to leave it as you wrote it, or **Ignore All** if the word occurs several times

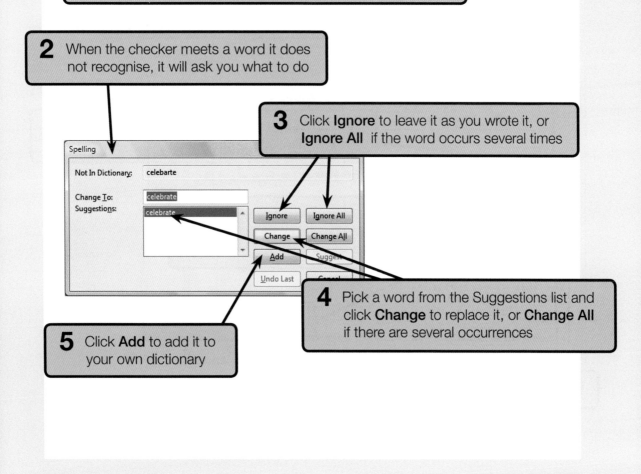

4 Pick a word from the Suggestions list and click **Change** to replace it, or **Change All** if there are several occurrences

5 Click **Add** to add it to your own dictionary

Replying to an e-mail

Replying to someone else's e-mail is the simplest and most reliable way to send a message, because the address is already there for you.

When you start to reply, the original text may be copied into your message. You can decide whether or not this should happen, and how the copied text is to be displayed – this is a Send option (see p. 188).

1 After reading the message, click 📧 Reply – the New Message window will open

2 The **To:** field will have the e-mail address in it – though it may display the person's name. Don't worry about that

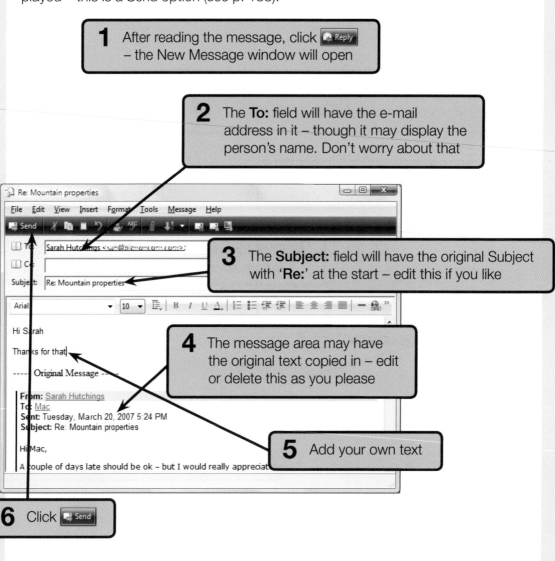

3 The **Subject:** field will have the original Subject with '**Re:**' at the start – edit this if you like

4 The message area may have the original text copied in – edit or delete this as you please

5 Add your own text

6 Click 📧 Send

Forwarding a message

If someone sends you a message that you would like to share with other people, you can do this easily by forwarding. The subject and message are copied into the New Message window, so all you have to do is add the address(es) of the recipient(s) and any comments of your own.

1 Select the message and click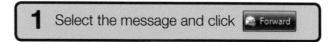

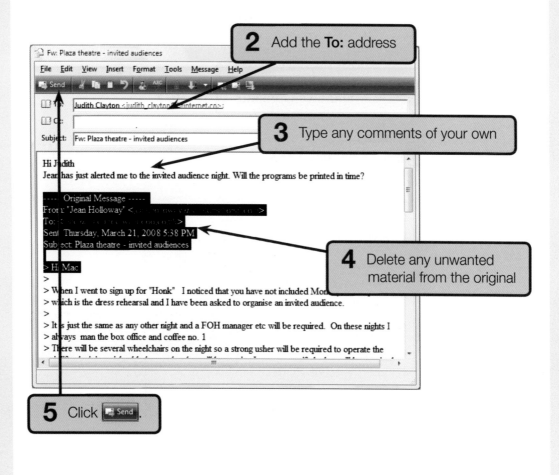

2 Add the **To:** address

3 Type any comments of your own

4 Delete any unwanted material from the original

5 Click [Send].

Windows Contacts

Windows Contacts is an essential tool for e-mail. Addresses are not often easy to remember and if you get just one letter wrong, the message won't get through. If an address is stored in your Contacts, you do not need to remember it because you can select it from there whenever you need it.

Addresses can be added to the Contacts in two ways: you can type them in, or if you are replying to people who have written to you, you can get Windows Mail to copy their addresses into the Contacts.

Contacts can store more than just the e-mail address. You can also add other contact information – home and business addresses and phone number, or other details – whatever is relevant; there is also space for the names of your contact's spouse and children, and even their birthday and anniversary dates. How much you put here is entirely up to you.

1 Click the **Contacts** button or open the **Tools** menu and select **Windows Contacts**

2 When the address list opens, click **New Contact**

Continued…

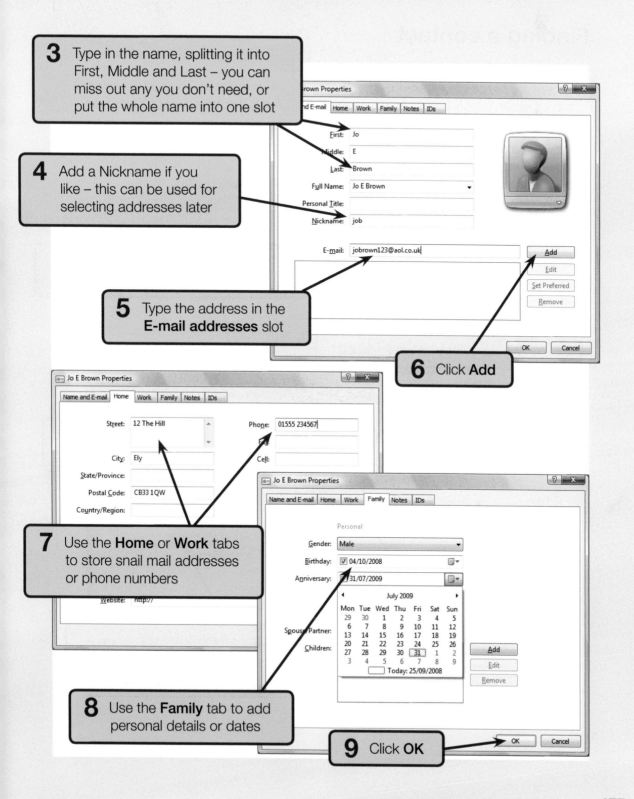

3 Type in the name, splitting it into First, Middle and Last – you can miss out any you don't need, or put the whole name into one slot

4 Add a Nickname if you like – this can be used for selecting addresses later

5 Type the address in the **E-mail addresses** slot

6 Click **Add**

7 Use the **Home** or **Work** tabs to store snail mail addresses or phone numbers

8 Use the **Family** tab to add personal details or dates

9 Click **OK**

Finding a contact

If there are only a couple of dozen entries in your Contacts, you should be able to find a person simply by scrolling through the list. As the numbers rise, it can take longer to spot the entry you need. Searching is the answer.

If you type a few letters of the name into the Search box, Contacts will filter the list to display only those that match. As you type more of the name, so the displayed list will shrink down until you should be able to spot the one you want.

1 Open the Contacts folder

2 Type the first letters – or any part – of the name into the Search box

3 Check the display as it is filtered, to see if the entry has been found

4 Type more of the name if necessary

5 Click on the entry to preview it

6 Double-click to open the file for editing

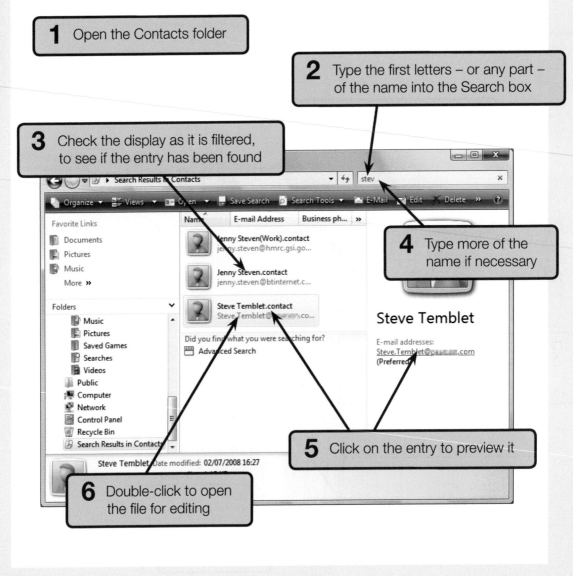

Attaching a file to a message

Images, documents, music, programs and other non-text files can be e-mailed, attached to messages. As the mail system was designed for transmitting plain text, other files have to be converted to text for transfer, and back to binary on receipt. Windows Mail handles these conversions for you, but you need to be aware of the conversion, because it increases the size of a file by about 50 per cent. This can create a problem. Many mail services set a limit of 10Mb for any single message. If you have a large image, complex Word document or movie clip with a file size of 6.5Mb or more, then it will make an attachment of 10Mb – and may well get blocked.

1 Start a new message as usual

2 Open the **Insert** menu and select **FileAttachment...** or click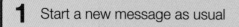

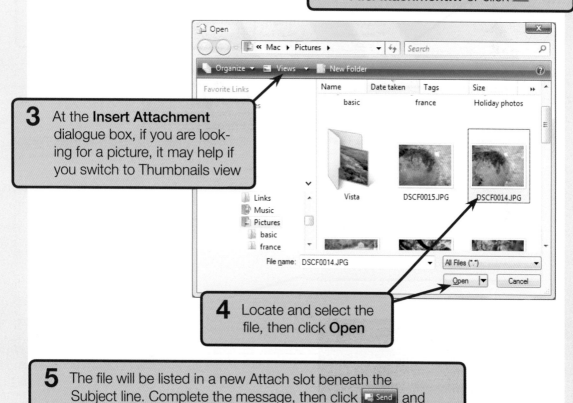

3 At the **Insert Attachment** dialogue box, if you are looking for a picture, it may help if you switch to Thumbnails view

4 Locate and select the file, then click **Open**

5 The file will be listed in a new Attach slot beneath the Subject line. Complete the message, then click **Send** and wait – it takes a few moments for the system to convert the file

Saving an attached file

You'll know if an incoming message has an attachment as there will be a paperclip icon beside it in the Header list. If you have opted to show the Preview pane header, you will also find a larger clip icon there.

For this you need a message with an attached file. So, you can either wait until someone sends you one, or attach a file to a message, set it to send later – so that it is in the Outbox – and then open the message. (Don't forget to delete it if you only created the message to test the procedure!)

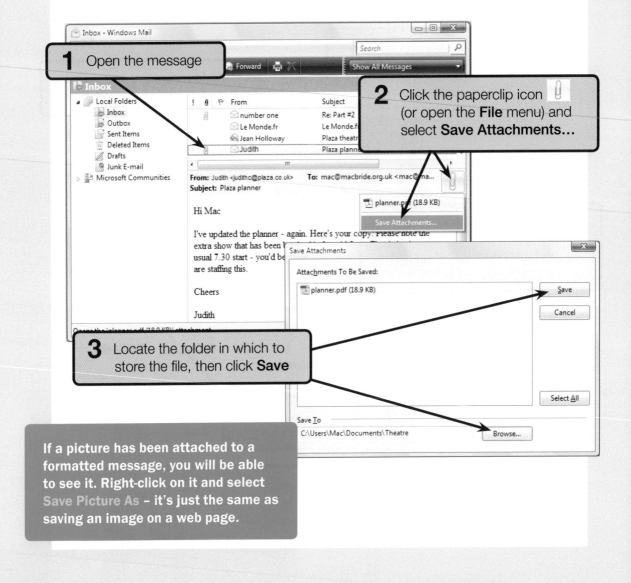

1 Open the message

2 Click the paperclip icon (or open the **File** menu) and select **Save Attachments...**

3 Locate the folder in which to store the file, then click **Save**

If a picture has been attached to a formatted message, you will be able to see it. Right-click on it and select Save Picture As – it's just the same as saving an image on a web page.

Opening an attachment

You can open an attachment directly from a message, without saving it. But take care. Some very nasty viruses are spread through attachments. You get a message, apparently from a friend, and when the you open it, the virus is activated. Typically, it will go through your Contacts list, sending virus-laden messages to your contacts, and it may also destroy the files on the hard drive.

Any executable file (program) may be a virus. Viruses can also be hidden in macros – programs that run within applications. These can be a problem in Word documents. Make sure that Word is set for high macro security. Go to the Tools menu, point to Macros, select Security… and set the level to High.

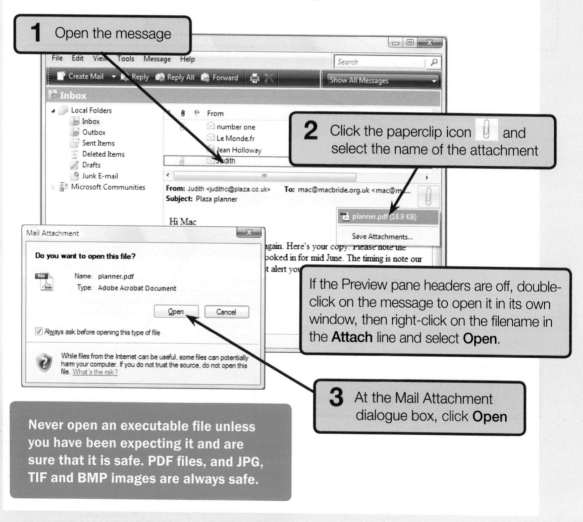

1 Open the message

2 Click the paperclip icon and select the name of the attachment

If the Preview pane headers are off, double-click on the message to open it in its own window, then right-click on the filename in the **Attach** line and select **Open**.

3 At the Mail Attachment dialogue box, click **Open**

Never open an executable file unless you have been expecting it and are sure that it is safe. PDF files, and JPG, TIF and BMP images are always safe.

Organising your old mail

E-mail can clog up your system, mainly because we tend to leave old messages in the Inbox. Think about what we do with paper letters. After reading, we normally answer them if necessary, then bin them, or file them – either straight away or when we get round to it. Why don't we do the same with e-mail? Tidying up your Inbox takes very little time and makes it easier to find those messages that you do want to keep.

Create one or more folders for storage using the File > New Folder command, then go through your messages, deleting them or moving them to appropriate folders.

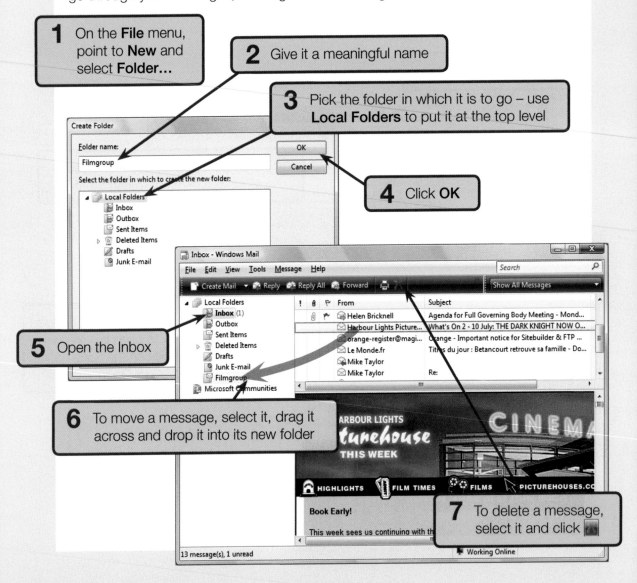

1 On the **File** menu, point to **New** and select **Folder...**

2 Give it a meaningful name

3 Pick the folder in which it is to go – use **Local Folders** to put it at the top level

4 Click **OK**

5 Open the Inbox

6 To move a message, select it, drag it across and drop it into its new folder

7 To delete a message, select it and click

Customising the toolbar

As with most other Windows programs, you can adjust the contents and appearance of the Windows Mail toolbar to suit your needs. You can add or remove buttons, set the size of the icons and choose whether to show text labels on all buttons, on a selected few, or on none.

1 Open the **View** menu, select **Layout...** and click **Customize Toolbar**

2 To add a button, select it from the left-hand pane and click **Add** – it will go above (i.e. to the left) of the selected item in the Current list

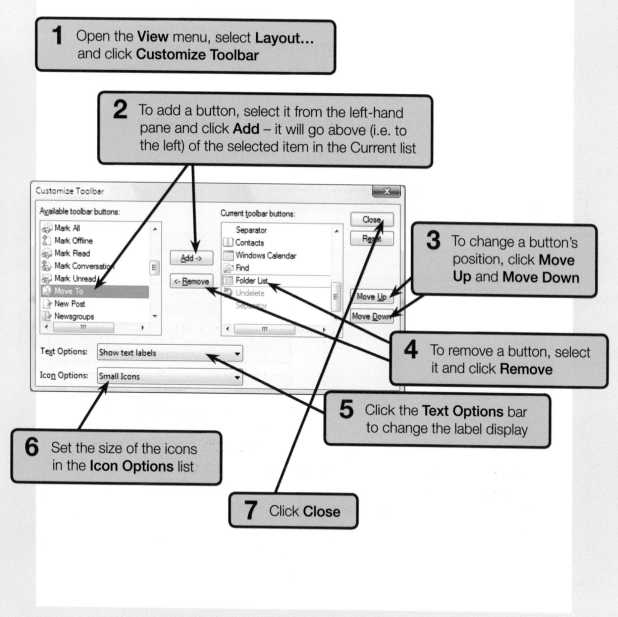

3 To change a button's position, click **Move Up** and **Move Down**

4 To remove a button, select it and click **Remove**

5 Click the **Text Options** bar to change the label display

6 Set the size of the icons in the **Icon Options** list

7 Click **Close**

Changing the Headers pane

You can change the selection and layout of the columns in the Headers pane, so that you can see the information that you need. These are the main columns, listed in order of how useful I find them:

- **From** – who sent it
- **Subject** – the contents of the subject line
- **Received** – when it arrived in the mailbox at your service provider
- **Size** – how big it is
- **Sent** – when it was sent
- **Attachment** – indicates that a file is attached to the message
- **Flag** – for you to mark the message
- **Priority** – messages can be marked as high or low priority.

1 Open the **View** menu and select **Columns**

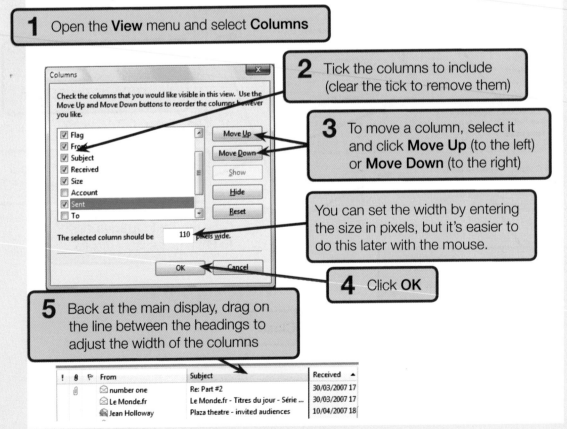

2 Tick the columns to include (clear the tick to remove them)

3 To move a column, select it and click **Move Up** (to the left) or **Move Down** (to the right)

You can set the width by entering the size in pixels, but it's easier to do this later with the mouse.

4 Click **OK**

5 Back at the main display, drag on the line between the headings to adjust the width of the columns

Sorting the headers

You can change the order of messages so that you can find (old) messages more easily. They can be sorted by the contents of any column and in either ascending or descending order. If you sort by From, for example, the messages will be grouped by sender's name in alphabetical (or reverse) order; sort them by Received and they will be in date order.

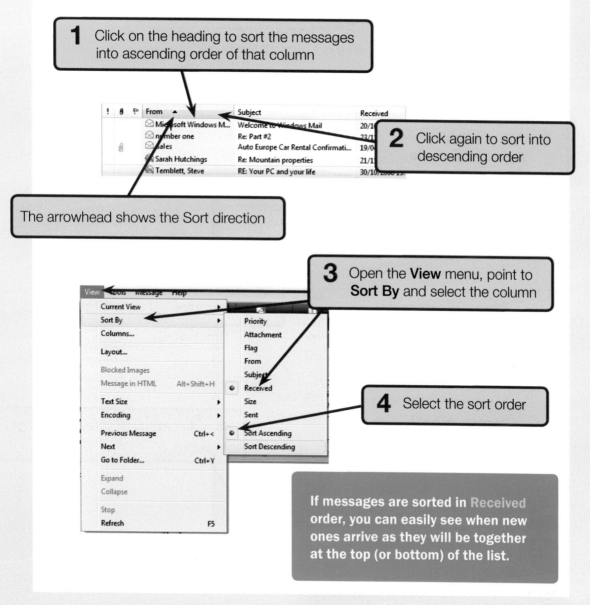

1 Click on the heading to sort the messages into ascending order of that column

2 Click again to sort into descending order

The arrowhead shows the Sort direction

3 Open the **View** menu, point to **Sort By** and select the column

4 Select the sort order

If messages are sorted in Received order, you can easily see when new ones arrive as they will be together at the top (or bottom) of the list.

Setting the options

There are 10 sets of options, which together allow you to customise just about every aspect of Windows Mail. We'll cover the five most important sets here.

The General options

These control what happens when you start Windows Mail, and how you send and receive mail. When setting them, the key questions are:

- Do you use the newsgroups? If not, turn off Notify me...
- Do you want to send and receive messages automatically, on start-up and/or at regular intervals?

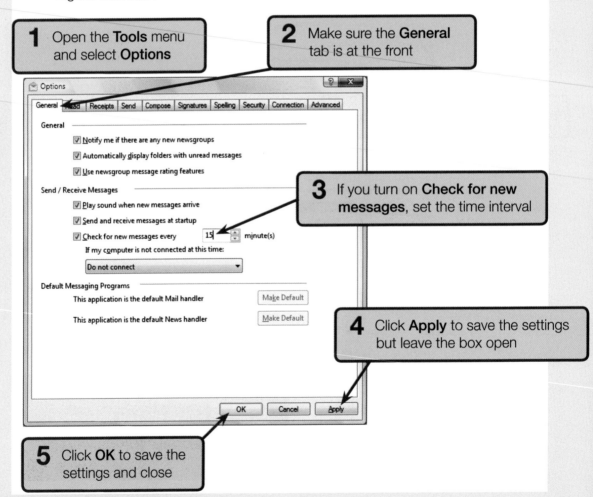

1 Open the **Tools** menu and select **Options**

2 Make sure the **General** tab is at the front

3 If you turn on **Check for new messages**, set the time interval

4 Click **Apply** to save the settings but leave the box open

5 Click **OK** to save the settings and close

Setting the Read options

The Read options control how incoming messages are handled. The key points are:

- Header lines are shown in bold until they have been marked as read. You can mark them yourself, using the Mark as Read command on the Edit menu, or you can have them marked automatically after a short delay.

- You can set the font in which messages are displayed. This will override whatever font – and font size – used when the message was written.

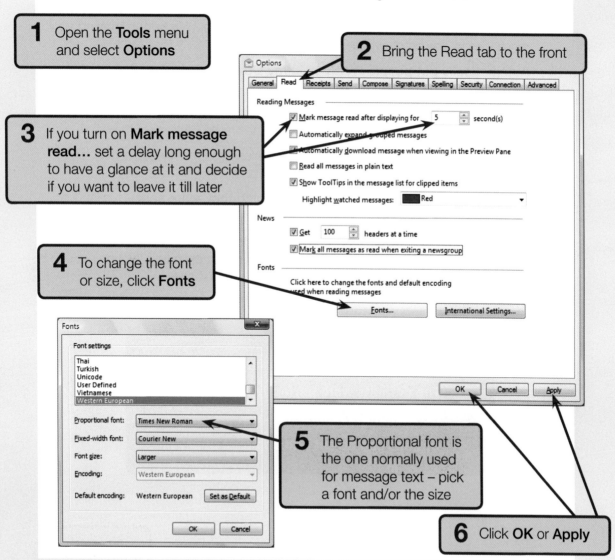

1 Open the **Tools** menu and select **Options**

2 Bring the Read tab to the front

3 If you turn on **Mark message read...** set a delay long enough to have a glance at it and decide if you want to leave it till later

4 To change the font or size, click **Fonts**

5 The Proportional font is the one normally used for message text – pick a font and/or the size

6 Click **OK** or **Apply**

Setting the Send options

The options on this tab are all quite important. You should make sure that you set them to match the way you use Windows Mail, but you will not know that at first, of course. So, after you have been using it for a few days or weeks – long enough to have handled a few dozen messages – come back to this page and set the options.

- **Save copy of sent messages in the Sent Items folder** – mainly for business users who need to keep a record of everything.

- **Send messages immediately** – turn this on if you have broadband. With a dial-up connection, turn this off, and use the Send/Receive button to send your messages in one batch when you go online.

- **Automatically put people I reply to in my Contacts list** – turn this on. You can always delete unwanted addresses later.

- **Automatically complete e-mail addresses when composing** – turn this on. You can then enter a **To:** address by typing the first few letters of the name.

- **Include messages in reply** – turn this off, unless you mainly use e-mail for work and need to reply to message point by point.

- **Reply to messages using the format in which they were sent** – turn this on. It avoids sending formatted replies to people who can only use plain text.

- The **Mail Sending Format** – is the default mode for new messages – i.e. those that aren't sent in reply to others. Set this to HTML or plain text, as you prefer. Click the Settings button if you want to specify the text style.

> When setting options remember that:
>
> **The defaults work perfectly well**
>
> **No option will do any damage**
>
> **Options can be set and changed at any time.**

Continued…

1 Open the **Tools** menu and select **Options**

2 Switch to the Send tab

3 Set the options as required

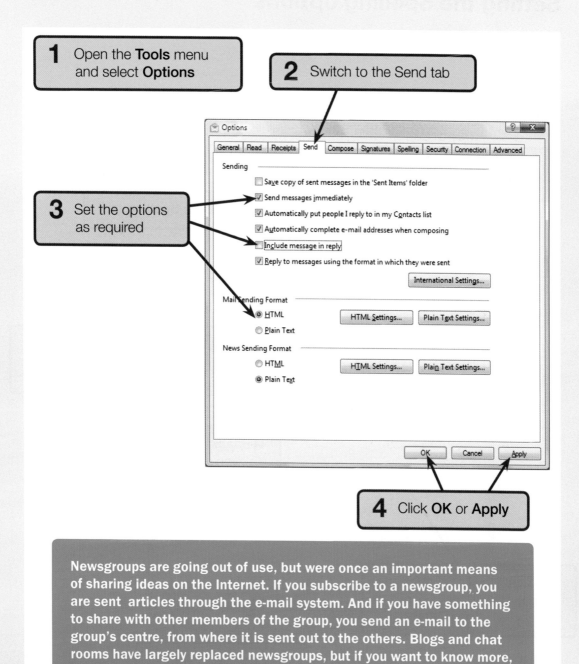

4 Click **OK** or **Apply**

Newsgroups are going out of use, but were once an important means of sharing ideas on the Internet. If you subscribe to a newsgroup, you are sent articles through the e-mail system. And if you have something to share with other members of the group, you send an e-mail to the group's centre, from where it is sent out to the others. Blogs and chat rooms have largely replaced newsgroups, but if you want to know more, go to Google and search for 'newsgroups'.

Setting the Spelling options

Not all of us are good spellers, and even the best make typing mistakes, but when you have a good spell-checker at hand, there is really no excuse for sending badly spelled (or typed) messages. The only questions are whether or not to set the spell-check to start automatically, and what sort of words to ignore. (There's no point in spell-checking Internet addresses, or the original text when replying to a message.)

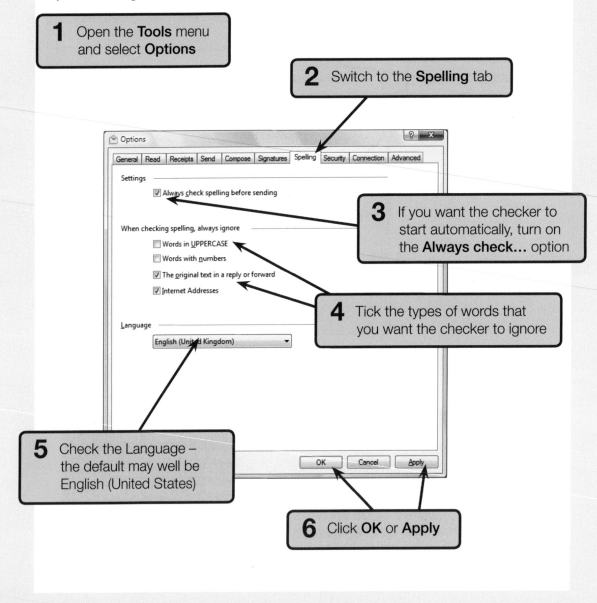

1 Open the **Tools** menu and select **Options**

2 Switch to the **Spelling** tab

3 If you want the checker to start automatically, turn on the **Always check...** option

4 Tick the types of words that you want the checker to ignore

5 Check the Language – the default may well be English (United States)

6 Click **OK** or **Apply**

Setting the Security options

Security restricts. The more secure you make your system, the less chance there is that viruses and spyware will get in and cause damage, but equally, the less you will be able to do. The trick is to find a happy medium.

If you have a good ISP, they will run virus-checking software on all your e-mail before it gets to your mailbox, and remove any viruses that they find. That is your first line of defence. The second line of defence is in the Security options. Go for the most secure settings at first, reducing the level only if you find it is too restricting.

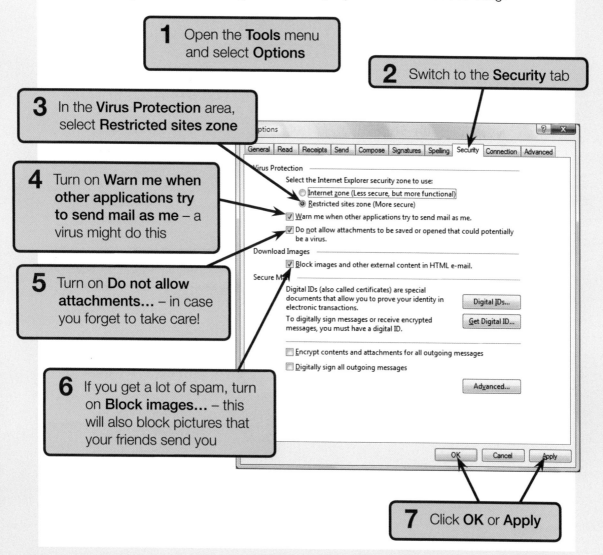

1 Open the **Tools** menu and select **Options**

2 Switch to the **Security** tab

3 In the **Virus Protection** area, select **Restricted sites zone**

4 Turn on **Warn me when other applications try to send mail as me** – a virus might do this

5 Turn on **Do not allow attachments...** – in case you forget to take care!

6 If you get a lot of spam, turn on **Block images...** – this will also block pictures that your friends send you

7 Click **OK** or **Apply**

5 Working with photographs

Most of us have by now discovered the delights of digital cameras, but if you don't yet have one, you can still explore photography on the PC using the photos in the Sample Pictures folder.

This chapter covers:

- Vista's Photo Gallery
- How to edit and crop a photo
- How to adjust the brightness, contrast and colour ranges
- How to get rid of red eye
- Importing images from a digital camera
- Burning a CD of images
- Sending images by e-mail
- How to set up a screensaver slide show of your favourite photos

Photo Gallery

The Photo Gallery can be used for viewing, organising and editing your photos. The first time that you run it, the Gallery will scour through your Pictures folders and add in every picture it finds. It will then display thumbnails of them all, and list the tags, dates, star rating and other properties that you can use to sort them.

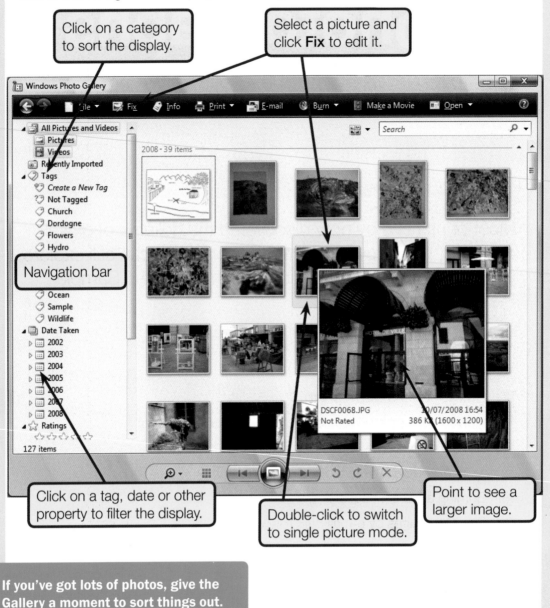

Click on a category to sort the display.

Select a picture and click **Fix** to edit it.

Navigation bar

Click on a tag, date or other property to filter the display.

Double-click to switch to single picture mode.

Point to see a larger image.

If you've got lots of photos, give the Gallery a moment to sort things out.

Single picture mode

If you double-click on a picture, or right-click and select Preview, the Gallery will switch to single picture mode. In this mode, you can add tags or a caption, and change the star rating of the current picture. With the tools at the bottom, you can zoom in and out, view other pictures, rotate the image or delete it.

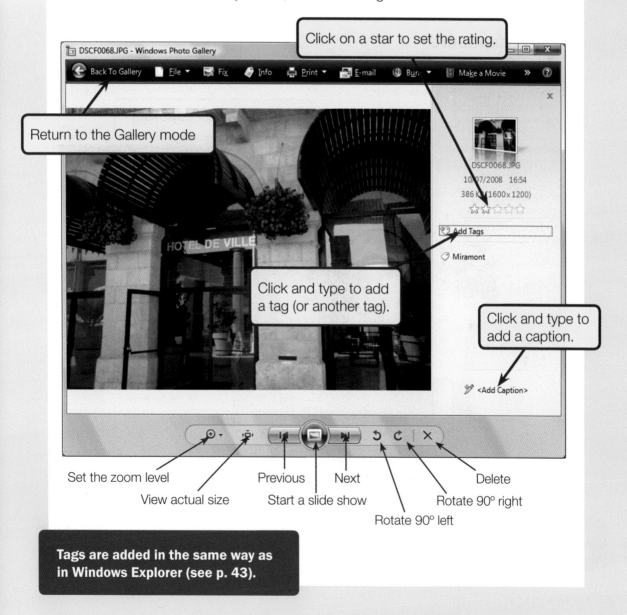

Click on a star to set the rating.

Return to the Gallery mode

Click and type to add a tag (or another tag).

Click and type to add a caption.

Set the zoom level

View actual size

Previous

Next

Start a slide show

Rotate 90° left

Rotate 90° right

Delete

Tags are added in the same way as in Windows Explorer (see p. 43).

Editing a photo

Photo Gallery offers a number of editing tools.

●   To take a picture into Editing mode, select it and click **Fix**.

There is an Auto Adjust feature which will adjust the different colour and brightness levels to get calculated 'best'. This often does a very good job, but you may prefer to set the levels yourself.

Adjust exposure

Start with the exposure. This is where you set the brightness and contrast levels.

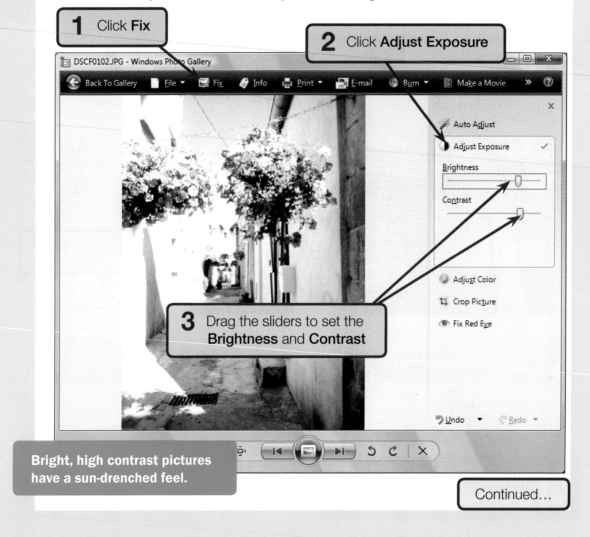

1   Click **Fix**

2   Click **Adjust Exposure**

3   Drag the sliders to set the **Brightness** and **Contrast**

Bright, high contrast pictures have a sun-drenched feel.

Continued…

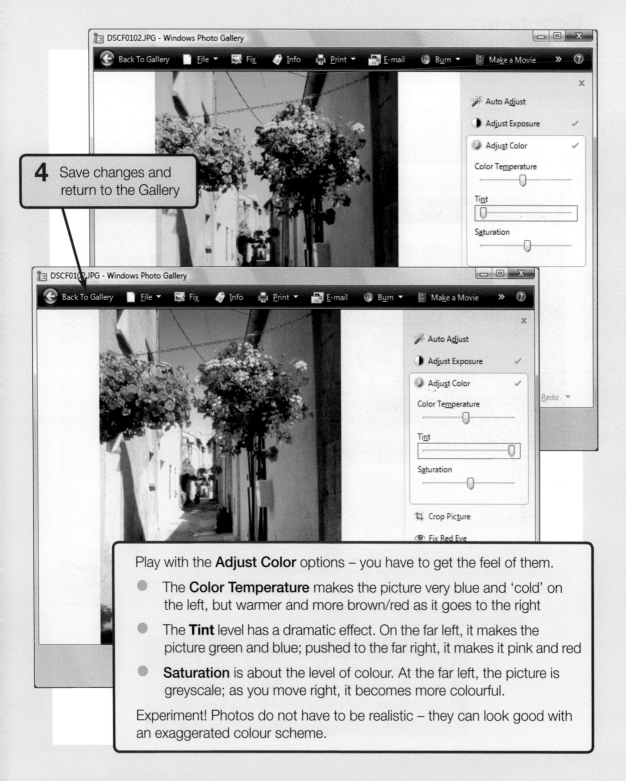

4 Save changes and return to the Gallery

Play with the **Adjust Color** options – you have to get the feel of them.

- The **Color Temperature** makes the picture very blue and 'cold' on the left, but warmer and more brown/red as it goes to the right

- The **Tint** level has a dramatic effect. On the far left, it makes the picture green and blue; pushed to the far right, it makes it pink and red

- **Saturation** is about the level of colour. At the far left, the picture is greyscale; as you move right, it becomes more colourful.

Experiment! Photos do not have to be realistic – they can look good with an exaggerated colour scheme.

Cropping

If a photograph has unwanted material around the intended subject, it can be cropped.

1 Click the **Crop Picture** button to display the cropping tools

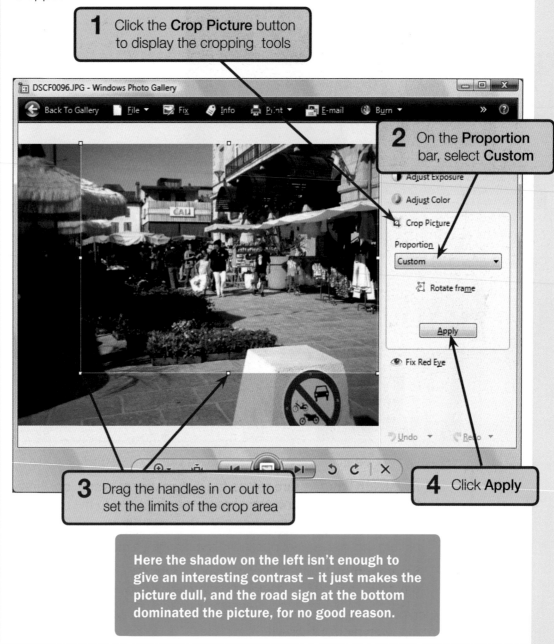

2 On the **Proportion** bar, select **Custom**

3 Drag the handles in or out to set the limits of the crop area

4 Click **Apply**

Here the shadow on the left isn't enough to give an interesting contrast – it just makes the picture dull, and the road sign at the bottom dominated the picture, for no good reason.

Cropping can also be used where a photo is to be printed on a particular size of paper. The question then is, which part of the photo is to be printed?

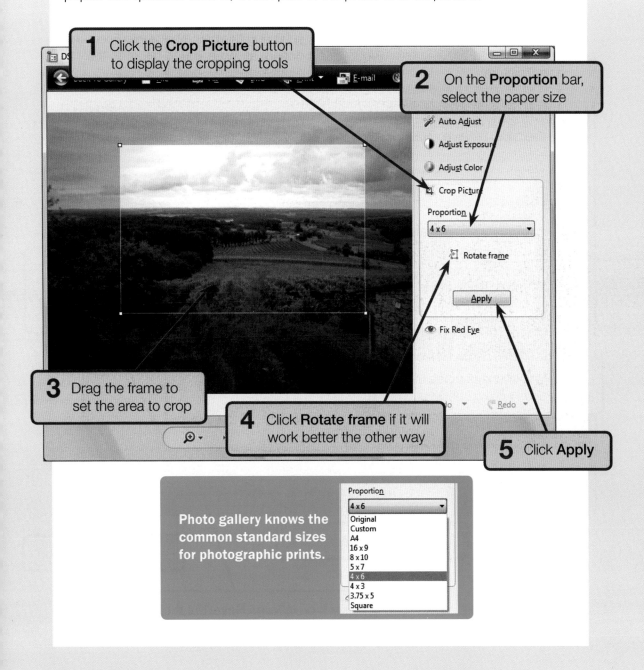

1 Click the **Crop Picture** button to display the cropping tools

2 On the **Proportion** bar, select the paper size

Auto Adjust

Adjust Exposure

Adjust Color

Crop Picture

Proportion

4 x 6

Rotate frame

Apply

Fix Red Eye

3 Drag the frame to set the area to crop

4 Click **Rotate frame** if it will work better the other way

5 Click **Apply**

Proportion

4 x 6

Original
Custom
A4
16 x 9
8 x 10
5 x 7
4 x 6
4 x 3
3.75 x 5
Square

Photo gallery knows the common standard sizes for photographic prints.

Undo and Revert

Like all good editing software, Photo Gallery has an Undo facility, which means that you can try out ideas without ruining your photo.

Undo will undo the changes made during an editing session. When you return to the Gallery, any edits will be saved – however, if you bring the photo back into Fix mode, the Undo button will then offer you a Revert option, allowing you to return to the original picture.

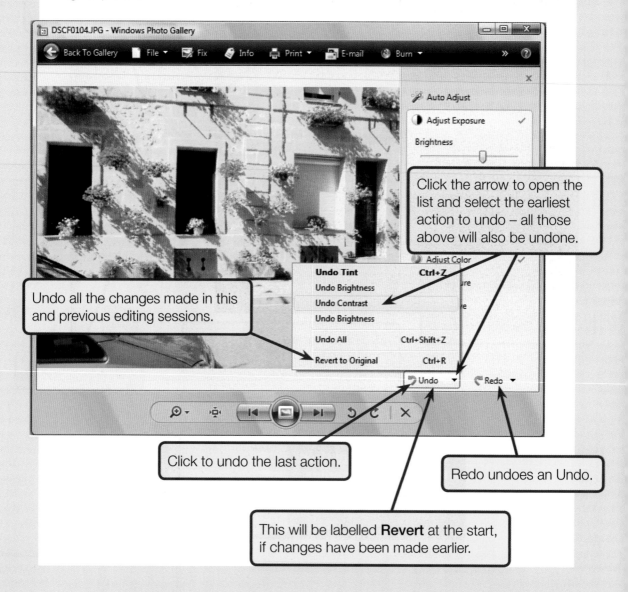

Click the arrow to open the list and select the earliest action to undo – all those above will also be undone.

Undo all the changes made in this and previous editing sessions.

Click to undo the last action.

Redo undoes an Undo.

This will be labelled **Revert** at the start, if changes have been made earlier.

Red eye

'Red eye' is a common problem in photos of people taken with flash. It is caused by reflection of light from the back of the eye, and is worse when the pupils are dilated – and if it's dark enough to need flash, people's pupils are likely to be wide open. Some modern cameras have a red eye reduction feature – there is an initial flash which causes pupils to shrink, before the main flash. If you don't have that facility, or you get red eye anyway, it can be fixed in Photo Gallery.

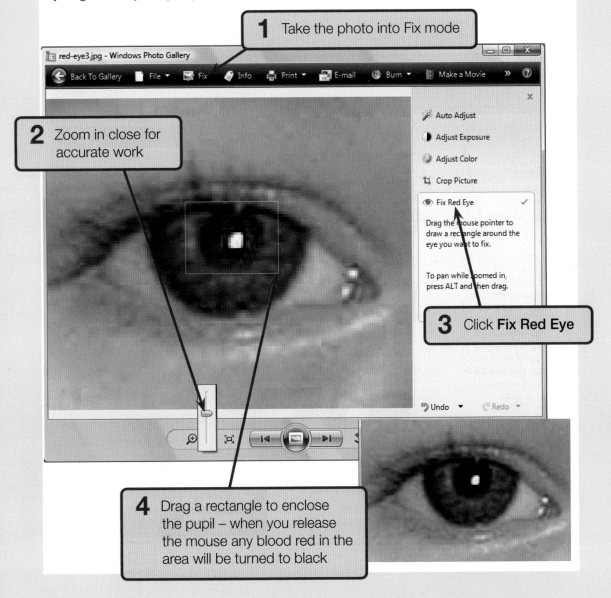

1 Take the photo into Fix mode

2 Zoom in close for accurate work

3 Click **Fix Red Eye**

4 Drag a rectangle to enclose the pupil – when you release the mouse any blood red in the area will be turned to black

Digital cameras and Windows Explorer

When you connect your camera to a USB port on your PC, and turn it on in view mode, two things may happen.

- The camera's own editing/management software may start up. If it does, shut it down unless you really like it. Vista does the job better!

- Vista will recognise that it is there and run Windows Explorer, with the camera as the current drive. If you simply want to copy photos onto your PC, this will do the job nicely. Here's how:

1 Windows Explorer will open at the top level folder of the camera's storage

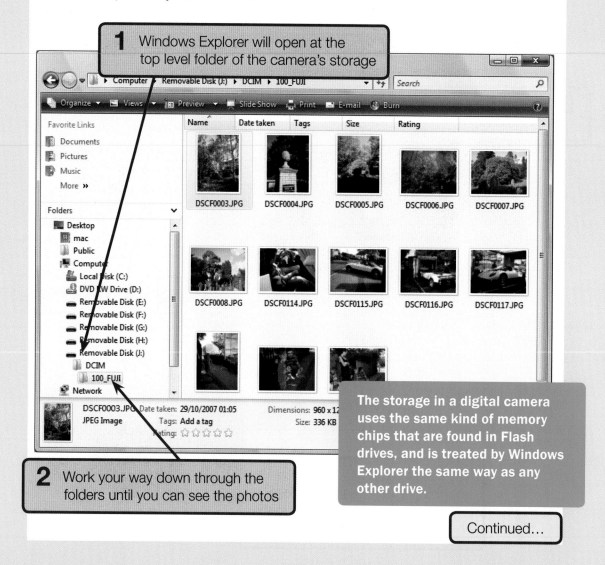

2 Work your way down through the folders until you can see the photos

The storage in a digital camera uses the same kind of memory chips that are found in Flash drives, and is treated by Windows Explorer the same way as any other drive.

Continued...

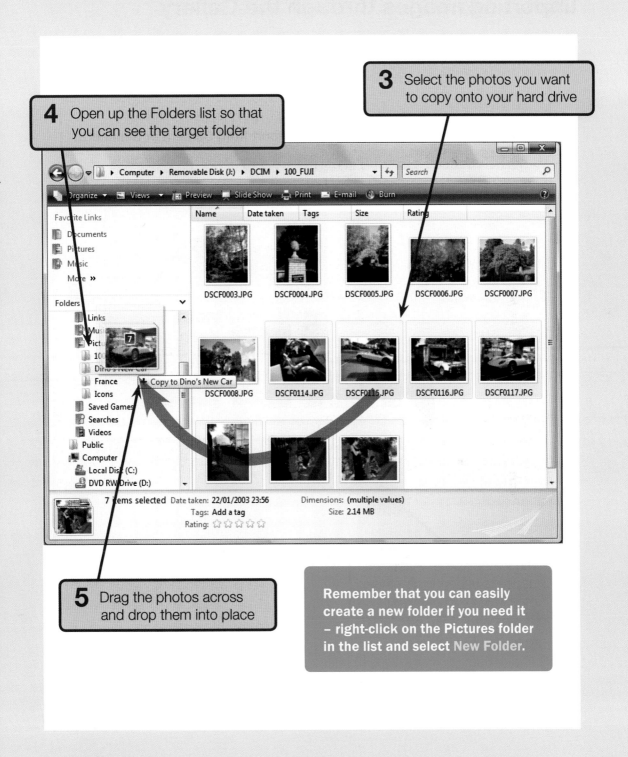

3 Select the photos you want to copy onto your hard drive

4 Open up the Folders list so that you can see the target folder

5 Drag the photos across and drop them into place

Remember that you can easily create a new folder if you need it – right-click on the Pictures folder in the list and select New Folder.

Importing images through the Gallery

If you want to edit your images, or add tags, after copying them onto your PC, then you may as well import them directly into the Gallery.

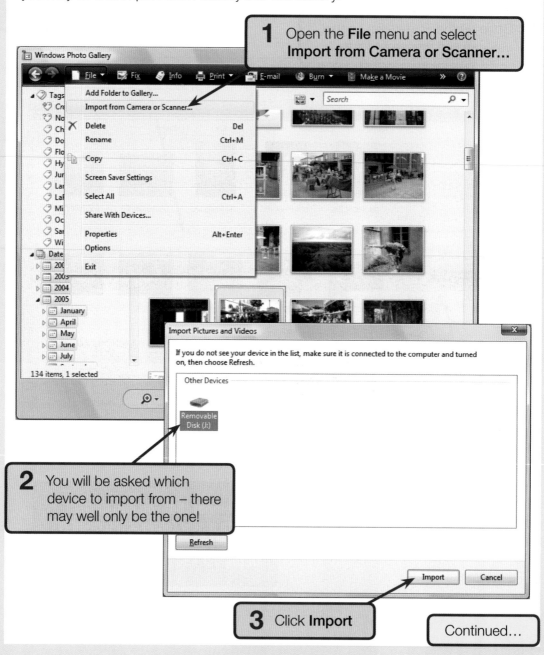

1 Open the **File** menu and select **Import from Camera or Scanner...**

2 You will be asked which device to import from – there may well only be the one!

3 Click **Import**

Continued...

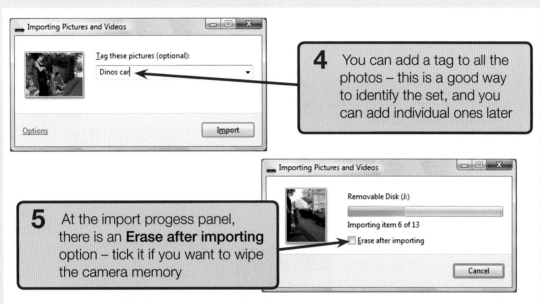

4 You can add a tag to all the photos – this is a good way to identify the set, and you can add individual ones later

5 At the import progess panel, there is an **Erase after importing** option – tick it if you want to wipe the camera memory

6 Your new imports may be listed under their tag, but will certainly be in the **Recently Imported** set

Burning a CD or DVD

You might want to copy photos (or other files) onto a recordable CD or DVD:

● To give to a friend

● To take to the photo shop for printing – it typically costs about half as much to have them printed in a shop than to print them yourself, and you will usually get a better quality result

● As backup, in case your PC goes wrong – it happens! If you value your photos, keep copies on discs.

You can burn your disks, either through Windows Explorer or through Photo Gallery. Here's how it works in Explorer:

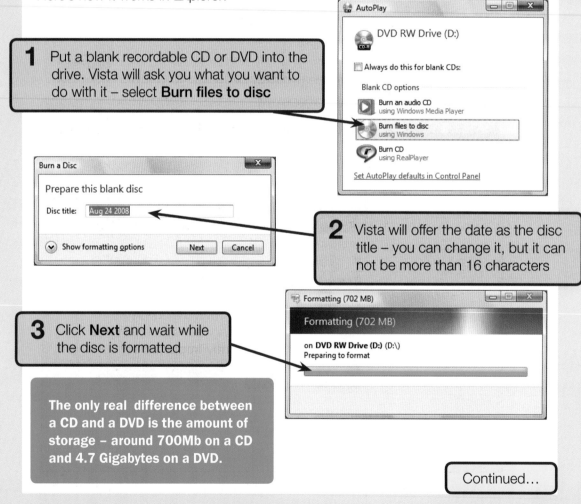

1 Put a blank recordable CD or DVD into the drive. Vista will ask you what you want to do with it – select **Burn files to disc**

2 Vista will offer the date as the disc title – you can change it, but it can not be more than 16 characters

3 Click **Next** and wait while the disc is formatted

The only real difference between a CD and a DVD is the amount of storage – around 700Mb on a CD and 4.7 Gigabytes on a DVD.

Continued...

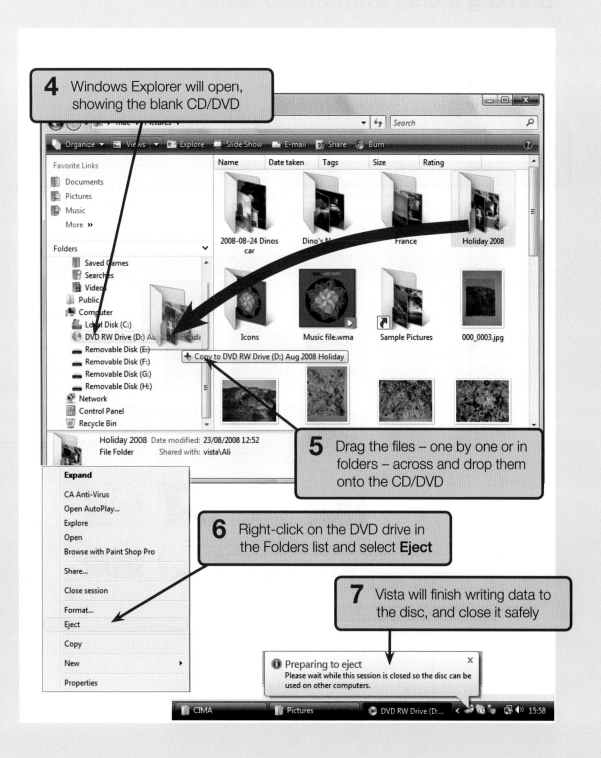

4 Windows Explorer will open, showing the blank CD/DVD

Search

Organize ▾ Views ▾ Explore Slide Show E-mail Share Burn

Favorite Links

Documents
Pictures
Music
More »

Name	Date taken	Tags	Size	Rating

Folders

Saved Games
Searches
Videos
Public
Computer
Local Disk (C:)
DVD RW Drive (D:) Aug 2008 Holida
Removable Disk (E:)
Removable Disk (F:)
Removable Disk (G:)
Removable Disk (H:)
Network
Control Panel
Recycle Bin

2008-08-24 Dinos car   Dino's N   France   Holiday 2008

Icons   Music file.wma   Sample Pictures   000_0003.jpg

＋ Copy to DVD RW Drive (D:) Aug 2008 Holiday

Holiday 2008 Date modified: 23/08/2008 12:52
File Folder Shared with: vista\Ali

5 Drag the files – one by one or in folders – across and drop them onto the CD/DVD

Expand

CA Anti-Virus
Open AutoPlay...
Explore
Open
Browse with Paint Shop Pro

Share...

Close session

Format...

Eject

Copy

New   ▸

Properties

6 Right-click on the DVD drive in the Folders list and select **Eject**

7 Vista will finish writing data to the disc, and close it safely

ⓘ Preparing to eject   ✕
Please wait while this session is closed so the disc can be used on other computers.

CIMA   Pictures   DVD RW Drive (D:...   15:58

Burning a disc from Photo Gallery

This is much the same as burning a disc through Explorer. The main difference is that you start by selecting the photos you want to copy. You do not have to add them all at once. You can select one set, burn them, then select and burn some more, until you have all the ones you want, or you run out of space.

1 Use the tags or other ways of sorting the photos to find the ones you want

2 Select the photos

3 If there is no CD/DVD in the drive, put one in now

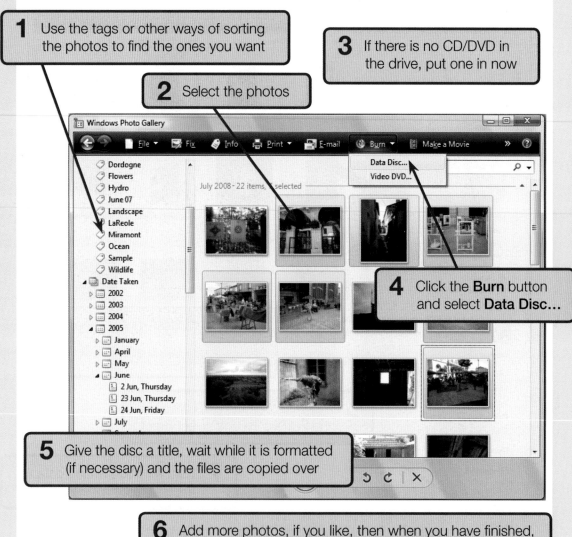

4 Click the **Burn** button and select **Data Disc...**

5 Give the disc a title, wait while it is formatted (if necessary) and the files are copied over

6 Add more photos, if you like, then when you have finished, press the button on the drive to eject the disc. Vista will make sure the files are safely stored before ejecting it

Sending by e-mail

You saw earlier how you could attach a file to an e-mail message, when writing one in Windows Mail. You can also attach a photo from within Photo Gallery, and doing it this way offers one big advantage – you can reduce its size before sending. Why might you want to do this? Because big files are slow to send (and to receive) and if the other person is going to view the photo onscreen, there is not much point in the picture being bigger than the screen. A 7Mb photo is about 3000 × 2500 pixels; how big is your screen? 1280 × 1024 is typical.

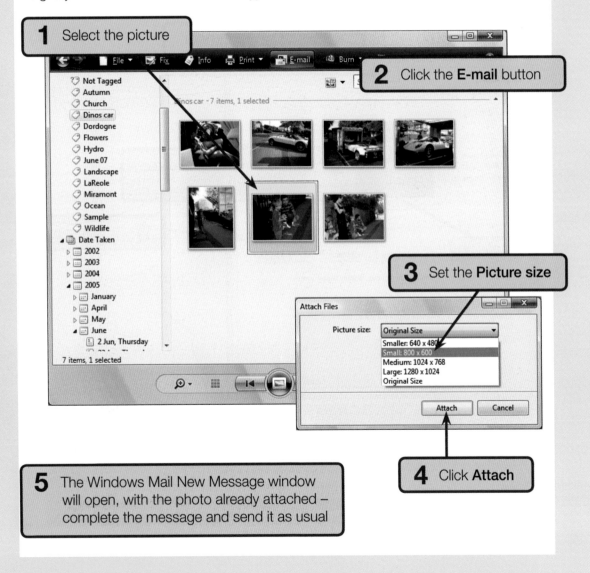

1 Select the picture

2 Click the **E-mail** button

3 Set the **Picture size**

4 Click **Attach**

5 The Windows Mail New Message window will open, with the photo already attached – complete the message and send it as usual

Creating a screen saver slide show

A screen saver is a moving or changing image that occupies the screen when the computer is not in use. A saver doesn't actually serve any useful purpose – it won't save the screen from anything – but it can be a neat way to display your photos. You can set the screen saver to show a selection of photos, in a variety of display styles, and at your chosen speed.

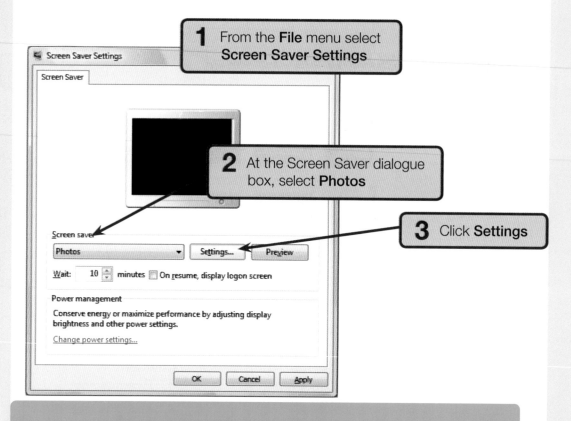

1 From the **File** menu select **Screen Saver Settings**

2 At the Screen Saver dialogue box, select **Photos**

3 Click **Settings**

Power saving

To save power, you should have your monitor set to go into sleep mode if the PC has not been used for 15 minutes (or however long). The screen saver will override this, and continue to display the slide show indefinitely. If you have finished with your PC for a while, and no one is going to be around to see the show, then use the Sleep option to turn the monitor off.

Continued...

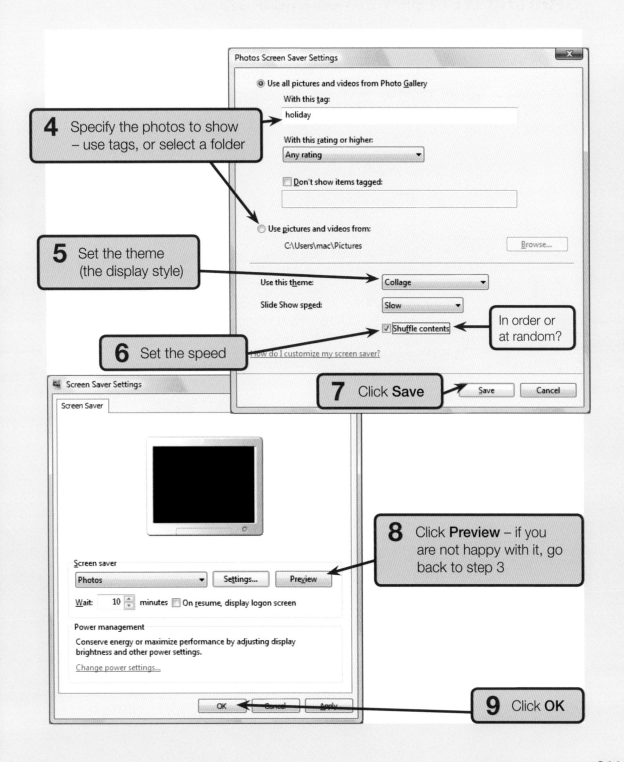

Photos Screen Saver Settings

◉ Use all pictures and videos from Photo Gallery

With this tag:

holiday

4 Specify the photos to show – use tags, or select a folder

With this rating or higher:

Any rating

☐ Don't show items tagged:

◯ Use pictures and videos from:

C:\Users\mac\Pictures   Browse...

5 Set the theme (the display style)

Use this theme: Collage

Slide Show speed: Slow

In order or at random?

☑ Shuffle contents

6 Set the speed

How do I customize my screen saver?

7 Click **Save**   Save   Cancel

Screen Saver Settings

Screen Saver

Screen saver

Photos   Settings...   Preview

Wait: 10 ⬍ minutes ☐ On resume, display logon screen

Power management

Conserve energy or maximize performance by adjusting display brightness and other power settings.

Change power settings...

8 Click **Preview** – if you are not happy with it, go back to step 3

OK   Cancel   Apply

9 Click **OK**

6 Music on your PC

To play CDs, your PC needs a decent set of speakers. Almost all desktop models come equipped with them. If yours does not, or if you have a laptop, you can add them cheaply and easily. You can buy good quality speakers for under £20, and to install them all you do is plug them into a USB port.

This chapter covers:

- Windows Media Player and its Library
- How to listen to an audio CD
- How to rip tracks from a CD
- How to burn an audio CD
- Copying tracks to an MP3 player
- Downloading music from the Internet
- iTunes software and the iTunes store

Media Player

You will have at least two, and possibly three or four, programs on your PC that can play music (and other audio files). These are supplied with the Vista package:

- Windows Media Center is an audio/video/live TV player. In theory, it will be the entertainment centre in your 'wired world', downloading content off the Web as well as playing and managing your audio and video discs. In practice, there is very little available online for use with it, and the software is unreliable.

- Windows Media Player is used for playing audio and video, and for copying files between CDs and the PC. It's simpler than Media Center – so it starts faster and there are fewer things to go wrong – but the output is every bit as good.

You may also have these:

- Real Player can play audio and video files from disc, but its main use is for playing 'streaming' content on web pages, i.e. audio and video files that you can watch as they download. You may well have had to install this so that you could watch a video at a website.

- QuickTime is another player that can handle files on web pages, as well as from disc. You may have installed this while browsing the Web.

When you put a CD into your drive, Vista will ask which player you want to use.

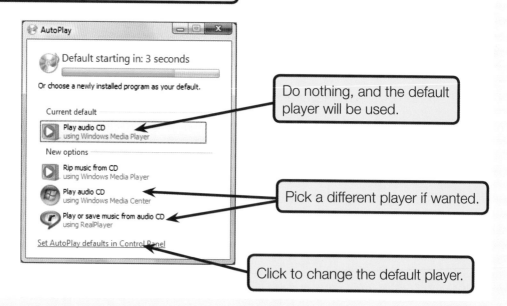

Do nothing, and the default player will be used.

Pick a different player if wanted.

Click to change the default player.

Listen to a CD

When a CD is passed to Media Player, the player first reads the data about the album and artist, and the track titles (if it's there – older CDs often do not have this). It then starts to play the first track, and runs a random, but synchronised, light show.

You can control which tracks are played, and their order, set the volume and shrink the Player down to a control bar.

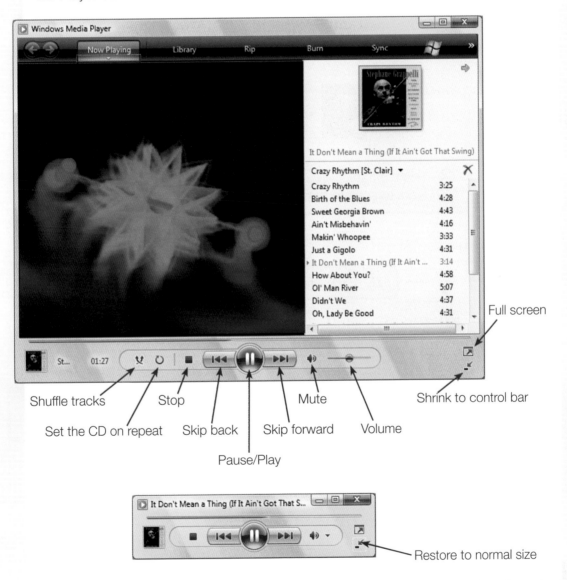

Full screen

Shrink to control bar

Shuffle tracks

Stop

Mute

Set the CD on repeat   Skip back   Skip forward   Volume

Pause/Play

Restore to normal size

Rip from a CD

'Ripping' means copying a file from a CD, converting it into a suitable format and storing it on the PC. It is a complicated technical process – which Media Player can do without blinking. All you have to do is tell it which files to rip.

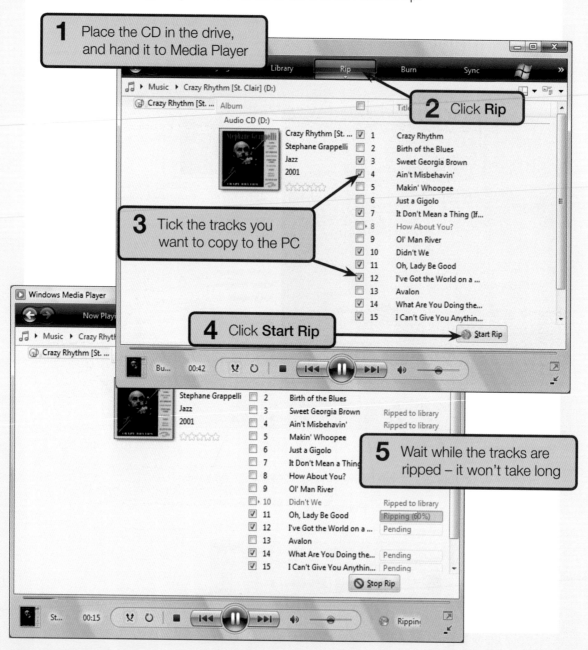

1 Place the CD in the drive, and hand it to Media Player

2 Click **Rip**

3 Tick the tracks you want to copy to the PC

4 Click **Start Rip**

5 Wait while the tracks are ripped – it won't take long

The Library

The audio files on your PC are catalogued and managed by the Library. In it, tracks are grouped into albums, but these can be sorted by artist, song title, genre or other details.

1 Click the Library button

2 Select a property to sort the music, then pick an album

3 Double-click (or right-click and select **Play**) on a track to play it

4 Use the controls as on any player

Respect copyright! It's OK to copy music from your own CDs onto your PC, to listen to there or to copy onto an MP3 for your own use. It's not OK to copy other people's CDs for your use, or to copy your CDs for other people to use. The same applies to music downloaded from the Internet, unless the artist has waived copyright.

Disc information

On most CDs, the album, artist, song title, genre and other data is stored on the disc and is picked up from here by the Library when the tracks are copied in. They are not present on some, mainly older, CDs, but you can add them easily enough.

1 Select the album

2 Click into the Album field and re-place 'Unknown Album' with its name

3 Do the same for the Artist, Genre and Year if you know them

4 Right-click on a track and select **Edit**, then type in the Track name

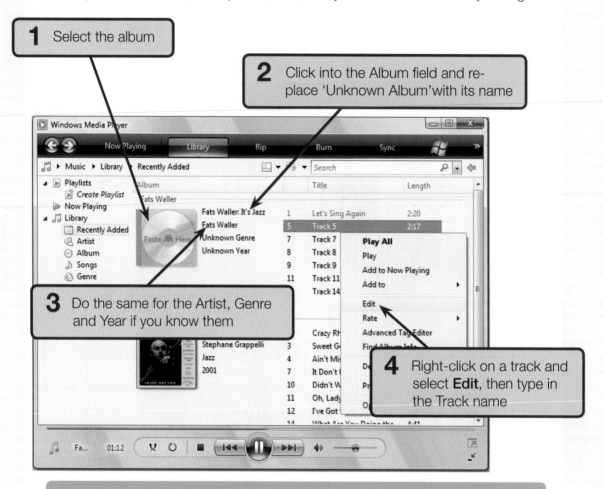

Play lists

A play list collects together tracks from one or more albums or other sources to be played as a set – either in sequence or shuffled randomly – or to be burned onto a CD for playing elsewhere.

A play list only contains links – the tracks themselves are not copied or moved from their original store – so the same track can be on as many lists as you like.

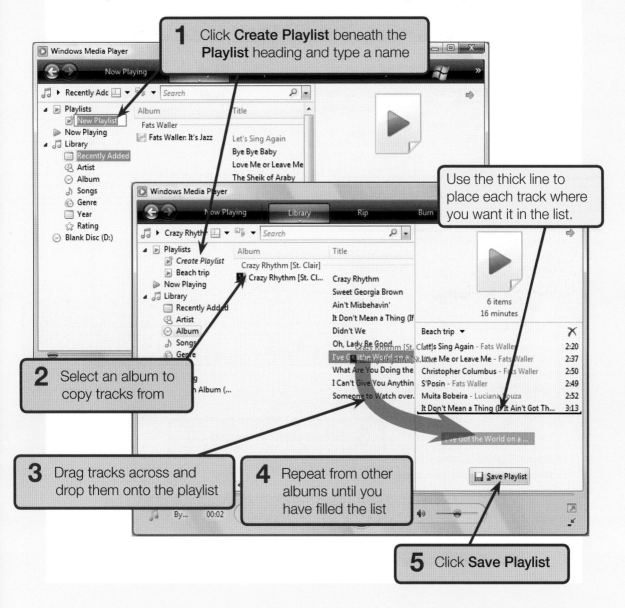

1 Click **Create Playlist** beneath the **Playlist** heading and type a name

Use the thick line to place each track where you want it in the list.

2 Select an album to copy tracks from

3 Drag tracks across and drop them onto the playlist

4 Repeat from other albums until you have filled the list

5 Click **Save Playlist**

Burn to CD

An album or playlist in your library, or a selection of individual tracks (or a combination of the three) can be copied onto CD.

1 Click the **Burn** button

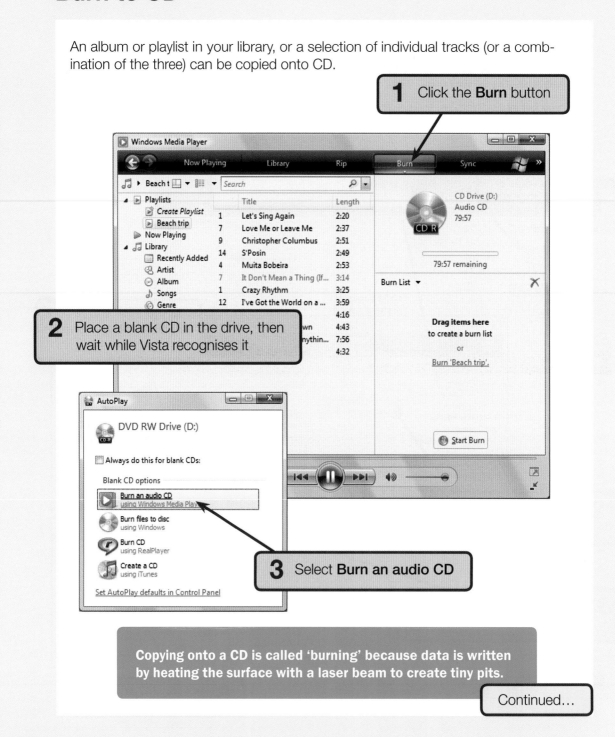

2 Place a blank CD in the drive, then wait while Vista recognises it

3 Select **Burn an audio CD**

Copying onto a CD is called 'burning' because data is written by heating the surface with a laser beam to create tiny pits.

Continued...

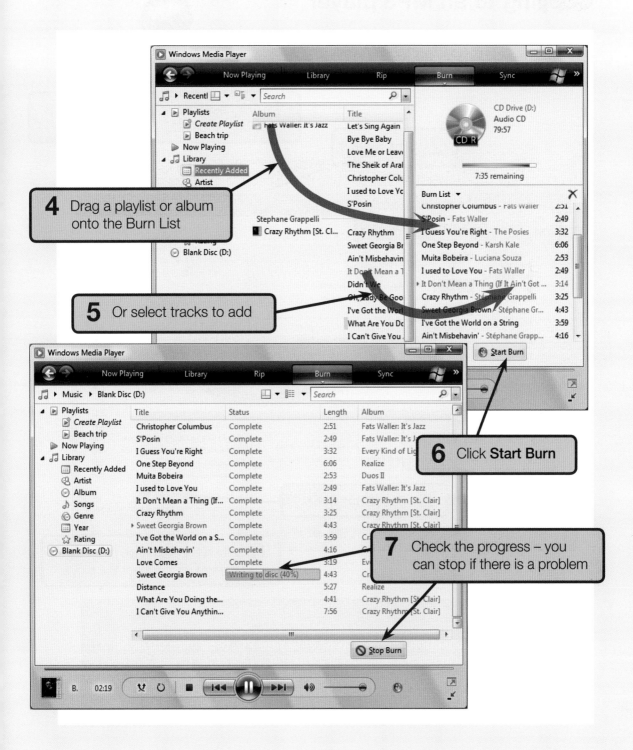

4 Drag a playlist or album onto the Burn List

5 Or select tracks to add

6 Click **Start Burn**

7 Check the progress – you can stop if there is a problem

Copying to an MP3 player

An MP3 player can play the MP3 and WMA audio files that Media Player has captured and stored. Copying files to an MP3 player is simplicity itself.

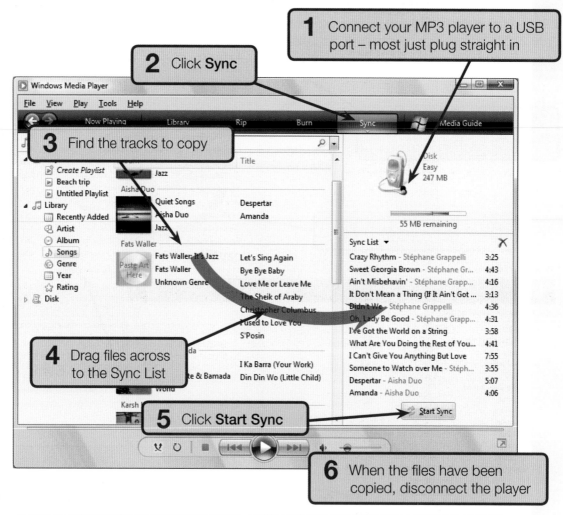

1 Connect your MP3 player to a USB port – most just plug straight in

2 Click **Sync**

3 Find the tracks to copy

4 Drag files across to the Sync List

5 Click **Start Sync**

6 When the files have been copied, disconnect the player

Vinyl to digital

Your old vinyl collection can be copied onto your PC, then onto CD or MP3 player, but you will need a digitiser – a special piece of kit to convert the analogue output from the record into digital form. They are very easy to use and cost under £100.

Music downloads

A vast amount of music, across the whole range from garage to medieval plainsong, is available for download over the Internet. Much of it has to be paid for (typically at around 60p a track), but there's a lot going free. Artists give away their music to build their audience, to encourage people to buy their other downloads and CD, and to come to their concerts. We'll have a look at two download sites in the next pages. To find others, go to Google and search for 'music downloads'.

1 Go to http://music.download.com

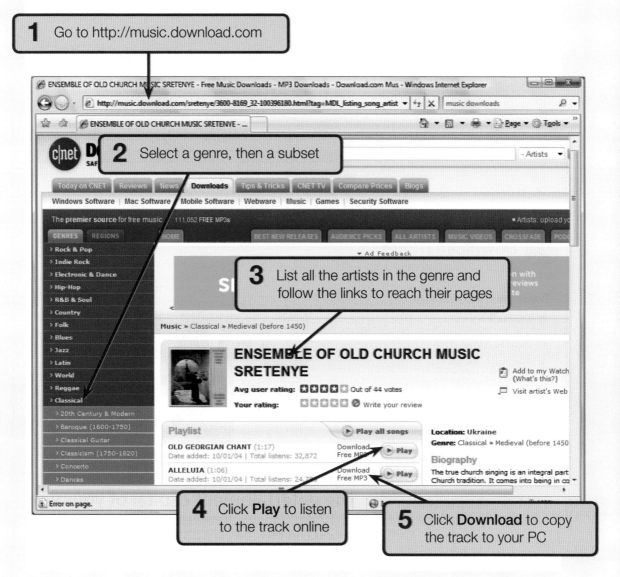

2 Select a genre, then a subset

3 List all the artists in the genre and follow the links to reach their pages

4 Click **Play** to listen to the track online

5 Click **Download** to copy the track to your PC

iTunes Store

Apple's iTunes site is currently the world's most-used download site – though others are competing hard for that title, so things may have changed by the time you read this. Its success has been fuelled by the success of the iPod. If you have an iPod, iTunes is the obvious place to go for your music.

You do not need an iPod to use iTunes, but you do need special software to access the site, and to download tracks. This software can also be used, instead of Media Player, to manage your music files.

Here's how to install the iTunes software.

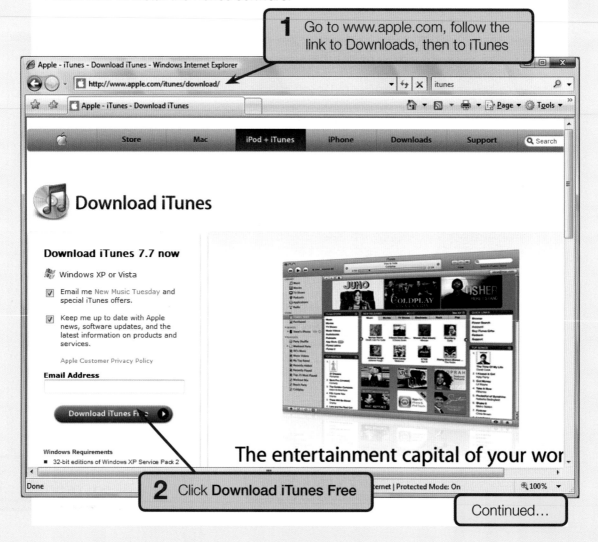

1 Go to www.apple.com, follow the link to Downloads, then to iTunes

2 Click **Download iTunes Free**

Continued...

3 At the Run or Save dialogue box, select Save – the installation software must be downloaded to your PC

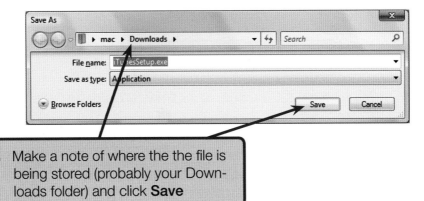

4 Make a note of where the the file is being stored (probably your Downloads folder) and click **Save**

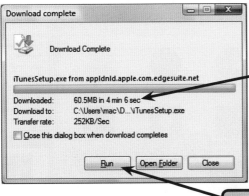

The Setup file is over 60Mb and takes three to five minutes to download over a broadband connection.

5 When the download is complete, click **Run** to start the installation

During installation follow the prompts. Agree to their terms and conditions (they are standard) and accept the suggestions for any settings. Installation will take a few minutes and you will have to restart the PC before you can use the software.

iTunes

The iTunes software is an alternative to Media Player for managing music on your PC (and if you have an iPod, it is the obvious one to use). It is essential for downloading tracks from the iTunes store.

1 Run iTunes

2 Go to the iTunes Store

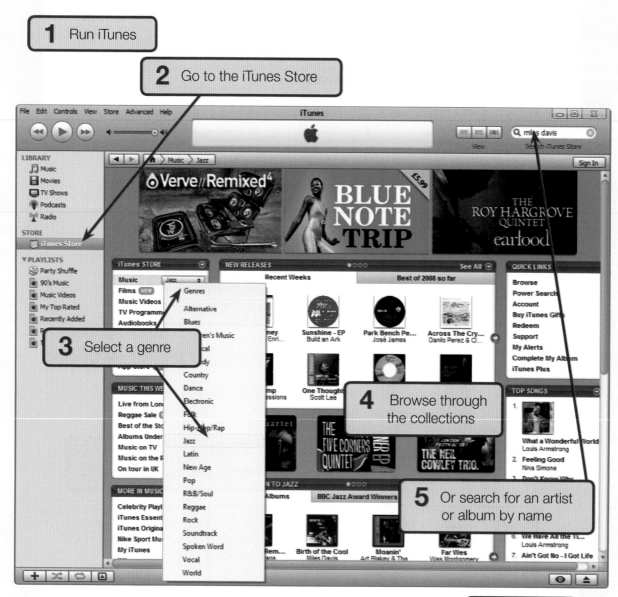

3 Select a genre

4 Browse through the collections

5 Or search for an artist or album by name

Continued...

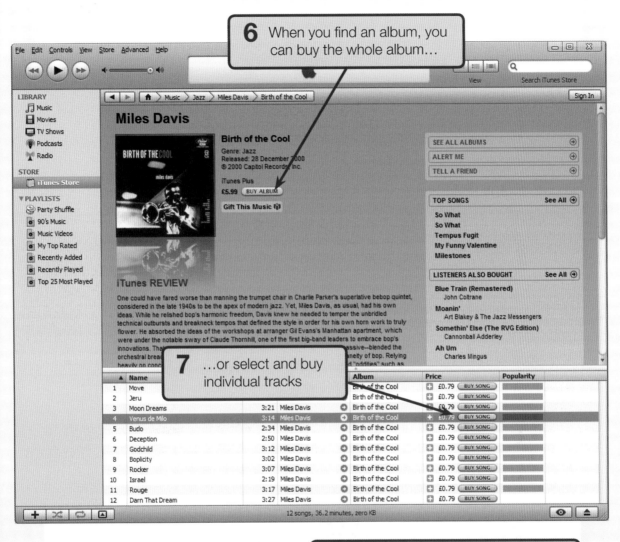

6 When you find an album, you can buy the whole album…

7 …or select and buy individual tracks

8 If you do not have an account with Apple, you will have to set one up to complete the transaction

7 watching and editing videos

You don't need a camcorder to shoot movies – most digital cameras can also take video. But if you do not have any video of your own, there are some clips in the Sample Videos folder which you can experiment with.

This chapter covers:

- Media Center and Media Player
- How to watch videos on your PC
- Windows Movie Maker, video editing software
- How to cut and splice video clips to make a movie
- How to add titles and credits to a video
- How to add voice-overs and music
- How to burn a movie file onto a DVD disc
- YouTube and publishing videos on the Internet
- Downloading videos from the Web

Playing a DVD

This has got to be the simplest thing that you can do with a PC! All you have to do is decide which player to use for showing the DVD – Media Player or the Media Center. Generally Media Player is the better bet – it starts faster and is more reliable.

When you place a DVD in the drive, the AutoPlay routine will swing into action. This will either ask you which player to use, or run the player if you have set that as the default action.

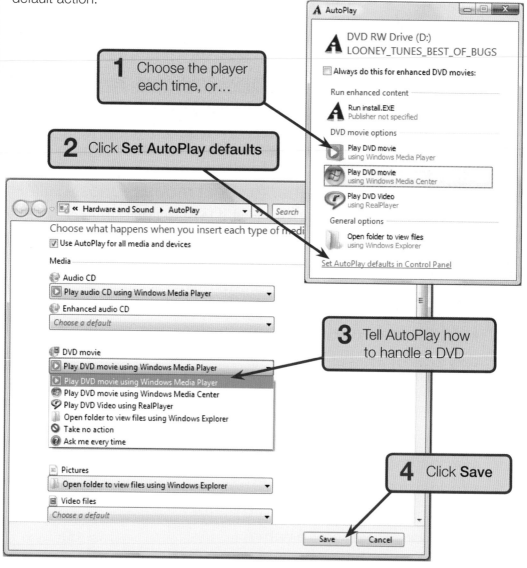

1 Choose the player each time, or...

2 Click **Set AutoPlay defaults**

3 Tell AutoPlay how to handle a DVD

4 Click **Save**

Watching a DVD

With a reasonable pair of speakers, and with Media Player running in full screen mode, a DVD is just as good on a PC as on a television.

Media Player does not have the full set of controls that you will find on a DVD player, and how they work varies a little with the DVD format, but a minute's playing with them should tell you all you need to know!

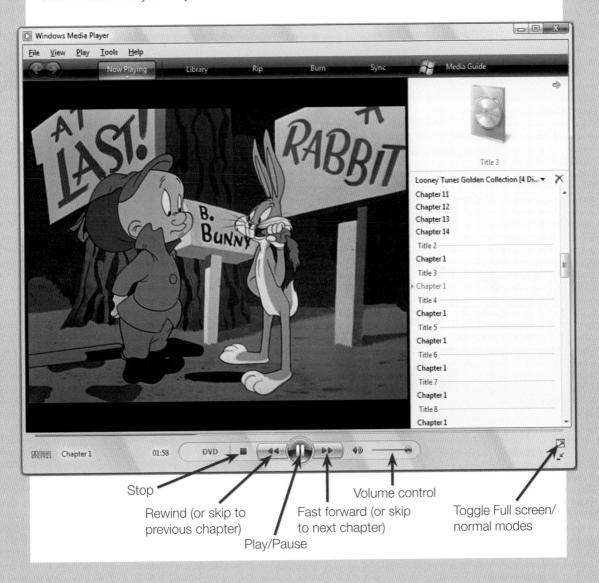

Stop

Rewind (or skip to previous chapter)

Play/Pause

Fast forward (or skip to next chapter)

Volume control

Toggle Full screen/ normal modes

Movie Maker

If you want to make a real movie, you'll need a script, a cast, a crew, sets, props and a few million dollars. If you just want to edit your family videos, Movie Maker is all that you need. You can use it to edit and splice video clips into a single movie, perhaps with transitions between scenes, and add titles and credits.

Import Media button – you will need this shortly

Imported clips are stored here

Current clip can be viewed and edited here

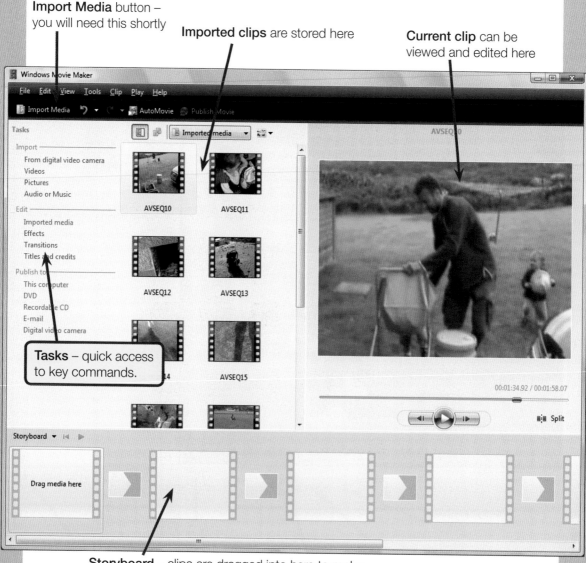

Tasks – quick access to key commands.

Storyboard – clips are dragged into here to make the movie. Their order can be changed if necessary.

The first job – assuming that you have shot or otherwise acquired all the clips that you will need for the movie – is to import the clips into Movie Maker.

Files can be imported directly from some digital cameras. With others, transfer them into your PC first, then import them from there.

1 In Movie Maker, click the **Import Media** button on the left of the toolbar

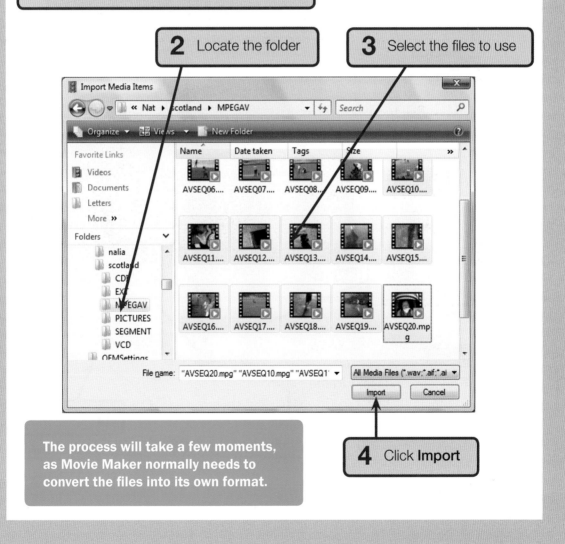

2 Locate the folder

3 Select the files to use

4 Click **Import**

The process will take a few moments, as Movie Maker normally needs to convert the files into its own format.

Edit video

Editing is essentially about cutting out the bits that don't work, then joining the good bits up in a way that makes sense. A clip can be split at any point. The front part gets (1) or (2) or (3) added to its name, and appears in the list of clips – and this is the part which stays in the viewer/editor. Either part can be split again, and you can do this as often as you need.

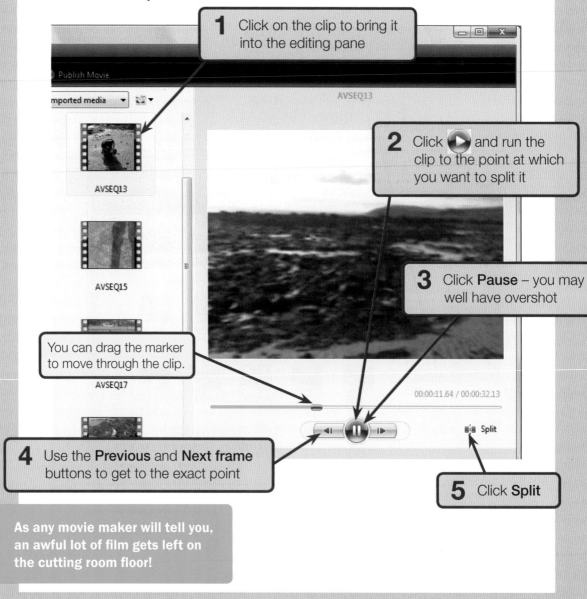

1 Click on the clip to bring it into the editing pane

2 Click ▶ and run the clip to the point at which you want to split it

3 Click **Pause** – you may well have overshot

You can drag the marker to move through the clip.

4 Use the **Previous** and **Next frame** buttons to get to the exact point

5 Click **Split**

As any movie maker will tell you, an awful lot of film gets left on the cutting room floor!

234

Adding to the Storyboard

Once you have trimmed your clips down to the good bits, you can start to assemble the movie. This is done in the Storyboard area. Drag clips onto the Storyboard to add them to the movie, and drag them into position there, to change their order.

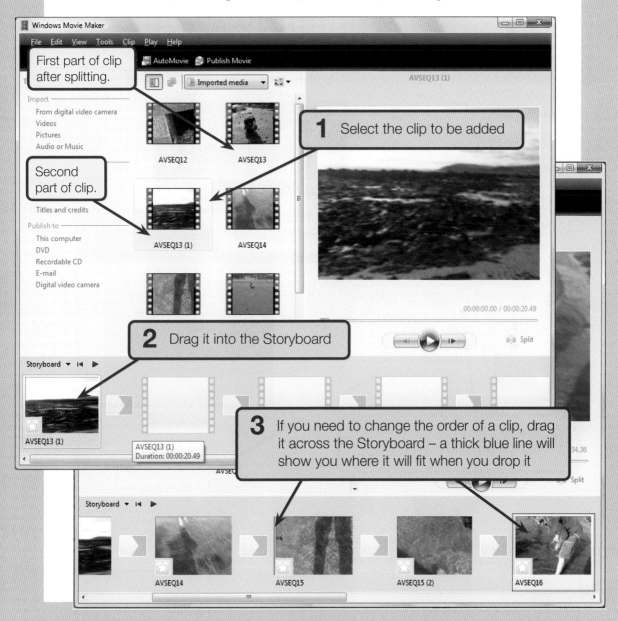

First part of clip after splitting.

Second part of clip.

1 Select the clip to be added

2 Drag it into the Storyboard

3 If you need to change the order of a clip, drag it across the Storyboard – a thick blue line will show you where it will fit when you drop it

Add titles

You can, of course, make your own movie title sequences, but Movie Maker has routines for adding a title screen and credits. All you need to do is type in the text, and pick the formatting, colour schemes and animation. Both the title and credits are clips, and can be viewed and edited as normal.

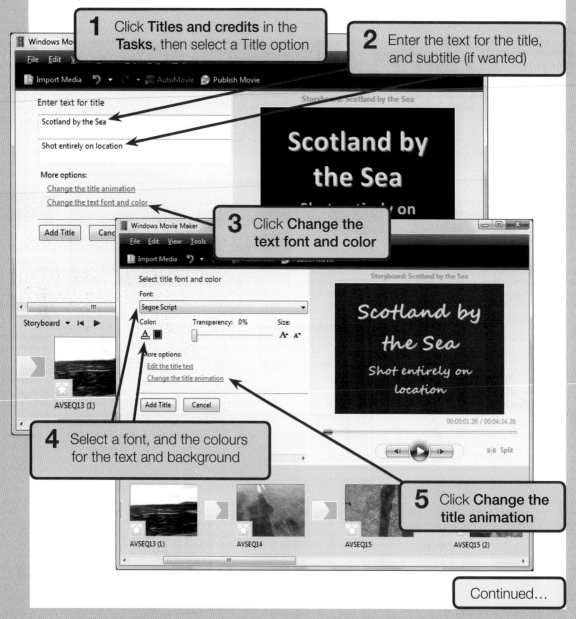

1 Click **Titles and credits** in the **Tasks**, then select a Title option

2 Enter the text for the title, and subtitle (if wanted)

3 Click **Change the text font and color**

4 Select a font, and the colours for the text and background

5 Click **Change the title animation**

Continued...

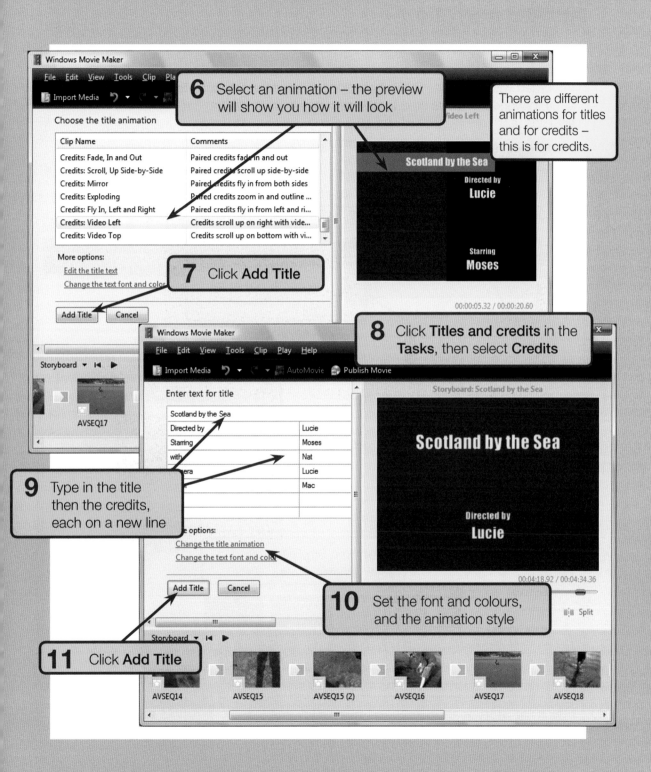

6 Select an animation – the preview will show you how it will look

There are different animations for titles and for credits – this is for credits.

Windows Movie Maker

File Edit View Tools Clip Pla

Import Media

Choose the title animation

Clip Name	Comments
Credits: Fade, In and Out	Paired credits fade in and out
Credits: Scroll, Up Side-by-Side	Paired credits scroll up side-by-side
Credits: Mirror	Paired credits fly in from both sides
Credits: Exploding	Paired credits zoom in and outline ...
Credits: Fly In, Left and Right	Paired credits fly in from left and ri...
Credits: Video Left	Credits scroll up on right with vide...
Credits: Video Top	Credits scroll up on bottom with vi...

More options:

Edit the title text

Change the text font and color

7 Click **Add Title**

Add Title   Cancel

Scotland by the Sea

Directed by
Lucie

Starring
Moses

00:00:05.32 / 00:00:20.60

8 Click **Titles and credits** in the **Tasks**, then select **Credits**

Windows Movie Maker

File Edit View Tools Clip Play Help

Import Media   AutoMovie   Publish Movie

Enter text for title

Storyboard: Scotland by the Sea

Scotland by the Sea	
Directed by	Lucie
Starring	Moses
with	Nat
era	Lucie
	Mac

9 Type in the title then the credits, each on a new line

e options:

Change the title animation
Change the text font and color

Add Title   Cancel

Scotland by the Sea

Directed by
Lucie

00:04:18.92 / 00:04:34.36

10 Set the font and colours, and the animation style

Split

Storyboard

AVSEQ17

11 Click **Add Title**

Storyboard

AVSEQ14   AVSEQ15   AVSEQ15 (2)   AVSEQ16   AVSEQ17   AVSEQ18

Adding narration

You can add a voice-over to your movie, to blend with or replace any sound recorded with the clips. This is best done after all the editing is finished. Take the time to work out your script, and to rehearse it while viewing the movie.

Don't try to record the whole script in one session. You cannot cut and splice audio clips, so work in self-contained units. If you mis-speak (and you will, unless you are a seasoned professional) you can record that unit again, without losing much work.

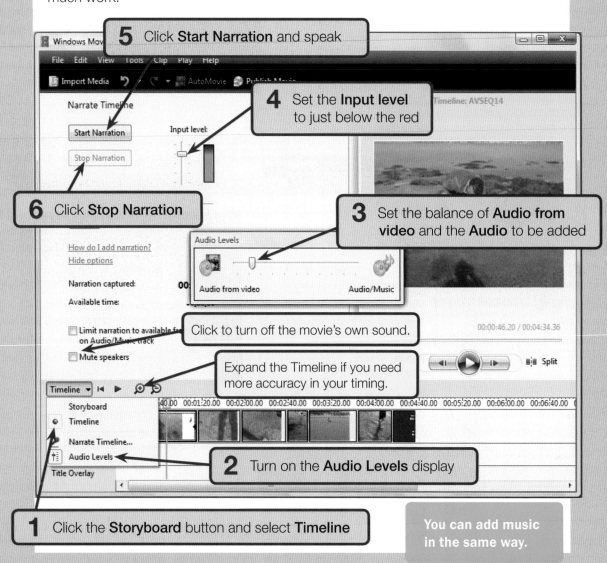

5 Click **Start Narration** and speak

4 Set the **Input level** to just below the red

6 Click **Stop Narration**

3 Set the balance of **Audio from video** and the **Audio** to be added

Click to turn off the movie's own sound.

Expand the Timeline if you need more accuracy in your timing.

2 Turn on the **Audio Levels** display

1 Click the **Storyboard** button and select **Timeline**

You can add music in the same way.

238

Transitions

How will you take your audience from one clip to the next? They can simply follow each other, or you can add transition effects to merge one into the next. There is a range of transitions, some of which work better than others in different situations. Try them – it's simple enough to remove them if they don't work.

1 Select **Transitions** in the **Tasks** menu

To preview a transition, click on it to pull it into the viewer, then play it.

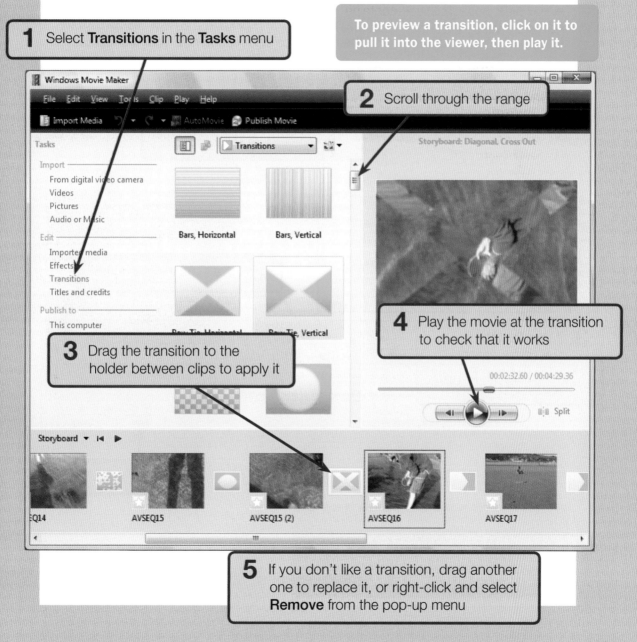

2 Scroll through the range

4 Play the movie at the transition to check that it works

3 Drag the transition to the holder between clips to apply it

5 If you don't like a transition, drag another one to replace it, or right-click and select **Remove** from the pop-up menu

Saving a movie project

As with any application, you must save your work as a file, if you don't want to lose it. But there is something different about movies which you need to note carefully. When you save a movie project, you do not save the movie itself. What you save is a list of the clips that you are using, details of which parts, the transitions and the title and credits text and formatting information. This is all that needs saving while you are working on the movie. When you re-open the project at the next session, Movie Maker will go off and track down the listed clips and reassemble your workspace.

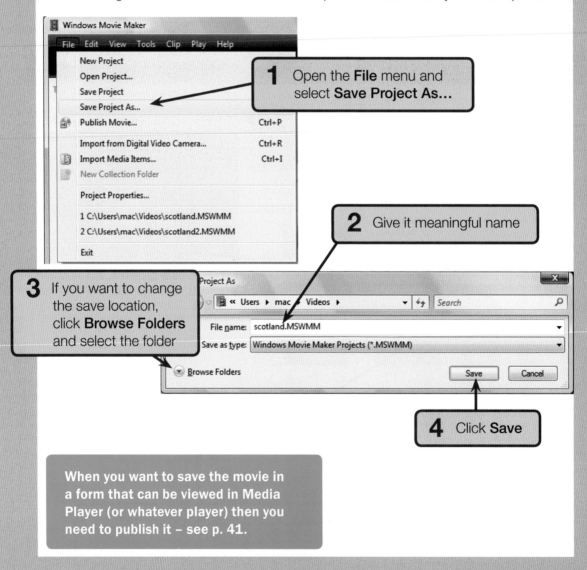

1 Open the **File** menu and select **Save Project As...**

2 Give it meaningful name

3 If you want to change the save location, click **Browse Folders** and select the folder

4 Click **Save**

When you want to save the movie in a form that can be viewed in Media Player (or whatever player) then you need to publish it – see p. 41.

Publishing your movie

When you publish a movie, Movie Maker takes all the clips, the transitions and the titles and forms them into one single file. The file can be in any of several formats, depending upon how you intend to publish it, and that depends upon how you intend to distribute it and what it will be played on. For example, the format used for sending by e-mail has a lower resolution and smaller file size.

1 Click **Publish Movie** on the toolbar

WMV (Windows Media Video) is the default format here, but you can change it for higher or lower resolutions – and therefore file size.

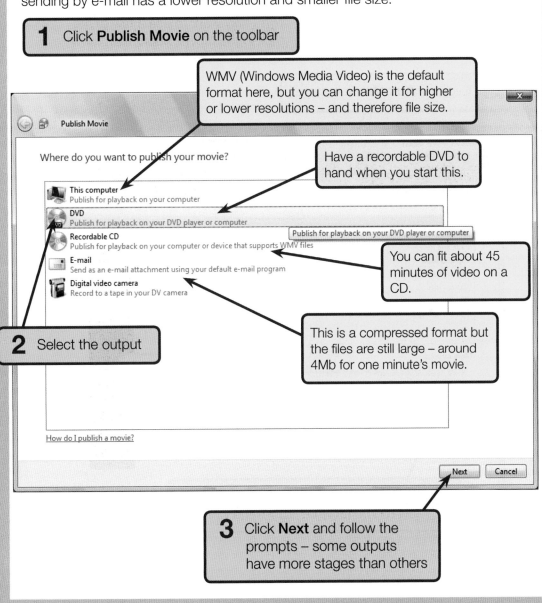

Publish Movie

Where do you want to publish your movie?

Have a recordable DVD to hand when you start this.

This computer
Publish for playback on your computer

DVD
Publish for playback on your DVD player or computer

Publish for playback on your DVD player or computer

Recordable CD
Publish for playback on your computer or device that supports WMV files

You can fit about 45 minutes of video on a CD.

E-mail
Send as an e-mail attachment using your default e-mail program

Digital video camera
Record to a tape in your DV camera

2 Select the output

This is a compressed format but the files are still large – around 4Mb for one minute's movie.

How do I publish a movie?

Next   Cancel

3 Click **Next** and follow the prompts – some outputs have more stages than others

AutoMovie

Here's a feature for people in a hurry. The AutoMovie routine will take your movie, slice out what it thinks are the best bits and make a movie for you – at a click of a button! All you will need to do is edit the title (maybe) and show it to your friends.

1 Import the clips

2 If you only want to use a few of the clips in the movie, select them now

3 Click the **AutoMovie** button

Windows Movie Maker

File   Edit   View   Tools   Clip   Play   Help

Import Media   AutoMovie   Publish Movie

Select an AutoMovie editing style   Automatically Create a Movie

Name	Description
Fade and Reveal	Applies fade and reveal transitions
Flip and Slide	Applies flip, slide, reveal, and page curl transitions
Highlights Movie	Cuts, fades, adds a title and credits
Music Video	Quick edits for fast beats and longer edits for slow b...
Old Movie	Film age effect applied to clips
Sports Highlights	Selects action clips and adds a title and credits

4 Pick an editing style

More options:

Enter a title for the movie

Select audio or background music

You could enter the title at this point.

Create AutoMovie   Cancel

5 Click **Create AutoMovie** – then wait a few moments while it does the work

Continued...

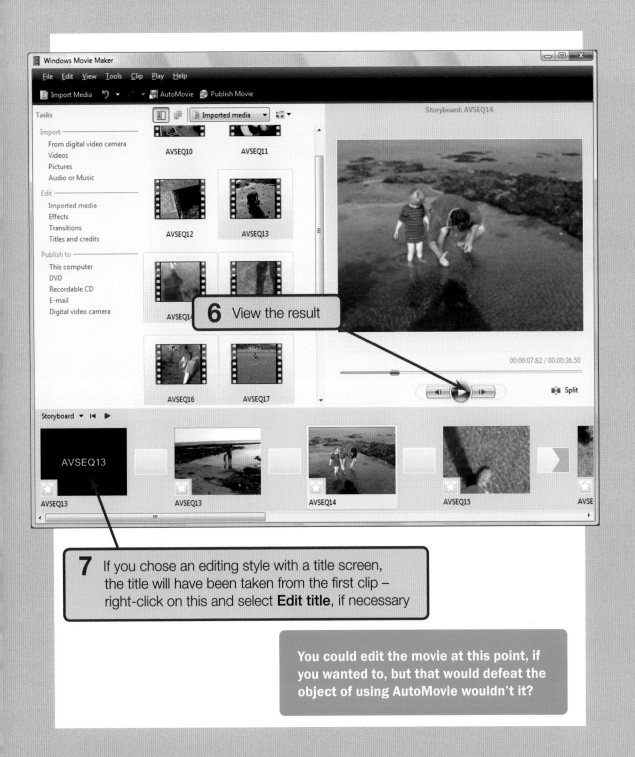

6 View the result

7 If you chose an editing style with a title screen, the title will have been taken from the first clip – right-click on this and select **Edit title**, if necessary

You could edit the movie at this point, if you wanted to, but that would defeat the object of using AutoMovie wouldn't it?

8 Organising your time

Calendar is part of the Vista package. To start it, click **Start**. It may be listed on the main menu. If not, point to **All Programs**. You should find it listed in the set of Windows programs.

This chapter covers:

- Windows Calendar
- The screen layout and elements
- How to record and keep track of appointments
- How Calendar can help you manage tasks
- How to set reminders
- Sharing calendars, so that you can co-ordinate your commitments with those of other people

Calendar screen and tools

Windows Calendar is supplied as part of the Vista package. You can use it to record and manage your appointments, meetings and other important dates, and to keep on top of the things you have to do.

Some of its features will only be of interest to people working in a business or other organisation where there is a local network and where easy access to other people's calendars makes it much simpler to set up meetings. Others are of value to us all. Use Calendar, and you need never again miss an appointment or a sports match, or forget a birthday!

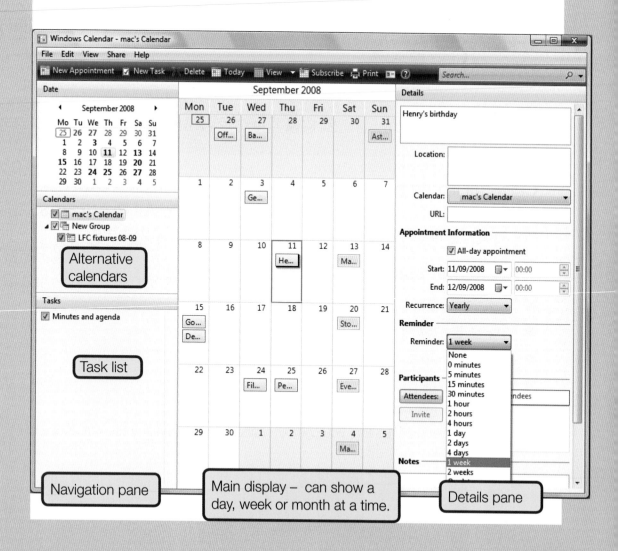

Changing the view

There are three aspects to this:

- The Navigation Pane and Details Pane are both optional. If you don't need them, turn them off and create more space for the main display

- The calendar can be shown one day, one week (work week, or full 7-day week) or one month at a time

- Today (this week/this month) is the default, but you can easily move through the calendar.

Most of these are controlled from the **View** menu.

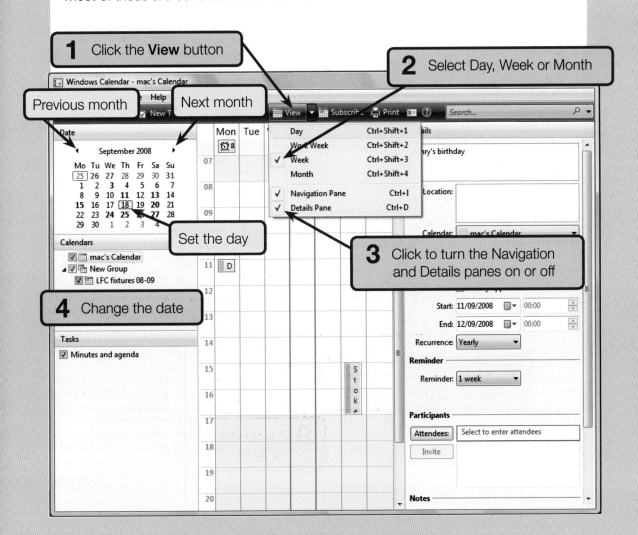

Make appointments and meetings

Setting up an appointment takes no more than two or three minutes. Arranging a meeting takes a little longer – but only because other people are involved. Both start the same way.

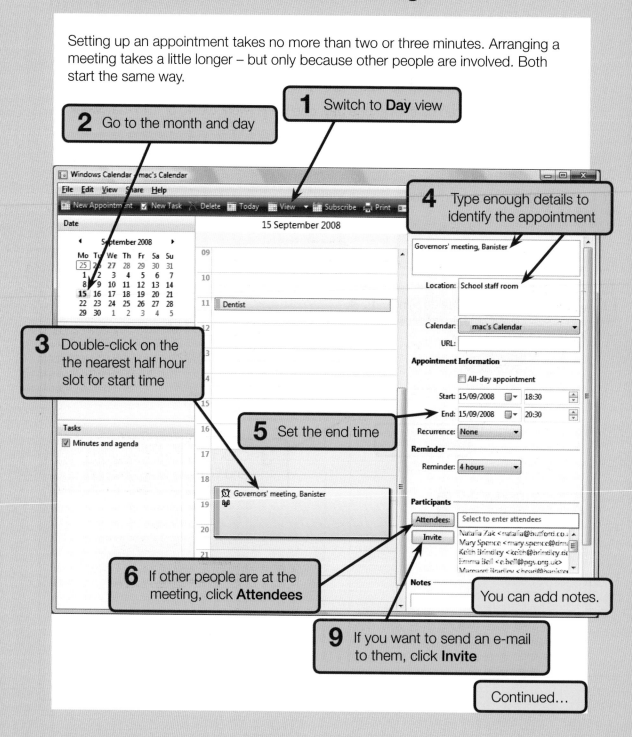

1 Switch to **Day** view

2 Go to the month and day

4 Type enough details to identify the appointment

3 Double-click on the the nearest half hour slot for start time

5 Set the end time

6 If other people are at the meeting, click **Attendees**

You can add notes.

9 If you want to send an e-mail to them, click **Invite**

Continued...

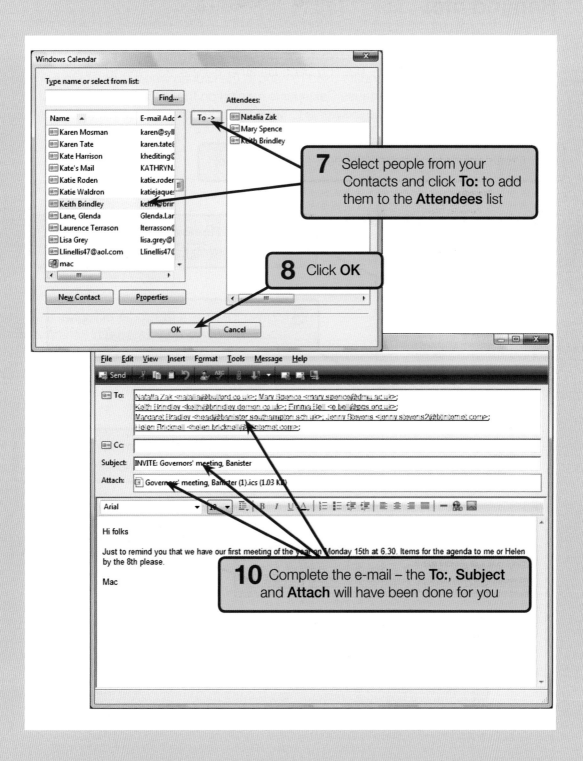

7 Select people from your Contacts and click **To:** to add them to the **Attendees** list

8 Click **OK**

10 Complete the e-mail – the **To:, Subject** and **Attach** will have been done for you

Remind me!

A calendar is no use if appointments can come and go by without you noticing, which is why my paper calendars used to hang in the kitchen where they would be seen every day. And just because Calendar is running on the PC, doesn't mean that you will refer to it in time. The answer is to set a reminder for anything that matters.

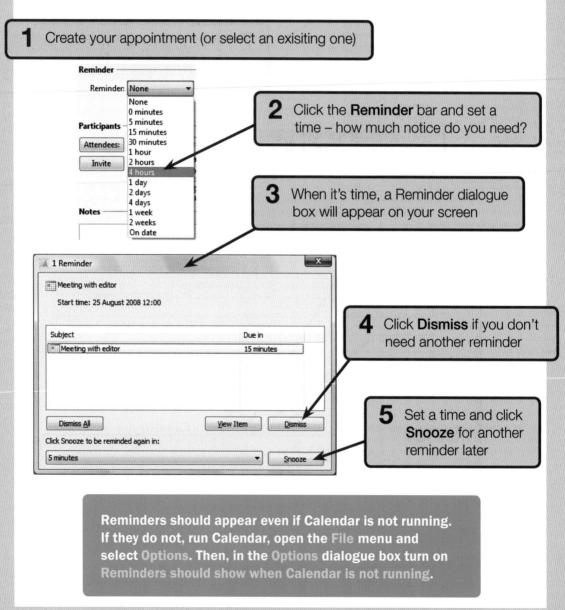

1 Create your appointment (or select an exisiting one)

2 Click the **Reminder** bar and set a time – how much notice do you need?

3 When it's time, a Reminder dialogue box will appear on your screen

4 Click **Dismiss** if you don't need another reminder

5 Set a time and click **Snooze** for another reminder later

Reminder
Reminder: None
None
0 minutes
5 minutes
15 minutes
30 minutes
1 hour
2 hours
4 hours
1 day
2 days
4 days
1 week
2 weeks
On date
Participants
Attendees:
Invite
Notes

1 Reminder
Meeting with editor
Start time: 25 August 2008 12:00
Subject | Due in
Meeting with editor | 15 minutes
Dismiss All | View Item | Dismiss
Click Snooze to be reminded again in:
5 minutes | Snooze

Reminders should appear even if Calendar is not running. If they do not, run Calendar, open the File menu and select Options. Then, in the Options dialogue box turn on Reminders should show when Calendar is not running.

As far as Calender is concerned, a task is the same as an appointment, but without a location or other people – the start and end times may also be more flexible.

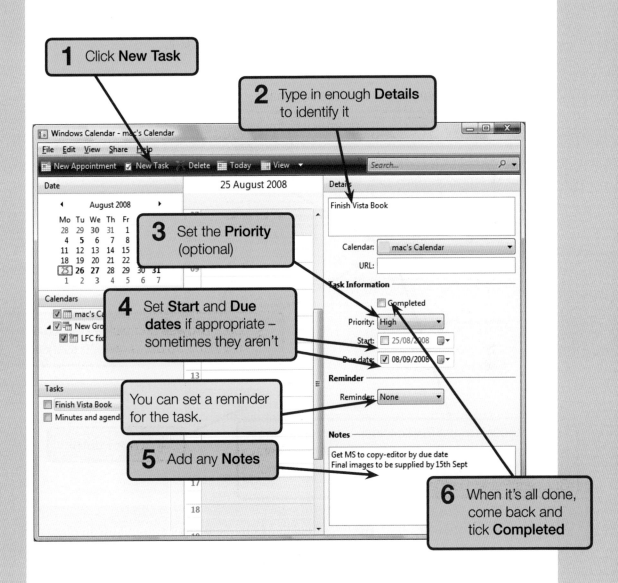

1 Click **New Task**

2 Type in enough **Details** to identify it

3 Set the **Priority** (optional)

4 Set **Start** and **Due** dates if appropriate – sometimes they aren't

You can set a reminder for the task.

5 Add any **Notes**

6 When it's all done, come back and tick **Completed**

Sharing calendars

Calendars can be shared with other people, across a network, over the Internet, or within the same PC. All you need is a place to store it, where others can access it. Here's how to share calendars with other users of the same PC.

- To make your calendar available to others, you **Publish** it
- To access another person's calendar, you **Subscribe** to it.

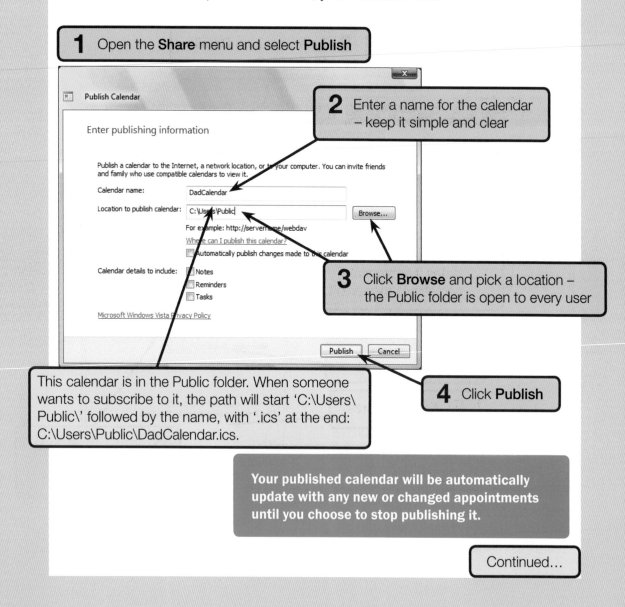

1 Open the **Share** menu and select **Publish**

Publish Calendar

Enter publishing information

Publish a calendar to the Internet, a network location, or to your computer. You can invite friends and family who use compatible calendars to view it.

Calendar name: DadCalendar

Location to publish calendar: C:\Users\Public

Browse...

For example: http://servername/webdav

Where can I publish this calendar?

☐ Automatically publish changes made to this calendar

Calendar details to include: ☐ Notes
☐ Reminders
☐ Tasks

Microsoft Windows Vista Privacy Policy

Publish   Cancel

2 Enter a name for the calendar – keep it simple and clear

3 Click **Browse** and pick a location – the Public folder is open to every user

This calendar is in the Public folder. When someone wants to subscribe to it, the path will start 'C:\Users\Public\' followed by the name, with '.ics' at the end: C:\Users\Public\DadCalendar.ics.

4 Click **Publish**

Your published calendar will be automatically update with any new or changed appointments until you choose to stop publishing it.

Continued...

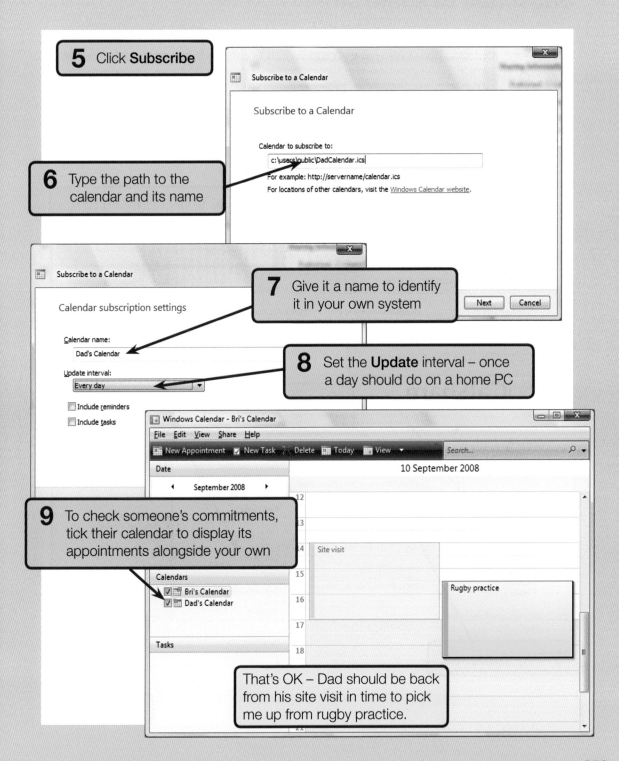

5 Click **Subscribe**

Subscribe to a Calendar

Subscribe to a Calendar

Calendar to subscribe to:

c:\users\public\DadCalendar.ics

6 Type the path to the calendar and its name

For example: http://servername/calendar.ics

For locations of other calendars, visit the Windows Calendar website.

Subscribe to a Calendar

Calendar subscription settings

7 Give it a name to identify it in your own system

Next   Cancel

Calendar name:

Dad's Calendar

8 Set the **Update** interval – once a day should do on a home PC

Update interval:

Every day

☐ Include reminders
☐ Include tasks

Windows Calendar - Bri's Calendar

File Edit View Share Help

New Appointment   New Task   Delete   Today   View ▼   Search...

Date

◄   September 2008   ►

10 September 2008

12

13

9 To check someone's commitments, tick their calendar to display its appointments alongside your own

14   Site visit

15

Rugby practice

Calendars

☑ Bri's Calendar
☑ Dad's Calendar

16

17

Tasks

18

That's OK – Dad should be back from his site visit in time to pick me up from rugby practice.

Subscribe to share site

In theory, you can share calendars via the Web. In practice there are two obstacles:

- You need access to a site where you can publish your calender
- Other people need a Vista PC or an Apple for easy access to your calendar.

But explore the idea. You might start by subscribing to some public calendars. There are thousands at iCalShare – if there's one for your club, you can have the fixtures in your own calendar.

1 Go to iCalShare at www.icalshare.com

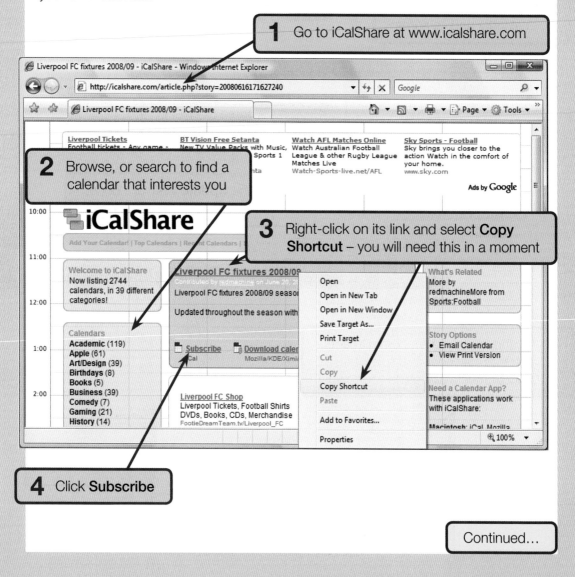

2 Browse, or search to find a calendar that interests you

3 Right-click on its link and select **Copy Shortcut** – you will need this in a moment

4 Click **Subscribe**

Continued...

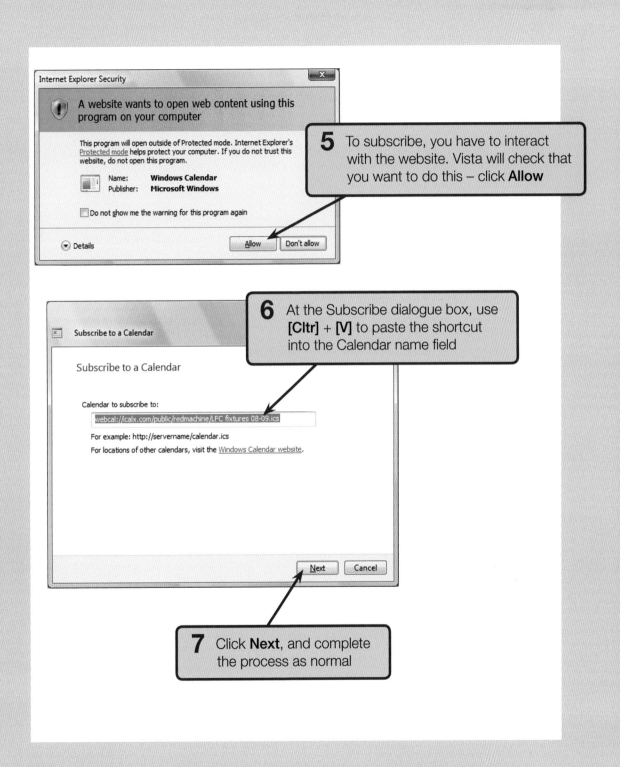

Internet Explorer Security

A website wants to open web content using this program on your computer

This program will open outside of Protected mode. Internet Explorer's Protected mode helps protect your computer. If you do not trust this website, do not open this program.

Name: **Windows Calendar**
Publisher: **Microsoft Windows**

Do not show me the warning for this program again

Details   Allow   Don't allow

5 To subscribe, you have to interact with the website. Vista will check that you want to do this – click **Allow**

6 At the Subscribe dialogue box, use [Cltr] + [V] to paste the shortcut into the Calendar name field

Subscribe to a Calendar

Subscribe to a Calendar

Calendar to subscribe to:

webcal://icalx.com/public/redmachine/LFC fixtures 08-09.ics

For example: http://servername/calendar.ics
For locations of other calendars, visit the Windows Calendar website.

Next   Cancel

7 Click **Next**, and complete the process as normal

9 Organising your money

In this chapter we will be using Excel 2007, part of the latest Microsoft Office suite, and present in all editions of the software. If you have Word 2007, you also have Excel 2007.

This chapter covers:

- Spreadsheets and the Microsoft Excel software
- How to move around a sheet and edit data
- Arithmetic and calculations
- Using cell references
- Copying values and using AutoFill
- How to build a simple budget system
- How to create invoices for a small business
- How to build a spreadsheet to keep track of your savings
- How to work out loan repayments – it's easy!

The Excel window

A spreadsheet is a system for storing data – mainly numbers – and for performing calculations. These can range from simple sums through to complex financial functions, such as mortgage repayment calculations.

The original spreadsheet was a large sheet of paper, ruled in rows and columns, and accountants would write into it their figures, and the results of their calculations (done by hand!). Excel has the same basic design, but add to this a large set of tools, which are all stored in the Ruler, above the sheet.

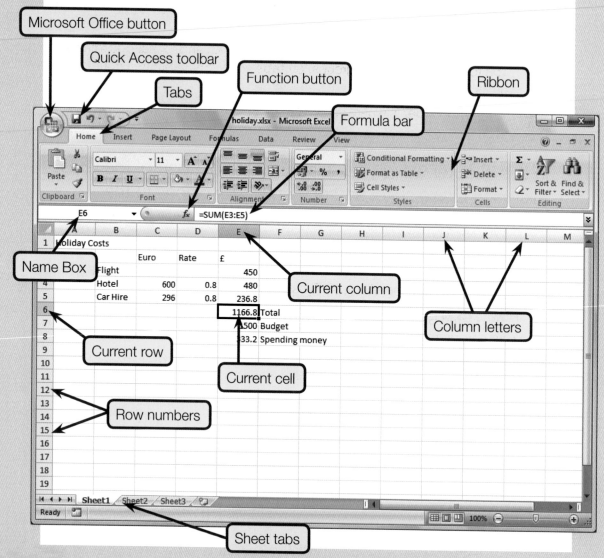

1 Run Excel. If you can't see it on the **Start** menu, look in **All Programs** in the **Microsoft Office** folder.

2 Identify these parts of the Excel window:

- The **Microsoft Office button** – click this to open the menu of filing commands

- The **Quick Access toolbar** – with shortcuts to selected commands. At first this will only have **Save**, **Undo** and **Redo**. You can add more shortcuts, just as you can in Word (see p. 63)

- The **Ribbon** holds the tools that you use to create and format documents. The tools are arranged in groups, on **tabs**. To bring a tab to the front, click on its name

- The **Formula bar** is where you edit data and formulae (see p. 262).

- The **Current cell** is the one that the cursor is in – you can recognise it by its thicker outline. This is linked to the Formula bar so that whatever is typed there goes into the current cell.

- **Column letters** are used to identify columns. They run through from A to Z, then start again from AA, AB and work through to ZZ, then start again from AAA and go on to a maximum of over 16,000! The letter of the **current column** (the one containing the current cell) is highlighted.

- **Row numbers** are used to identify rows. There can be up to 1,000,000 rows. The number of the **current row** is highlighted.

- The **Name Box** identifies the current cell. Cells can be given names, but are usually identified by their column letter and row number (see p. 264).

- A function is a ready-made formula, to which you just give the required data. The **Function button** is used for finding functions and working with them.

- An Excel file can have many separate worksheets. Together they are known as a workbook. Use the **sheet tabs** to switch between them.

The Microsoft Office button

There is a menu that opens from the Microsoft Office button. This holds commands which relate to the whole document – New, Open, Save, Print and the like. Some of these are simple one-job commands; others have options.

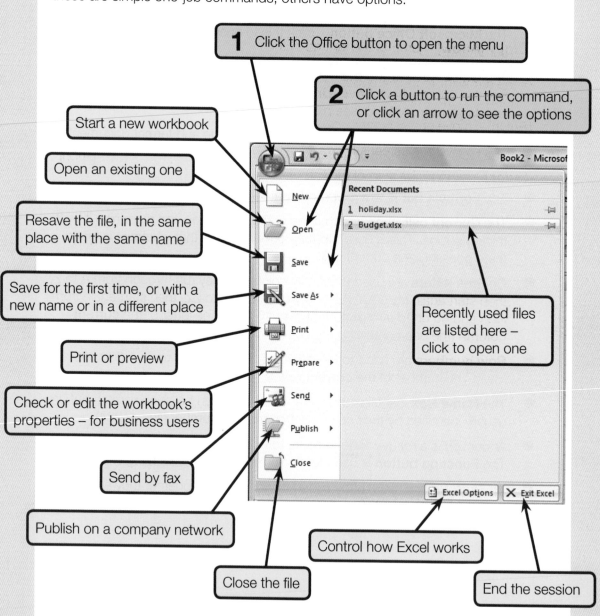

1 Click the Office button to open the menu

2 Click a button to run the command, or click an arrow to see the options

Start a new workbook

Open an existing one

Resave the file, in the same place with the same name

Save for the first time, or with a new name or in a different place

Print or preview

Check or edit the workbook's properties – for business users

Send by fax

Publish on a company network

Close the file

Recently used files are listed here – click to open one

Control how Excel works

End the session

Moving around the sheet

To make a different cell the current cell, you have to move the highlight to it. Much of the time, the simplest way to do this to click into the cell with the mouse. Sometimes it is simpler to move there with the keys. Learn these keystrokes:

- **[Arrows]** – one cell left, right, up or down

- **[Ctrl]** + **[Arrow]** – jump to the far end of the current block or the start of the next in the direction of the arrow (or to the far edges of the sheet if there is nothing in the way)

- **[PgUp]** – move one screenful up

- **[PgDn]** – move one screenful down

- **[Home]** – jump to the start of the line

- **[Ctrl]** + **[Home]** jump to cell A1 (the top left corner of the sheet)

- **[Ctrl]** + **[End]** – jump to the cell at the bottom right corner of the active sheet – i.e. where all the cells are empty further down and further to the right.

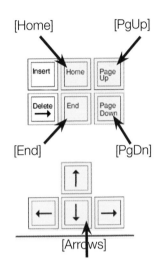

On a large sheet, use the scroll bars to move areas into view

[Ctrl] + [End] would take you here, on this sheet

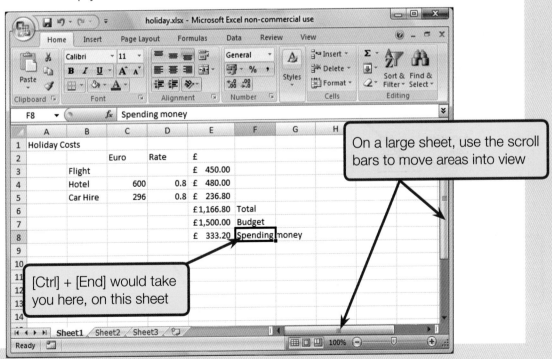

Data entry and edit

Start typing and your typing appears in two places – in the Formula bar and in the current cell. Watch whichever one works best for you.

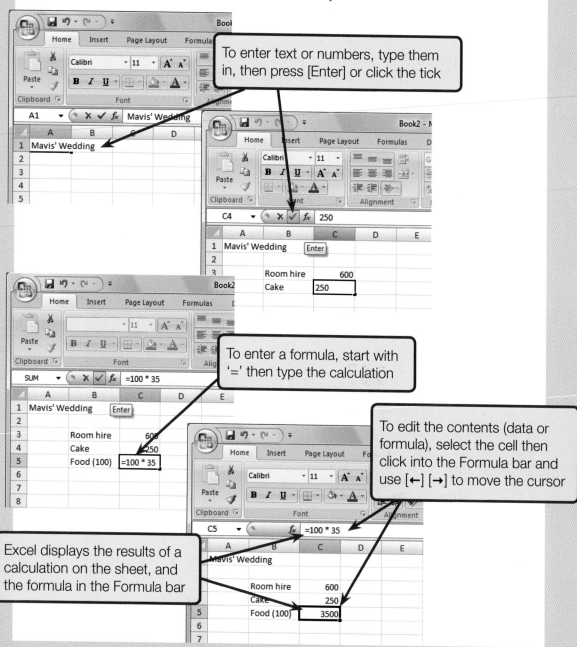

To enter text or numbers, type them in, then press [Enter] or click the tick

To enter a formula, start with '=' then type the calculation

To edit the contents (data or formula), select the cell then click into the Formula bar and use [←] [→] to move the cursor

Excel displays the results of a calculation on the sheet, and the formula in the Formula bar

Simple calculations

Excel use these arithmetic operators:

+ Add   – Subtract   * Multiply   / Divide   ^ Power   () Brackets

They can be used in any combination, and follow the normal rules of precedence. Where there are mixed operators, Excel calculates them in the order:

1   Expressions in brackets

2   Power

3   Multiply and divide, working left to right across the sum

4   Add and subtract, working left to right.

There are some examples in this screenshot.

- Column C shows what the formulae look like
- Column D shows the results of the calculations

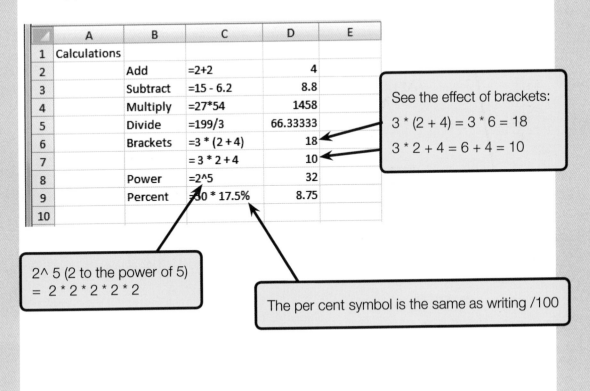

	A	B	C	D	E
1	Calculations				
2		Add	=2+2	4	
3		Subtract	=15 - 6.2	8.8	
4		Multiply	=27*54	1458	
5		Divide	=199/3	66.33333	
6		Brackets	=3 * (2 + 4)	18	
7			= 3 * 2 + 4	10	
8		Power	=2^5	32	
9		Percent	=50 * 17.5%	8.75	
10					

See the effect of brackets:

$3 * (2 + 4) = 3 * 6 = 18$

$3 * 2 + 4 = 6 + 4 = 10$

2^5 (2 to the power of 5)
= 2 * 2 * 2 * 2 * 2

The per cent symbol is the same as writing /100

Cells and ranges

Every cell has its own unique identifier or cell reference. It is made up of the column letter followed by the row number. The references are used in formulae to access the values in their cells.

Some calculations can be performed on **ranges** (blocks of cells) e.g. adding up the total of a column. To identify these, we give the references of the cells in the top left and bottom right corners, seperated by a colon, e.g. A1: B4.

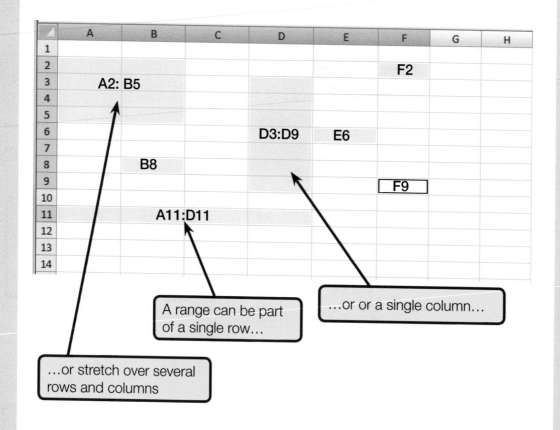

A range can be part of a single row...

...or or a single column...

...or stretch over several rows and columns

Cell references in formulae

While you can use a spreadsheet to calculate directly with numbers, that's not the best way to use it. Excel can work with the values in cells, and the beauty of this is that if you want to do the same calculation with different values, you can just change the values, and not rewrite the formula.

For example, what's €500 in pounds, if €1.00 = £0.82?

Try it, click into a cell and type = 500 * 0.82

But what if the exchange rate is €1.00 = £0.84?

Let's build a spreadsheet.

1 Click the Microsoft Office button and select **New**

New
Open
Save

Recent Documents
1 holiday.xlsx
2 Budget.xlsx

2 Click into cell A1 and type: Formulae

3 Type these headings into A3, A4 and A5

10 Click the tick

4 In B3 type: 500

SUM ▾ X ✓ *fx* =B3*B4

	A	B	C
1	Formulae		
2			
3	Price in Euros	500	
4	Exchange rate	0.82	
5	Price in Pounds	=B3*B4	
6			

7 Click into B3 – its reference will be added to the formula

6 In B5 type: = (to start the formula)

8 Type: * (multiply)

9 Click into B4, to add its reference to the formula

5 In B4 type: 0.82

If you have followed the steps correctly, you should see £410 in B5. Change the number of euros (in B3) – what does B5 show? Change the exchange rate (in B4) and see its effect.

Adjusting the rows and columns

Spreadsheet systems are flexible, in many ways. Rows and columns can be inserted if you need to add more between existing material (or deleted if you want to close up unused space).

Here's how to insert a single row:

1 Click on the number of the row you want to move down to make space for an extra one

2 Right-click anywhere on the highlighted row and select **Insert** from the menu

To delete unwanted rows, select **Delete.**

You can insert several rows at once. Here's how:

This is the **mini toolbar.**

3 Decide where you want to insert the rows and drag down the numbers of the rows at that point, to select them

4 Right-click on the highlighted rows and select **Insert**

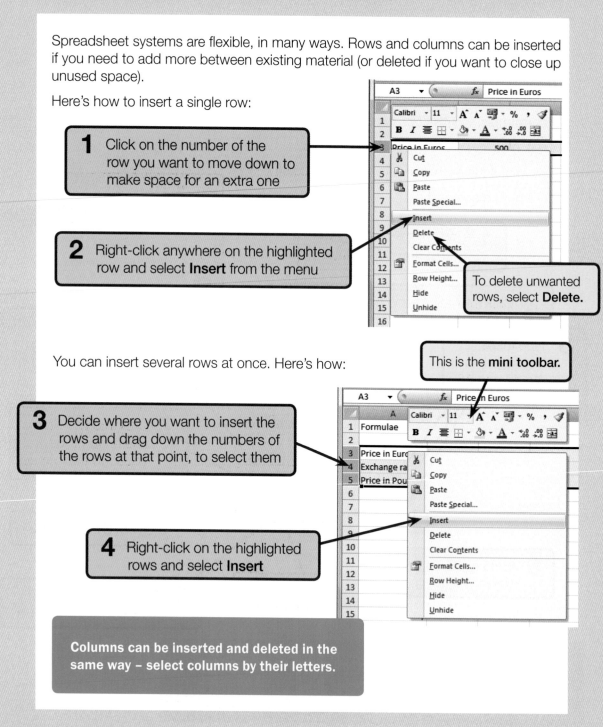

Columns can be inserted and deleted in the same way – select columns by their letters.

Column width

You will have noticed that if you type too much text into a cell it spills across into the next one. And that's OK, unless the next cell is occupied – and then the text gets chopped short. We can soon fix that. You can adjust the width of columns, to allow room for longer text labels. Here are two ways to do it.

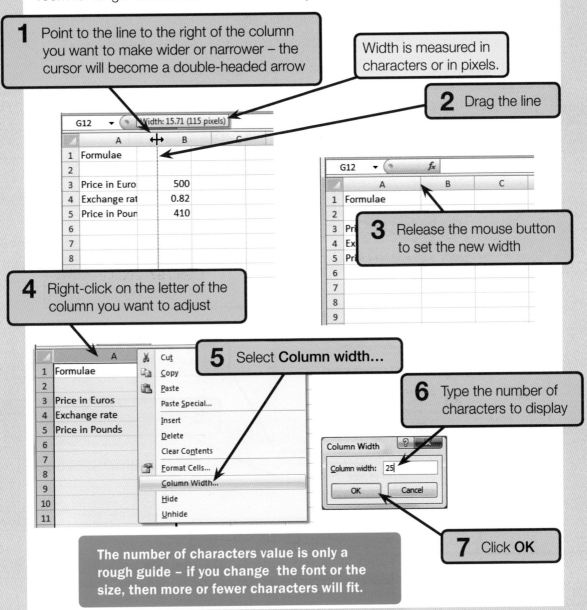

1 Point to the line to the right of the column you want to make wider or narrower – the cursor will become a double-headed arrow

Width is measured in characters or in pixels.

2 Drag the line

3 Release the mouse button to set the new width

4 Right-click on the letter of the column you want to adjust

5 Select **Column width...**

6 Type the number of characters to display

7 Click **OK**

The number of characters value is only a rough guide – if you change the font or the size, then more or fewer characters will fit.

Saving files

In Excel, as in most applications, anything that you enter into it will be lost when you exit – unless you save it as a file. There are three things to decide when saving:

- Which format to use – the Excel 2007 Workbook format cannot be read by people with earlier versions of the software. If the spreadsheet is to be shared with others, select the Excel 97–2003 format
- Where to save it – the simple solution is to put it in your Documents folder
- What to call it – the default names are Book1, Book2, etc.

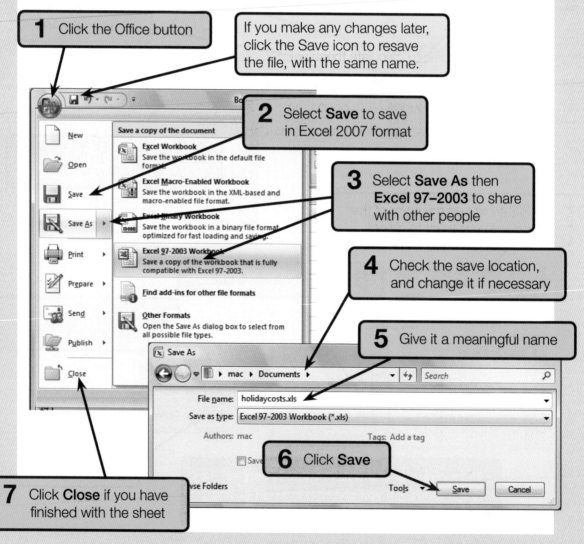

1 Click the Office button

If you make any changes later, click the Save icon to resave the file, with the same name.

2 Select **Save** to save in Excel 2007 format

3 Select **Save As** then **Excel 97–2003** to share with other people

4 Check the save location, and change it if necessary

5 Give it a meaningful name

6 Click **Save**

7 Click **Close** if you have finished with the sheet

Practice!

If you have got this far, then you will know enough to build a simple spreadsheet.

Here's the scenario. A group of you are going on holiday and will be hiring a car and splitting the costs between you. The variables (the values which might change) are:

- the daily hire rate
- the number of days
- the insurance surcharge (fixed no matter how long the hire)
- the exchange rate (the hire will be priced in euros, but you want it in pounds)
- the number in the group (Charlie can't make his mind up).

You need formulae to calculate these values:

- The price in euros (daily rate times number of days plus insurance)
- The price in pounds (euro price times the exchange rate)
- The cost for each member (pounds divided by number in the group).

The finished sheet should look like this.

	A	B	C
1	Car Hire		
2			
3	Daily rate	25	
4	Number of days	18	
5	Insurance	50	
6	Price in Euros	500	
7	Exchange rate	0.82	
8	Price in Pounds	410	
9	Number in party	4	
10	Cost for each	102.5	

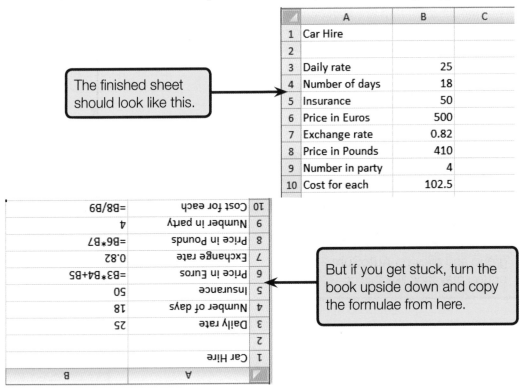

But if you get stuck, turn the book upside down and copy the formulae from here.

	A	B
1	Car Hire	
2		
3	Daily rate	25
4	Number of days	18
5	Insurance	50
6	Price in Euros	=B3*B4+B5
7	Exchange rate	0.82
8	Price in Pounds	=B6*B7
9	Number in party	4
10	Cost for each	=B8/B9

The SUM function

If you want to add up a set of numbers, you can do it in two ways.

- Write a formula to add the values in each cell. This is OK where there are only a few cells, and you are not likely to change them. Building a formula using '+' and cell references is hard work when there are more than a few cells

- Use the SUM function. This will add up all the values in a range of cells. The range can be any size, and it can be stretched, if necessary, to add in more cells.

Here's how to use SUM:

1 Set up a spreadsheet like this one – it doesn't have to have the costs for Mavis' wedding, but it should have a set of values in C3 down to C8

2 Select the range of cells with the values (C3:C8) and the next two beyond

3 On the Ribbon, look in the **Editing** group and click on **AutoSum** – the button may look like this ∑ ▾

If you are adding values in a row, include the next two cells on the right.

Continued...

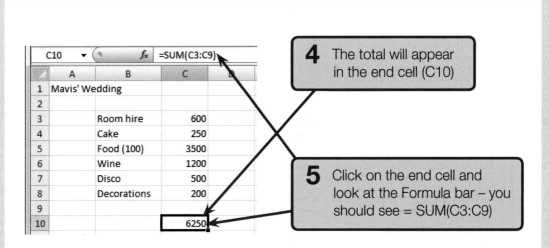

4 The total will appear in the end cell (C10)

5 Click on the end cell and look at the Formula bar – you should see = SUM(C3:C9)

Stretching a range

The range in the example SUM function was C3:C9. If rows are inserted between 3 and 9, the range will adjusted. As there is a blank row between the last cell in the range and the formula, we can insert a new row there without changing the existing order of things. (Which is why you should always leave a blank at the end.)

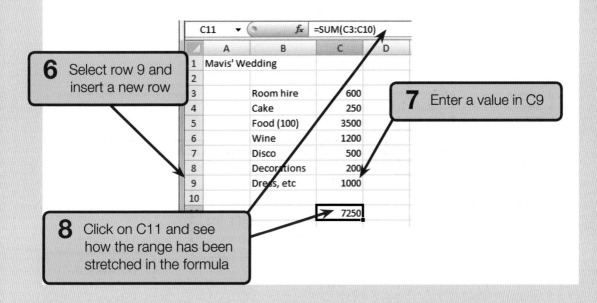

6 Select row 9 and insert a new row

7 Enter a value in C9

8 Click on C11 and see how the range has been stretched in the formula

Copying

Building a spreadsheet typically involves a lot of copying. If you were setting up a budgeting sheet, for example (as we are here), many of the costs are the same every month, and the same calculations are needed – add up all the outgoings and subtract them from the incoming. Excel recognises this and provides some very neat tools for copying data and formulae. Work through this next example and you will see. It creates a six-month budget – I've based the figures on a student. Use your own figures or headings, but keep the structure the same.

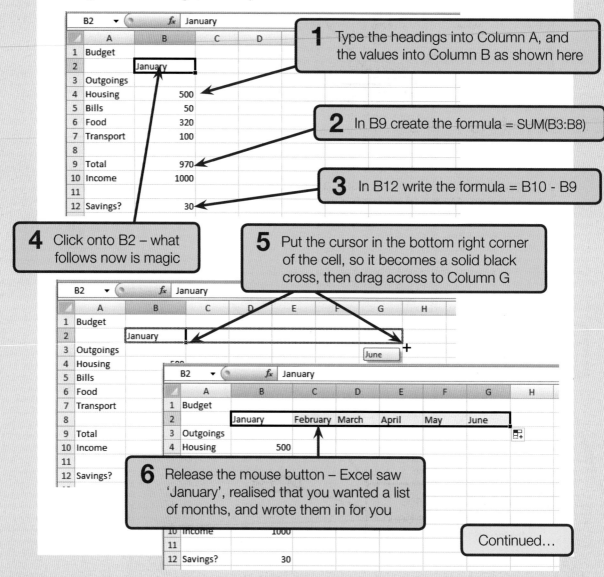

1 Type the headings into Column A, and the values into Column B as shown here

2 In B9 create the formula = SUM(B3:B8)

3 In B12 write the formula = B10 - B9

4 Click onto B2 – what follows now is magic

5 Put the cursor in the bottom right corner of the cell, so it becomes a solid black cross, then drag across to Column G

6 Release the mouse button – Excel saw 'January', realised that you wanted a list of months, and wrote them in for you

Continued...

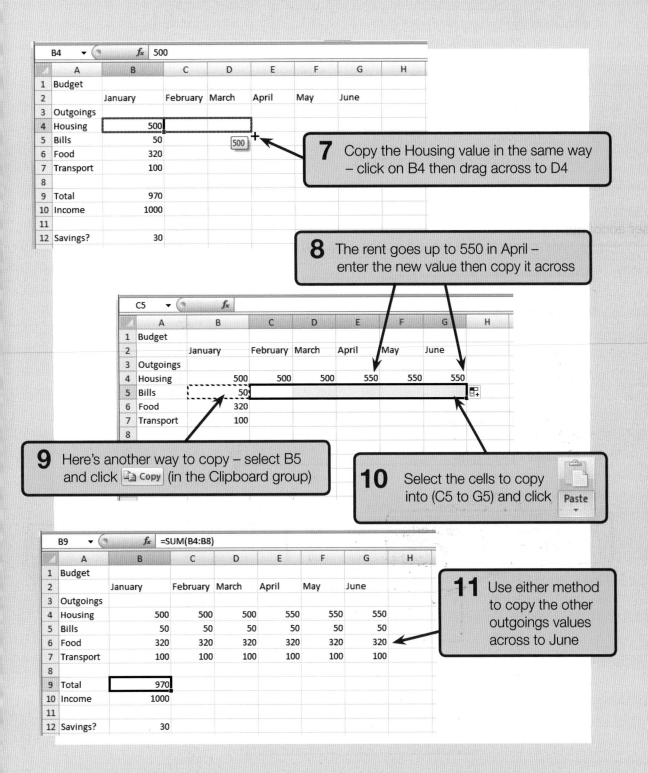

B4 | *fx* 500

	A	B	C	D	E	F	G	H
1	Budget							
2		January	February	March	April	May	June	
3	Outgoings							
4	Housing	500						
5	Bills	50						
6	Food	320						
7	Transport	100						
8								
9	Total	970						
10	Income	1000						
11								
12	Savings?	30						

500

7 Copy the Housing value in the same way – click on B4 then drag across to D4

8 The rent goes up to 550 in April – enter the new value then copy it across

C5 | *fx*

	A	B	C	D	E	F	G	H
1	Budget							
2		January	February	March	April	May	June	
3	Outgoings							
4	Housing	500	500	500	550	550	550	
5	Bills	50						
6	Food	320						
7	Transport	100						
8								

9 Here's another way to copy – select B5 and click 🗐 Copy (in the Clipboard group)

10 Select the cells to copy into (C5 to G5) and click Paste

B9 | *fx* =SUM(B4:B8)

	A	B	C	D	E	F	G	H
1	Budget							
2		January	February	March	April	May	June	
3	Outgoings							
4	Housing	500	500	500	550	550	550	
5	Bills	50	50	50	50	50	50	
6	Food	320	320	320	320	320	320	
7	Transport	100	100	100	100	100	100	
8								
9	Total	970						
10	Income	1000						
11								
12	Savings?	30						

11 Use either method to copy the other outgoings values across to June

AutoFill

You have already seen AutoFill at work – that was what created the January to June series. AutoFill will take a value in one cell and fill the adjacent cells (across the row or down the column) with:

- a series of dates or numbers

- the number, without changing it.

The question is, how does it know what to do? The answer is, it takes a guess, but it gives you the final say. AutoFIll can also take a formula, and copy it, adjusting the cell references to fit.

You can see both of these things at work in this example.

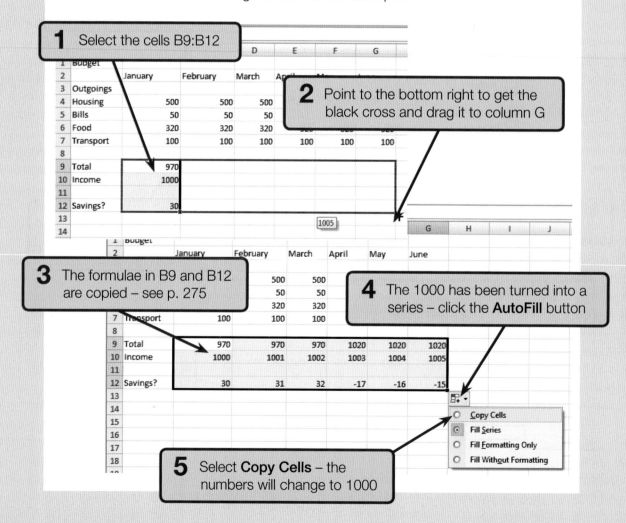

1 Select the cells B9:B12

2 Point to the bottom right to get the black cross and drag it to column G

3 The formulae in B9 and B12 are copied – see p. 275

4 The 1000 has been turned into a series – click the **AutoFill** button

5 Select **Copy Cells** – the numbers will change to 1000

References in formulae

When Excel copies a formula, it automatically adjusts the cell references to match the position of the new copies. In the Budget spreadsheet, the formula in B9 is:

= SUM(B4:B8)

and Excel understands this to mean, add up the values in the 5 cells above the one holding the formula. So, when it copies the formula over to G9, it adjusts it to read:

= SUM(G4:G9)

so that it still refers to the cells above the SUM.

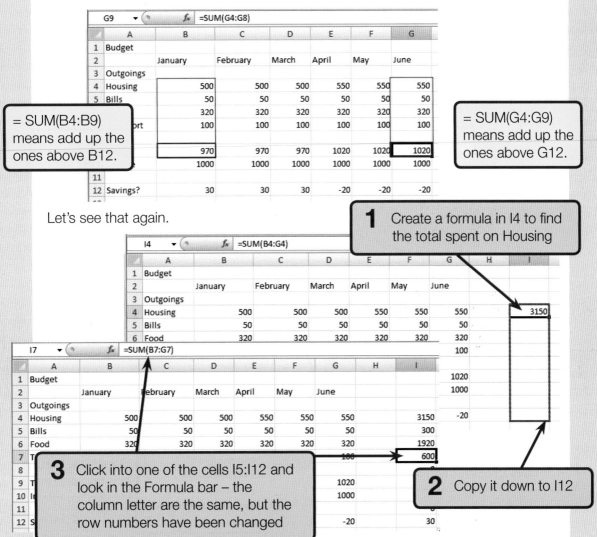

= SUM(B4:B9)
means add up the
ones above B12.

= SUM(G4:G9)
means add up the
ones above G12.

Let's see that again.

1 Create a formula in I4 to find the total spent on Housing

2 Copy it down to I12

3 Click into one of the cells I5:I12 and look in the Formula bar – the column letter are the same, but the row numbers have been changed

Formatting in Excel

You have many of the same formatting options in Excel as in Word. You can set the font, size, colour and style, and align it to the left, right or centre of the cells. And then there are more, because spreadsheets have different layout needs. You can:

- Set the vertical alignment – putting text in the top, bottom or middle of the cell
- Display the text at an angle or vertical – for headings to narrow columns
- Add a range of lines and borders – thin, thick or double underlines are often put below ranges of values, and/or their totals
- Make one heading span several columns – this is 'Merge and Center'.

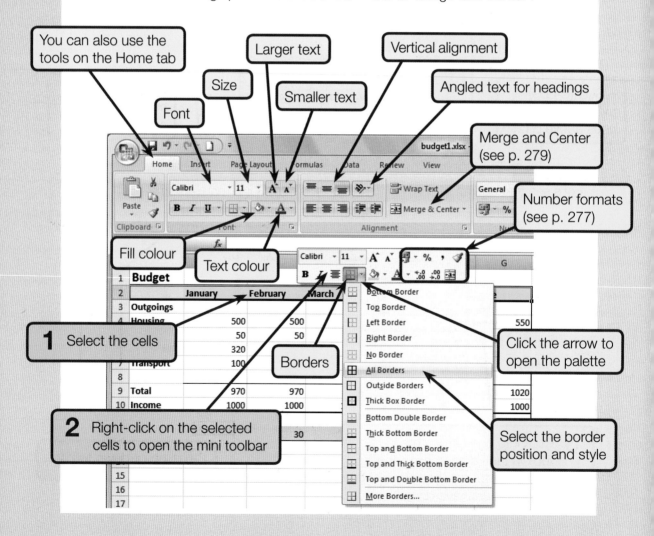

Number formats

What does a number look like? It depends on what sort of number it is – it could be a simple or currency, or a percentage, or a date, or an astronomical figure that is best expressed in scientific notation. Excel can handle all of these. Below the surface of the sheet, all numbers are treated the same way, but they can be formatted different ways for display. The options are in the **Number** group on the **Home** tab.

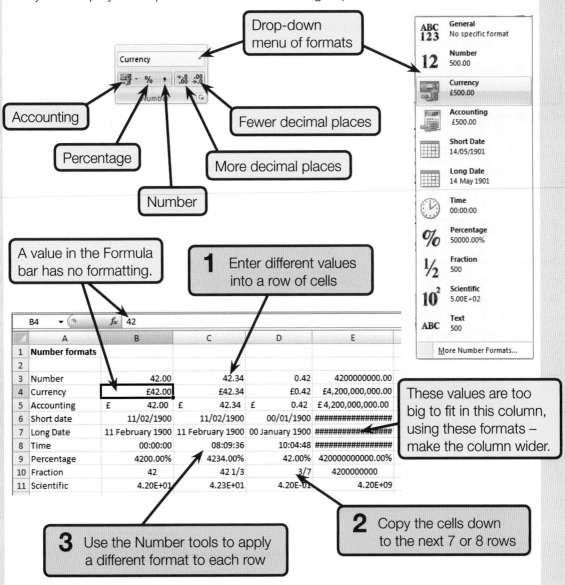

Drop-down menu of formats

Accounting

Percentage

Number

Fewer decimal places

More decimal places

A value in the Formula bar has no formatting.

1 Enter different values into a row of cells

	General	No specific format
ABC 123		
12	Number	500.00
	Currency	£500.00
	Accounting	£500.00
	Short Date	14/05/1901
	Long Date	14 May 1901
	Time	00:00:00
%	Percentage	50000.00%
½	Fraction	500
10²	Scientific	5.00E+02
ABC	Text	500

More Number Formats...

B4		fx	42		
	A	B	C	D	E
1	**Number formats**				
2					
3	Number	42.00	42.34	0.42	4200000000.00
4	Currency	£42.00	£42.34	£0.42	£4,200,000,000.00
5	Accounting	£ 42.00	£ 42.34	£ 0.42	£ 4,200,000,000.00
6	Short date	11/02/1900	11/02/1900	00/01/1900	#################
7	Long Date	11 February 1900	11 February 1900	00 January 1900	#################
8	Time	00:00:00	08:09:36	10:04:48	#################
9	Percentage	4200.00%	4234.00%	42.00%	420000000000.00%
10	Fraction	42	42 1/3	3/7	4200000000
11	Scientific	4.20E+01	4.23E+01	4.20E-01	4.20E+09

These values are too big to fit in this column, using these formats – make the column wider.

2 Copy the cells down to the next 7 or 8 rows

3 Use the Number tools to apply a different format to each row

Worked example: an estimate

Because Excel can format the text and the layout, as well as do calculations, it can be used to create things like estimates and invoices. No special techniques are needed – there are only one new things used in this example: Merge and Center and the TODAY() function.

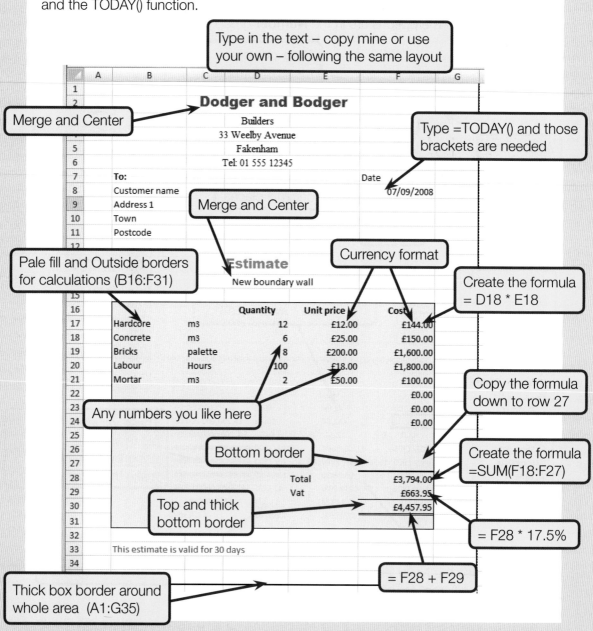

Type in the text – copy mine or use your own – following the same layout

Merge and Center

Type =TODAY() and those brackets are needed

Merge and Center

Pale fill and Outside borders for calculations (B16:F31)

Currency format

Create the formula = D18 * E18

Any numbers you like here

Copy the formula down to row 27

Bottom border

Create the formula =SUM(F18:F27)

Top and thick bottom border

= F28 * 17.5%

Thick box border around whole area (A1:G35)

= F28 + F29

Merge and Center

This formatting option stretches a heading across several columns, and is very useful where you have large text, or a lot of text, but want to keep narrower columns further down the sheet. It doesn't matter which of the cells the text is in – but the other cells must be empty.

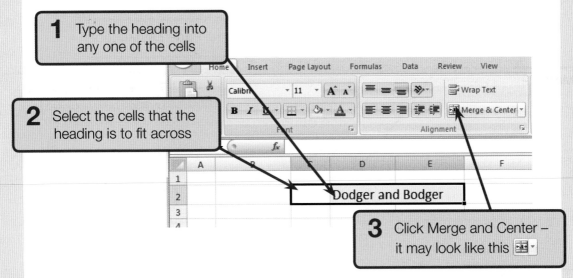

1 Type the heading into any one of the cells

2 Select the cells that the heading is to fit across

3 Click Merge and Center – it may look like this

= TODAY()

This function produces the current date. It will initially appear in the Long Date format (e.g. 7 September 2008). For a more compact display, use the Short Date format (e.g.07/09/2008).

Applying borders

Each of the four borders around a cell is also a border of one of the four surrounding cells. When you apply a border to one cell, it may have an unwanted impact on another. Inserting and deleting rows and columns can also affect the borders. So, leave the borders until last, and be ready to redo them.

The Print Area

Excel will normally print from A1 to the lowest cell on the right which has anything in it, i.e. the active part of the sheet. You can set a more limited print area if there are parts that you do not want to print.

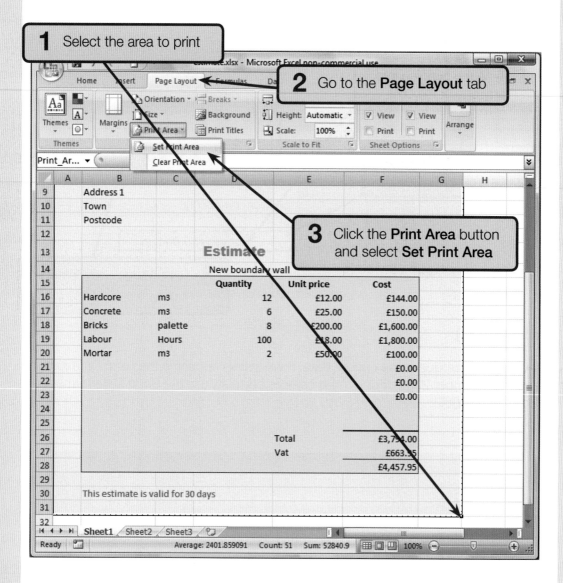

1 Select the area to print

2 Go to the **Page Layout** tab

3 Click the **Print Area** button and select **Set Print Area**

Print preview

It's not easy to tell how a spreadsheet will look when it is printed, so it's always worth previewing it. When layout matters, as it does with our estimate, or when it is a large sheet that will be printed over several pages, previewing is essential.

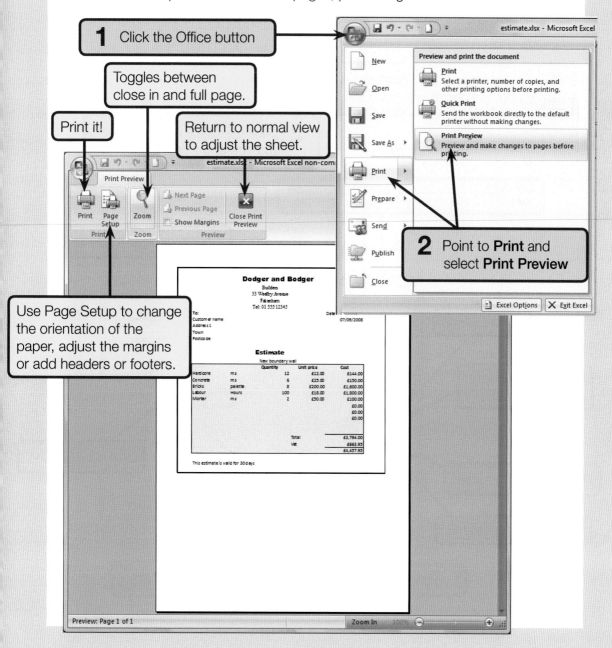

1 Click the Office button

Toggles between close in and full page.

Print it!

Return to normal view to adjust the sheet.

Use Page Setup to change the orientation of the paper, adjust the margins or add headers or footers.

2 Point to **Print** and select **Print Preview**

Preview and print the document

Print
Select a printer, number of copies, and other printing options before printing.

Quick Print
Send the workbook directly to the default printer without making changes.

Print Preview
Preview and make changes to pages before printing.

Printing

If you have set the print area, and you only want one copy, from the usual printer, use **Print** > **Quick Print** on the Office button menu to output your sheet.

If you want to print a selected part of the sheet, or a few pages of a large one, or have multiple copies, or use a different printer, then you need to go through the Print dialogue box.

1 If you want to print a special part of the sheet, select it now

2 Click the Office button, point to **Print** and select **Print**

3 Set the output options as required

Choose a different printer.

Print the entire sheet.

Print a set of pages of a large sheet.

Print the selected area.

Print all the active area.

How many copies?

You can preview from here.

4 Click **OK**

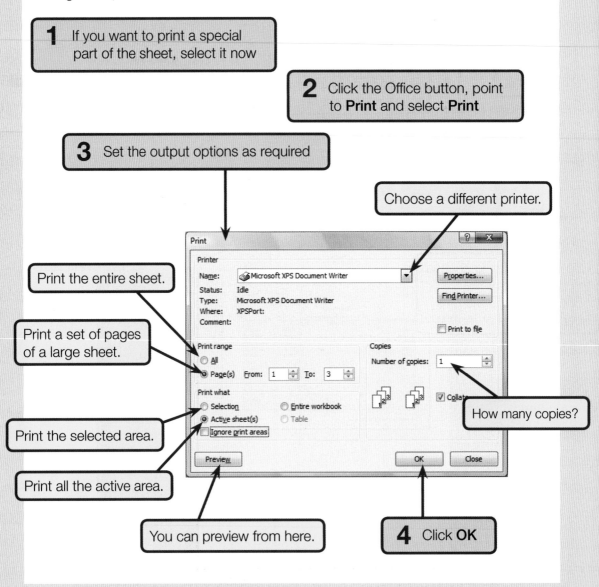

Spreadsheets from templates

When you start a new file, using the **New** command on the Office button menu, you will see the New Workbook window. There is a **Blank Workbook** option, if you want to start a sheet from scratch, but there are also a lot of templates. These have structure, layout and formulae in place, ready for you to enter your own data, and are often a better bet than writing your own. Even if none will do exactly what you want, you should be able to find one to provide a good base – and in most cases, all you will have to do is simply ignore those features which you do not need.

1 Click the Office button and select **New**

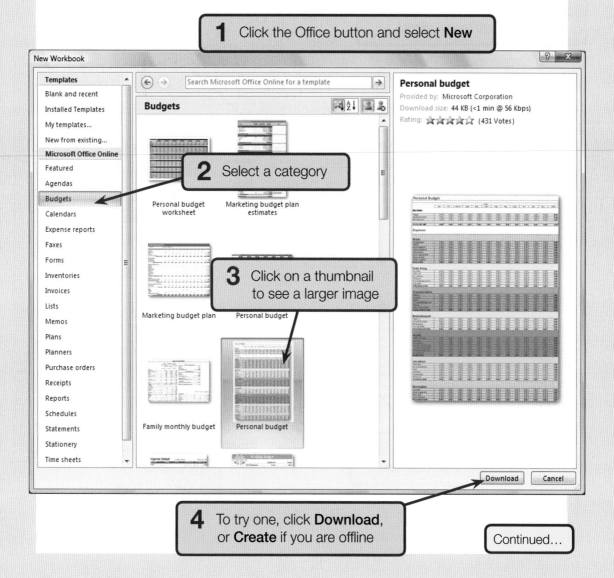

2 Select a category

3 Click on a thumbnail to see a larger image

4 To try one, click **Download**, or **Create** if you are offline

Continued...

As well as its formulae and formatting, a template-based spreadsheet will normally also have some sample data, to show how it is used. Obviously, you will need to remove this before using the sheet, but you do not want to lose the formulae.

Try one of the budget templates – there are lots to chose from – and see if you can take better control of your household finances!

5 Study the sheet, so that you understand how it works

6 Identify the cells with formulae – they will be a different colour or be marked in other ways

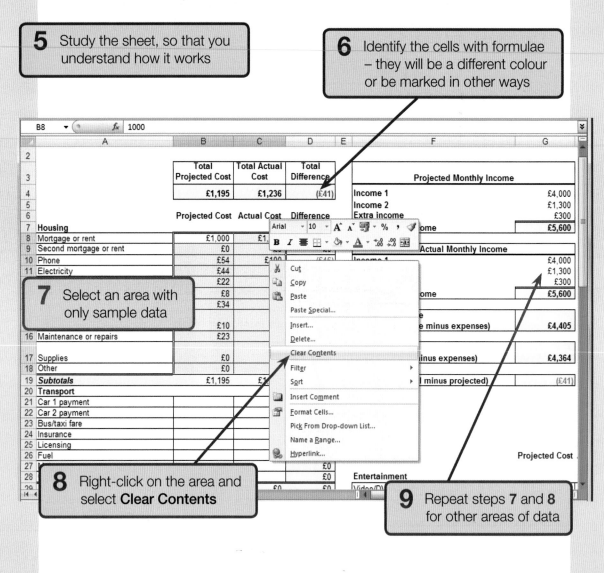

7 Select an area with only sample data

8 Right-click on the area and select **Clear Contents**

9 Repeat steps **7** and **8** for other areas of data

Other templates

Amongst the many templates, you will find a whole set of calendars, some of which are multiple-sheet versions. A workbook file can have many sheets. These would typically relate to different aspects of the same things, and would be interlinked, with values and calculations on one sheet being used in others. The calendar workbooks are much simpler – they just use a different sheet for each month. They are designed to be printed, and each sheet must be printed separately.

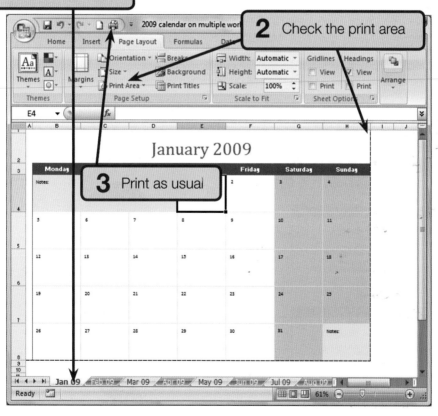

1 Click a tab to bring its sheet to the front

2 Check the print area

3 Print as usual

Templates for business

If you are in business, or have anything to do with financial decisions in an organisation, do take time to explore the templates, and make sure that you look in the **More Categories** section, especially in the Analysis, Calculators and Forecasts sets. There are many here that could be immediately useful in your financial decision-making.

This is an example of a workbook from the Analysis set. This does a thorough job of collecting data (there's much more to this sheet than can be seen here), processing it and outputting the results both as figures and as graphs.

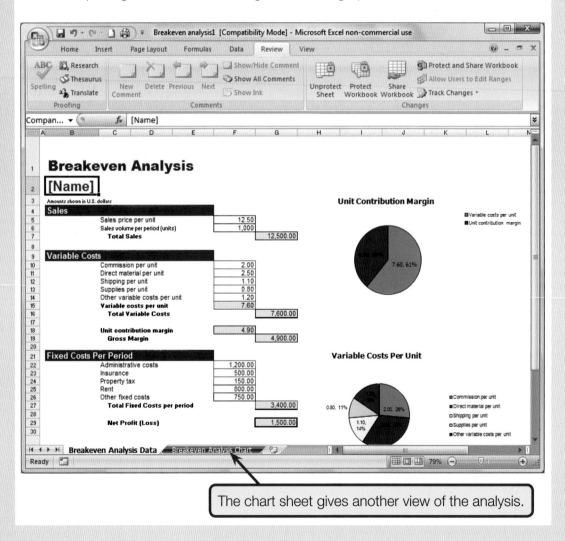

The chart sheet gives another view of the analysis.

Practice!

Using what you have learnt so far, you could now build a spreadsheet to track your savings and investments. It's not much more than a matter of recording changing values at regular intervals, and totalling them up. The data could then be charted to give a visual display – and we will do that next.

Savings

Use =SUM(…) and copy the formula across.

Time interval – I'm recording values quarterly, but this could be daily, weekly, monthly, or whatever.

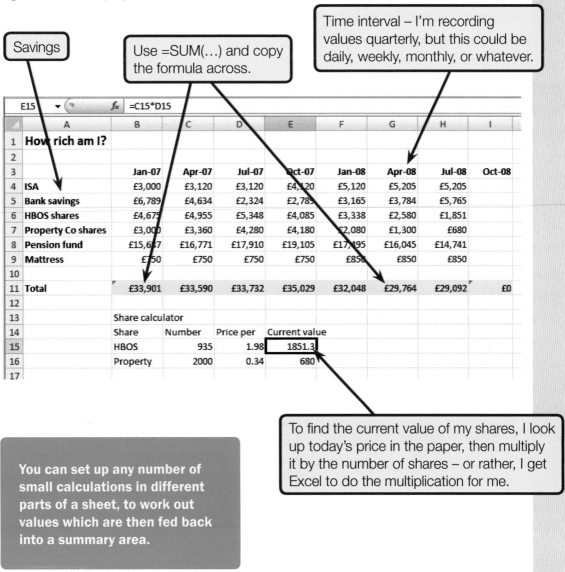

E15		fx	=C15*D15					
	A	B	C	D	E	F	G	H	I
1	How rich am I?								
2									
3		Jan-07	Apr-07	Jul-07	Oct-07	Jan-08	Apr-08	Jul-08	Oct-08
4	ISA	£3,000	£3,120	£3,120	£4,120	£5,120	£5,205	£5,205	
5	Bank savings	£6,789	£4,634	£2,324	£2,785	£3,165	£3,784	£5,765	
6	HBOS shares	£4,675	£4,955	£5,348	£4,085	£3,338	£2,580	£1,851	
7	Property Co shares	£3,000	£3,360	£4,280	£4,180	£2,080	£1,300	£680	
8	Pension fund	£15,687	£16,771	£17,910	£19,105	£17,495	£16,045	£14,741	
9	Mattress	£750	£750	£750	£750	£850	£850	£850	
10									
11	Total	£33,901	£33,590	£33,732	£35,029	£32,048	£29,764	£29,092	£0
12									
13		Share calculator							
14		Share	Number	Price per	Current value				
15		HBOS	935	1.98	1851.3				
16		Property	2000	0.34	680				
17									

To find the current value of my shares, I look up today's price in the paper, then multiply it by the number of shares – or rather, I get Excel to do the multiplication for me.

You can set up any number of small calculations in different parts of a sheet, to work out values which are then fed back into a summary area.

Charts

Creating charts in Excel is simple – and can be very quick. (It can be also be time-consuming because there is a real temptation to play with all the display options!)

Ideally, the data to be charted should be in a solid block (i.e. with no unwanted stuff between the rows) with headings along the top and on the left. Less well-organised data can be used, but it takes more setting up.

1 Select the data, along with its headings

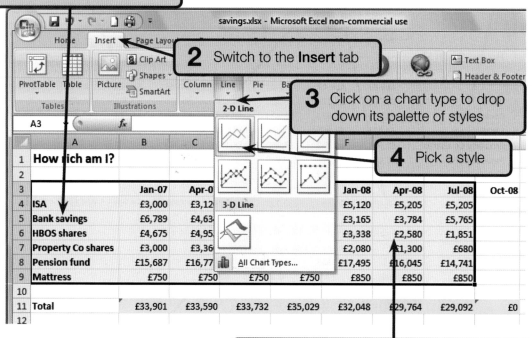

2 Switch to the **Insert** tab

3 Click on a chart type to drop down its palette of styles

4 Pick a style

	Jan-07	Apr-0				Jan-08	Apr-08	Jul-08	Oct-08
1 How rich am I?									
4 ISA	£3,000	£3,12				£5,120	£5,205	£5,205	
5 Bank savings	£6,789	£4,63				£3,165	£3,784	£5,765	
6 HBOS shares	£4,675	£4,95				£3,338	£2,580	£1,851	
7 Property Co shares	£3,000	£3,36				£2,080	£1,300	£680	
8 Pension fund	£15,687	£16,77				£17,495	£16,045	£14,741	
9 Mattress	£750	£750	£750	£750		£850	£850	£850	
11 Total	£33,901	£33,590	£33,732	£35,029		£32,048	£29,764	£29,092	£0

Each row of data is a **Data Series** and will be drawn as a line on a graph. The headings along the top will be used to label the **horizontal (X) axis**. The headings on the left wil be used in the **Legend** to identify the lines.

If you are not sure which style to use, don't worry, you can change it at any time and try a different one.

The Chart Design tools

When a chart is first inserted it appears in a small window, on top of the data area (it can be moved), and the Chart Design tools will come to the front of the Ribbon. The chart can be formatted and adjusted in many ways.

Excel assumes the data are in rows, click here if they are in columns.

Variations on the type.

To be used with scattered data.

Colour schemes.

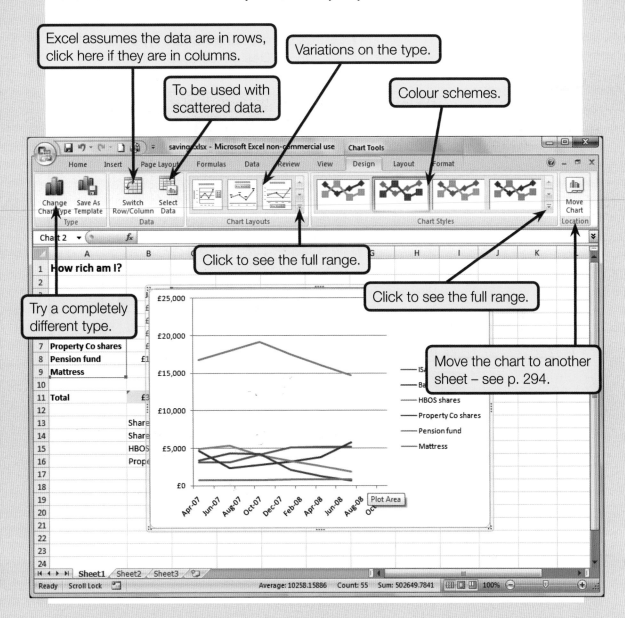

Click to see the full range.

Click to see the full range.

Try a completely different type.

Move the chart to another sheet – see p. 294.

Chart types

Excel offers a choice of over 70 different types of charts, grouped into 12 categories. And that's by no means the end of the choices, because each of these has variations of layout and styles. You should be able to find something suitable for any job!

You can change the type of an existing chart at any time.

1 Click the **Change Chart Type** tool on the **Design** tab of the Ribbon

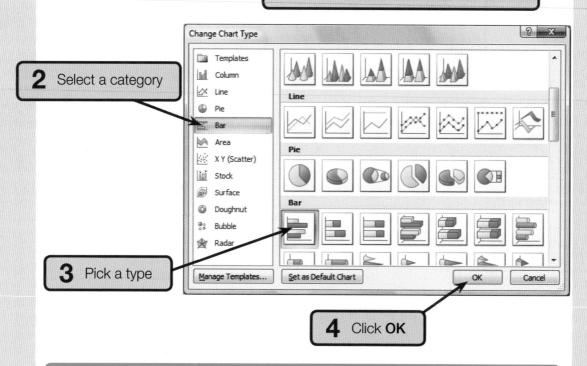

2 Select a category

3 Pick a type

4 Click **OK**

Note that not all types can be used for all sets of data. Column, line, bar and area charts can be used where you have several rows or columns of data – see p. 291. Pie charts can only be used where there is a single data series. The XY (Scatter), Stock and Radar charts all have special uses and are designed to bring out different aspects of the relationships between values.

Line charts

These are good where you want to show change over time, and to compare sets of data. The 3-D versions may look smarter, but the simpler 2-D charts are often easier to read – compare this with the one on p. 295.

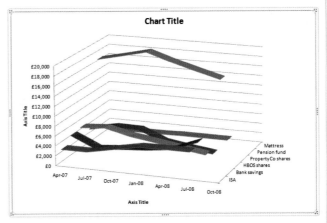

Bar charts

These highlight the differences between the values at each point in time, but make it harder to see the changes in any given data series.

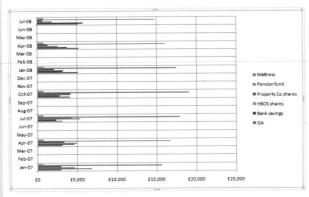

Column charts

These are essentially the same as bar charts, except that here the bars, rods, cones or columns are vertical instead of horizontal.

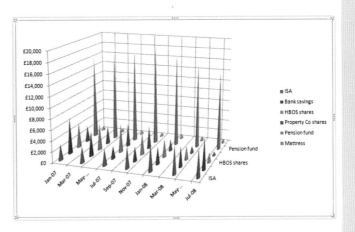

Stacked charts

These stack the series on top of each other, so that you can see how much each contributes to the total. There are also stacked versions of Line charts – these do not usually work that well.

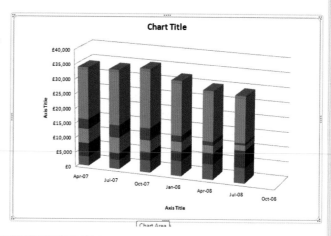

Area charts

These are development of the stacked line – filling in the space between the lines with slabs of colour. They help to bring out both change over time and how much each contributes to the total.

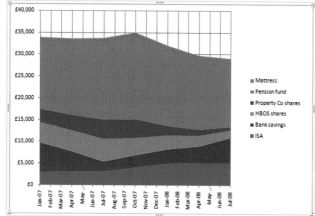

100% charts

There are 100% versions of line, bar, column and area charts. They convert the actual values to percentages, so that the total at each point is always 100. It gives you another way to look at relative contributions.

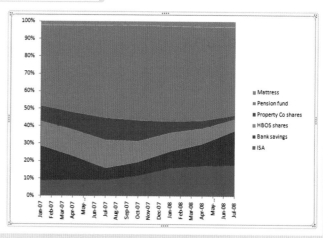

Pie charts

These are the classic way of showing how values contribute to the total, but can only be used with a single data series. Of course, there is nothing to stop you setting up a pie chart for each of several series, then setting them next to each other on the sheet.

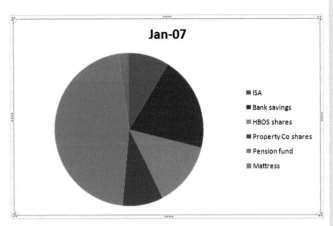

Mixed charts

Sometimes it is useful to pick out one set of data, and Excel gives you a neat way to do this – you can mixed display types in a chart.

1 Click on a set of data to select it

2 Right-click on the series and select **Change Series Chart Type**

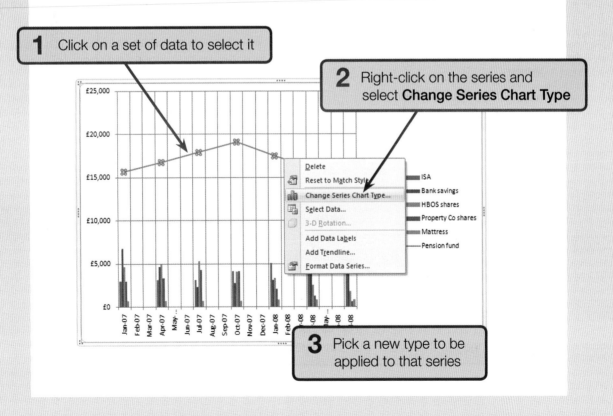

3 Pick a new type to be applied to that series

Moving a chart

When the chart first appears on your sheet, it will probably be in just the wrong place – covering some or all of the data that it is based on. But, it's easily moved. You can relocate it within the sheet, or move it to a new chart sheet (which has no gridlines).

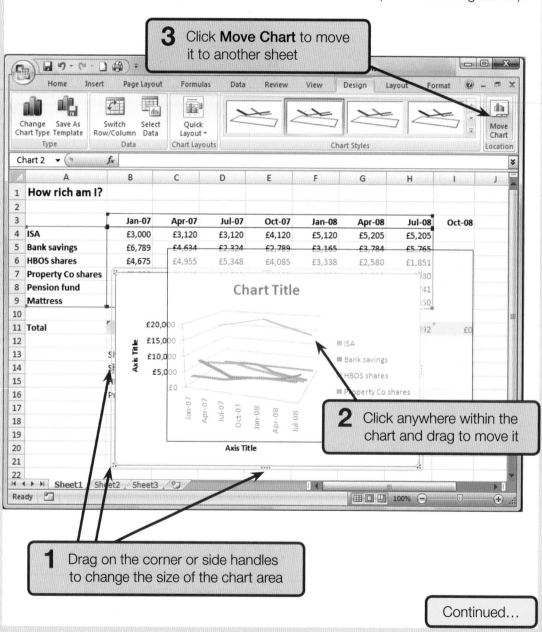

3 Click **Move Chart** to move it to another sheet

2 Click anywhere within the chart and drag to move it

1 Drag on the corner or side handles to change the size of the chart area

Continued...

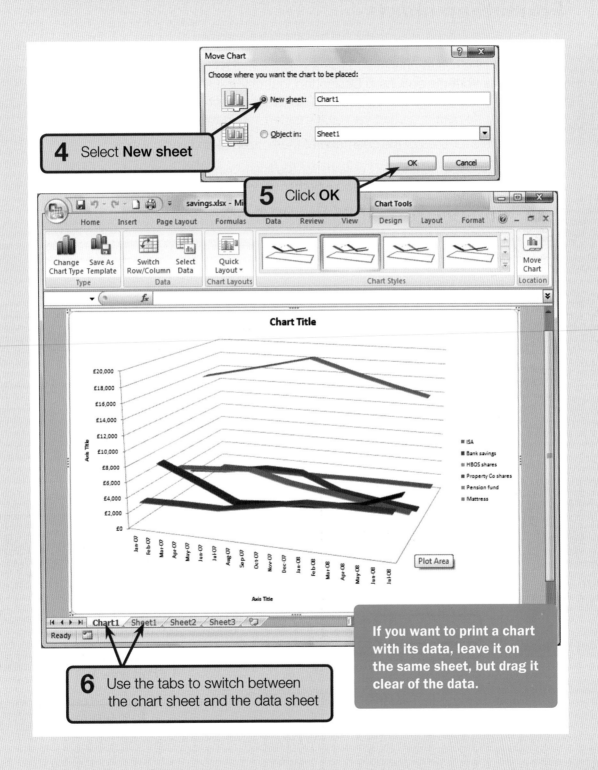

Move Chart

Choose where you want the chart to be placed:

○ New sheet: Chart1

4 Select **New sheet**

○ Object in: Sheet1

OK   Cancel

5 Click **OK**

savings.xlsx - Mi...   Chart Tools

Home   Insert   Page Layout   Formulas   Data   Review   View   Design   Layout   Format

Change Chart Type   Save As Template   Switch Row/Column   Select Data   Quick Layout   Move Chart

Type   Data   Chart Layouts   Chart Styles   Location

Chart Title

£20,000
£18,000
£16,000
£14,000
£12,000
£10,000
£8,000
£6,000
£4,000
£2,000
£0

Axis Title

■ ISA
■ Bank savings
■ HBOS shares
■ Property Co shares
■ Pension fund
■ Mattress

Plot Area

Axis Title

Chart1   Sheet1   Sheet2   Sheet3

Ready

6 Use the tabs to switch between the chart sheet and the data sheet

If you want to print a chart with its data, leave it on the same sheet, but drag it clear of the data.

295

Formatting charts

You can make overall changes to the appearance of a chart by selecting a new layout or style from the options in Design tab, but that is just the start of making your charts look good. You can use the full range of font formatting on any text, but then every element of a chart can be formatted in certain ways. You can set:

- The text for titles of the chart and of the horizontal and vertical axes
- The colour, style and 3-D options for the lines, bars, columns, dots or segments that represent data series, and whether or not values are displayed on them
- The spacing of divisions on the axes, and the display of gridlines
- The angle and tilt of 3-D charts
- The colour of the background, of the chart itself and the surrounding area.

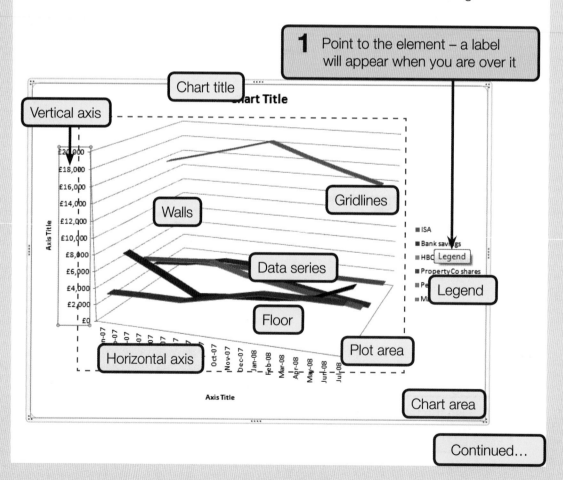

1 Point to the element – a label will appear when you are over it

Continued...

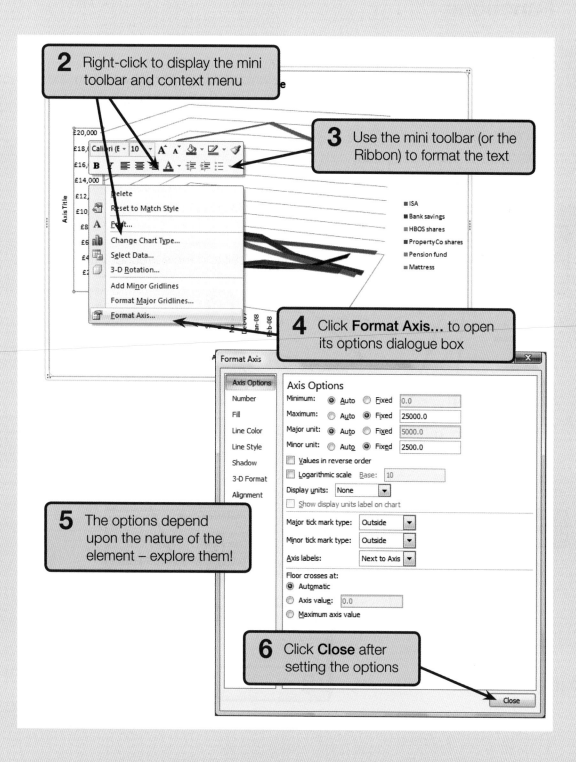

2 Right-click to display the mini toolbar and context menu

3 Use the mini toolbar (or the Ribbon) to format the text

Delete
Reset to Match Style
Font...
Change Chart Type...
Select Data...
3-D Rotation...
Add Minor Gridlines
Format Major Gridlines...
Format Axis...

4 Click **Format Axis...** to open its options dialogue box

Format Axis

Axis Options
Number
Fill
Line Color
Line Style
Shadow
3-D Format
Alignment

Axis Options

Minimum: ● Auto ○ Fixed 0.0
Maximum: ○ Auto ● Fixed 25000.0
Major unit: ● Auto ○ Fixed 5000.0
Minor unit: ○ Auto ● Fixed 2500.0

☐ Values in reverse order
☐ Logarithmic scale Base: 10
Display units: None

☐ Show display units label on chart

Major tick mark type: Outside
Minor tick mark type: Outside
Axis labels: Next to Axis

Floor crosses at:
● Automatic
○ Axis value: 0.0
○ Maximum axis value

5 The options depend upon the nature of the element – explore them!

6 Click **Close** after setting the options

Close

ISA
Bank savings
HBOS shares
PropertyCo shares
Pension fund
Mattress

Axis Title

£20,000
£18,000
£16,000
£14,000
£12,000
£10,000
£8,000
£6,000
£4,000
£2,000

Functions

A function is a kind of ready-made calculation. It will take data, process it and give you a result. We've met one function SUM(), which adds up the values. There are many more, some of which do some very complicated calculations – but which are all pretty straightforward to use. Let's explore some of the simpler ones. These four all work on the values in a range of cells:

- COUNT tells you how may cells in the range hold values
- AVERAGE works out the mean value = total/number of items
- MAX and MIN tell you the highest and lowest values in the range.

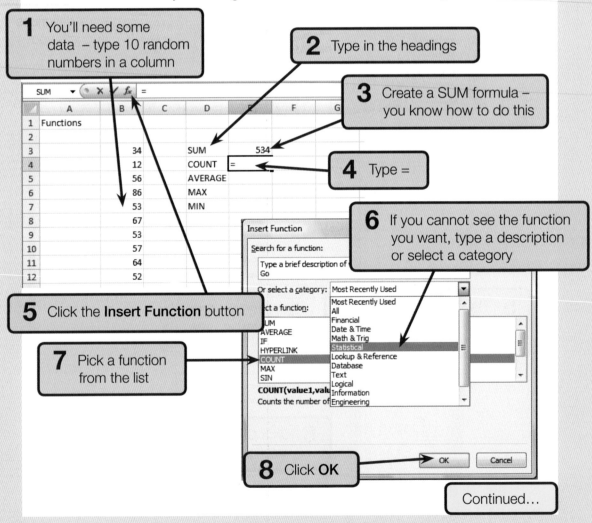

1 You'll need some data – type 10 random numbers in a column

2 Type in the headings

3 Create a SUM formula – you know how to do this

4 Type =

5 Click the **Insert Function** button

6 If you cannot see the function you want, type a description or select a category

7 Pick a function from the list

8 Click **OK**

Continued...

The items of data (values, or cell references) that you give to a function are called **Arguments**.

You can type the range here, or collect the references from the sheet.

9 Click to shrink the box so more of the sheet is visible

The dialogue box describes the function and tells you what arguments are needed – COUNT needs a range of cells.

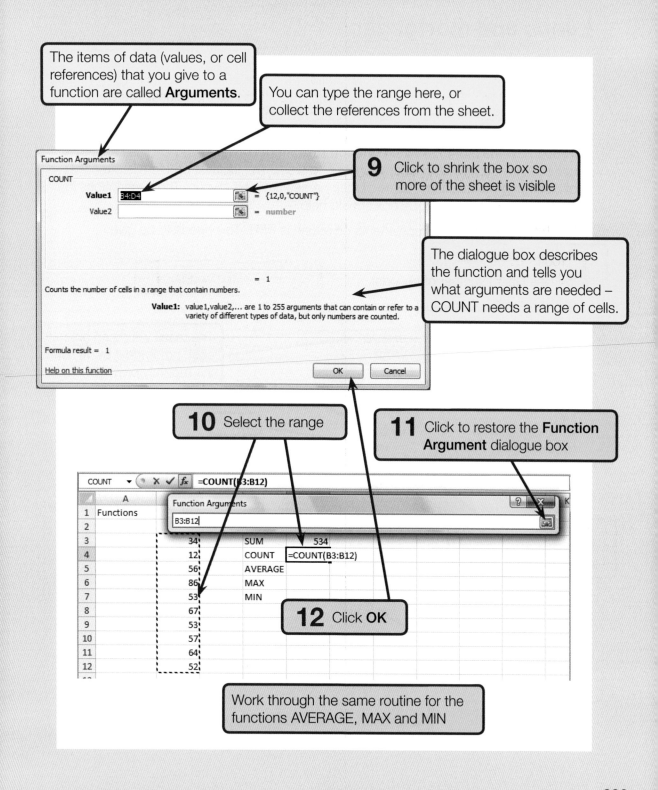

Function Arguments

COUNT

Value1	B4:D4		= {12,0,"COUNT"}
Value2			= number

= 1

Counts the number of cells in a range that contain numbers.

Value1: value1,value2,... are 1 to 255 arguments that can contain or refer to a variety of different types of data, but only numbers are counted.

Formula result = 1

Help on this function

OK   Cancel

10 Select the range

11 Click to restore the **Function Argument** dialogue box

COUNT ▾ X ✓ *fx* =COUNT(B3:B12)

	A	Function Arguments		? X K
1	Functions	B3:B12		
2				
3		34	SUM	534
4		12	COUNT	=COUNT(B3:B12)
5		56	AVERAGE	
6		86	MAX	
7		53	MIN	
8		67		
9		53		
10		57		
11		64		
12		52		

12 Click **OK**

Work through the same routine for the functions AVERAGE, MAX and MIN

Loans and mortgages

I've included this to show that something which may seem to be very complicated – like working out the repayments on a mortgage – can be done very simply in Excel. And of course, once you have got the calculation set up, you can experiment with different values.

If you follow the prompts in the **Function Argument** dialogue box, and use a bit of common sense, you can put any function to work. The trickiest problem is often that of identifying the function – some of their names are a bit cryptic. The descriptions in the **Insert Function** dialogue box should help.

The function to calculate repayments on a loan is PMT. This needs to be given:

- the interest rate
- the Nper (Number of periods)
- the PV (Present Value) – the amount you are borrowing.

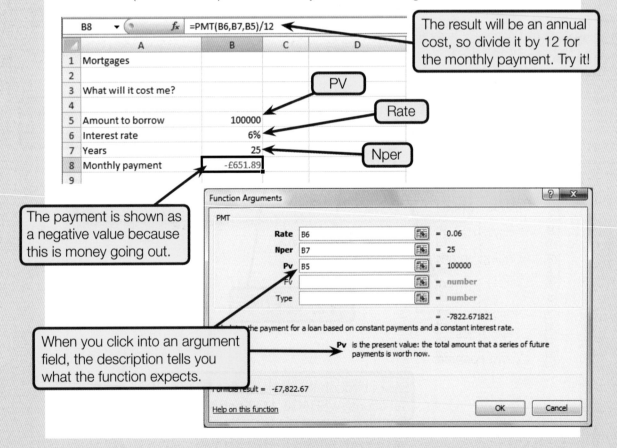

The result will be an annual cost, so divide it by 12 for the monthly payment. Try it!

PV

Rate

Nper

The payment is shown as a negative value because this is money going out.

When you click into an argument field, the description tells you what the function expects.

10 Sharing and networking your PC

Networking used to be a complicated business, but Vista makes it easy for people to to share a computer, and to share files and other resources between computers.

This chapter covers:

- How to create User Accounts
- Passwords for restricting access
- Logging on and off
- Simple networks
- How to let Vista set up a network for you
- Sharing files
- Sharing printers

User Accounts

Windows Vista makes it easy for several people to share the use of one PC. Each user has their own set of folders and their own customised Desktop and Start menu.

You can only create accounts if you have an Adminstrator level account, or if yours is the only account.

1 From the **Start** menu, open the **Control Panel**

2 In the **User Accounts** area, click **Add or remove user accounts** – Windows will ask you for permission – click **Continue**

3 Click **Create a new account**

4 Enter a name for the user

5 Set the account – Standard unless the user needs to be able to add software or make other changes to the system

Parental controls

6 Click **Create Account** – the user can later set a password or change their picture

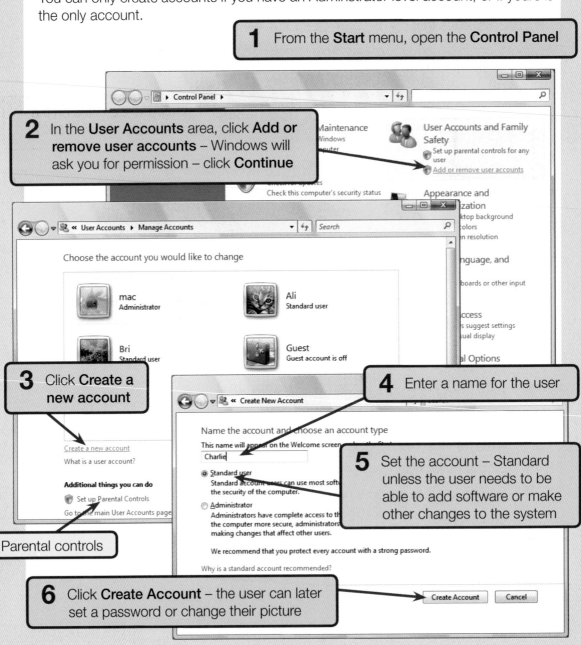

Parental controls

If the account is for a young child, parents can set up controls. These can restrict:

- the times of the day that the account can be used
- the programs that can be used
- the websites that can be accessed.

Parental controls can only be set by users with Administrator accounts, and passwords should be set on these.

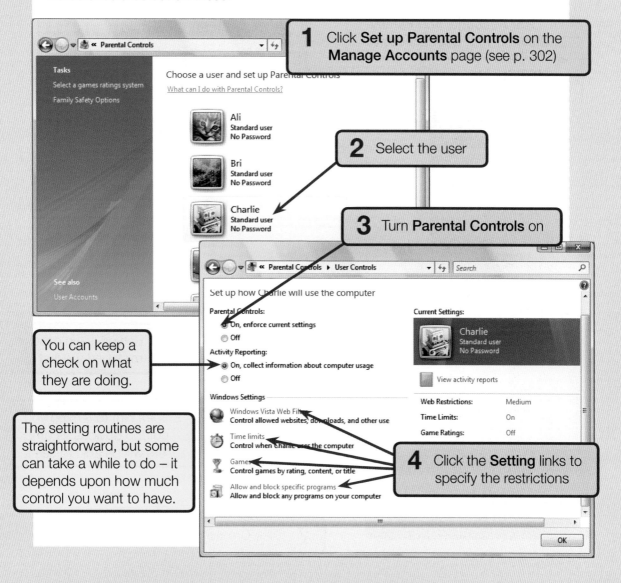

1 Click **Set up Parental Controls** on the **Manage Accounts** page (see p. 302)

2 Select the user

3 Turn **Parental Controls** on

You can keep a check on what they are doing.

The setting routines are straightforward, but some can take a while to do – it depends upon how much control you want to have.

4 Click the **Setting** links to specify the restrictions

Setting a password

Any user who feels the need to protect their files from prying eyes can set a password for their accounts. And users with Administrator status should set passwords, so that Standard users cannot log on as them and – accidentally or otherwise – change system settings or delete software.

The password should be something that you can remember, but that other people are not likely to guess. Mixing capitals, lower case and digits is a good idea.

1 Open the **Control Panel**, go to **User Accounts and Family Safety**, then to **User accounts**

2 Click **Create a password reset disk** and follow the instructions – you will need it when you forget your password

3 Click **Create a password**

4 Type a password – it will appear as a string of *

5 Retype it – in case you mistyped the first time

6 Enter a hint to remind you – not too obvious as other users will be able to see it

If you do not need a password, don't set one – it's just another thing to mistype and forget!

7 Click **Create password**

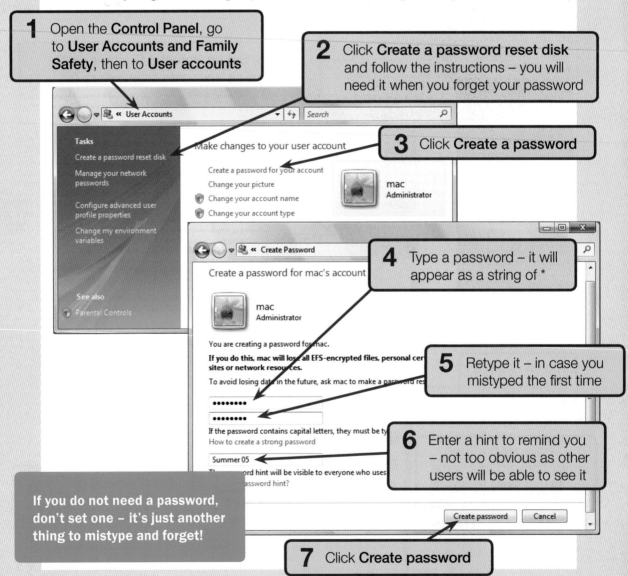

Logging on and off

If there are several user accounts, when you turn on the PC it runs through its basic start-up routine and stops when it reaches the log-on screen. The user then clicks their picture – and enters a password if one was set – to log on.

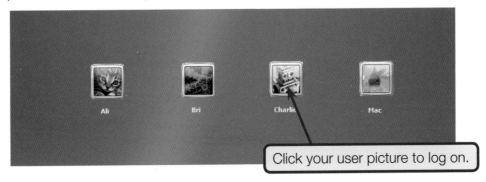

Click your user picture to log on.

At the end of a session, on a multi-user machine, you have two extra choices:

● Select **Switch User** to let someone else use the PC for a while. The programs that you are running and the documents that you have open will be put safely on hold. You can come back later and log on again, and everything will be just as you left it, ready to start straight back into work.

● Select **Log Off** if you have finished work for the day. If any programs are running, they will be shut down. If any documents are open, you will be prompted to save them before they are closed.

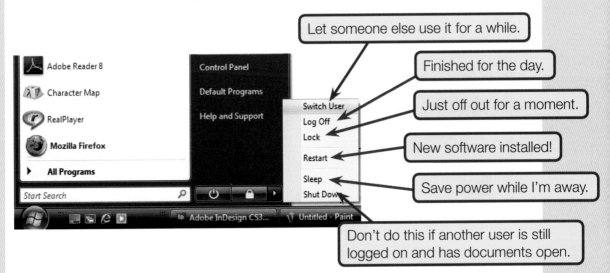

Let someone else use it for a while.

Finished for the day.

Just off out for a moment.

New software installed!

Save power while I'm away.

Don't do this if another user is still logged on and has documents open.

Home networks

It is not simple to set up and maintain a network in a business or organisation where data need to be protected, as there there must be very careful limits on who can access which files, folders, programs and printers on the network. At home or in a small office, you shouldn't have these problems, and with Windows Vista setting up a network is very easy.

If you have wireless broadband, the network can be set up through that (see page 306). Otherwise, you can join two PCs or laptops using their built-in Ethernet connections – all Vista machines have this. Buy a cable long enough to stretch between the two, and plug it into the Ethernet sockets. Vista can manage the rest, if you let it.

On each machine to be networked you need to turn on Network Discovery, which will allow a wizard to search for networks, and File sharing, so that other people can have some access to your machine.

1 On the **Start** menu, click **Network** to open the Network folder

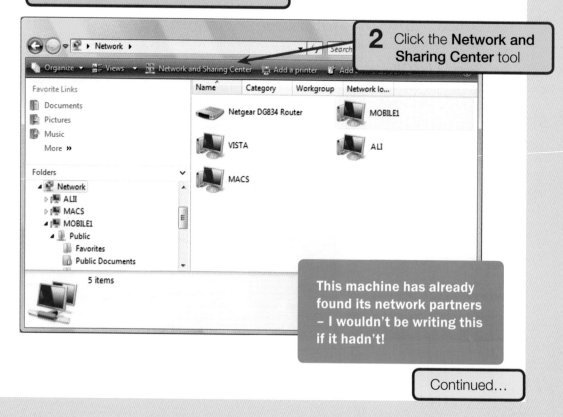

2 Click the **Network and Sharing Center** tool

This machine has already found its network partners – I wouldn't be writing this if it hadn't!

Continued...

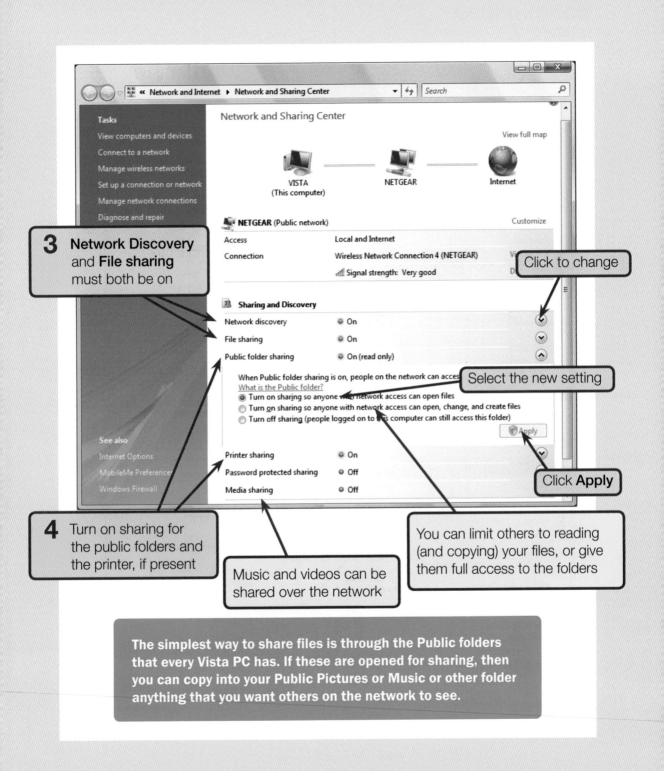

Sharing files

Once the network is in place, you can access its shared folders using Windows Explorer, just as if they were on your PC.

1 Start from the **Network** button on the Start menu, or...

Network ▸

Organize ▾   Views ▾   Network and Sharing Center   Add a printer   Add a wireless device

Name	Category	Workgroup	Network lo...

Favorite Links
- Documents
- Pictures
- Music

More »

Netgear DG834 Router

MOBILE1

2 ...if Explorer is running, select **Network** in the list

ALI

Folders
- Network
  - ALII
  - MACS
  - MOBILE1
    - Public
      - Favorites
      - Public Documents

MACS

3 Click on the machine you want to access

Network ▸ MOBILE1 ▸

Organize ▾   Views ▾   Network and Sharing Center

Favorite Links
- Documents
- Pictures
- Music

More »

Printers can also be shared.

Name	Type	Comments

Brother HL 2030

Microsoft Office Document Image Writer

Public

Send To OneNote 2007

Folders
- Network
  - ALI
  - MACS
  - MOBILE1
    - Public
      - Favorites
      - Public Documents

Users

Printers

4 Select the folder

Public (\\MOBILE1)

Continued...

Notice that only the Public folders are shown – the rest are not shared and are not visible over the network.

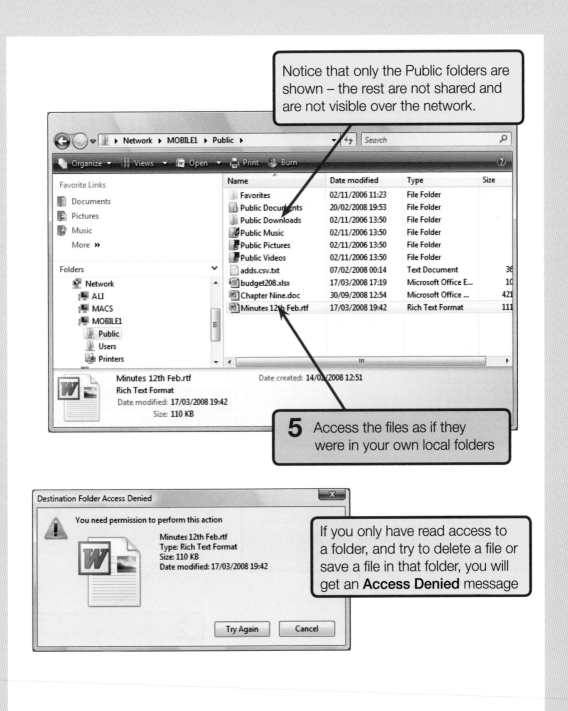

5 Access the files as if they were in your own local folders

If you only have read access to a folder, and try to delete a file or save a file in that folder, you will get an **Access Denied** message

Sharing a printer

If your computers are networked, any computer can print on any printer. This won't be worth doing if you've got the same sort of printer attached to every computer, but it will be if there's, for example, a black and white laser on one, and a colour ink jet on a second, and no printer at all on a third.

Some important points to note about sharing printers:

● Printing on a printer attached to another computer makes very little extra work for that computer

● If a computer is in Sleep mode, or turned off, its printer is not accessible over the network

● The driver for the printer must be installed on every computer that is to use it. Vista should do this for you when you first try to access a networked printer. If it doesn't, take the printer's installation disc and run it on every machine

● Someone – either you or the person on the other computer – is going to have make sure that there's paper and be ready to clear any paper jams!

Checking the printer

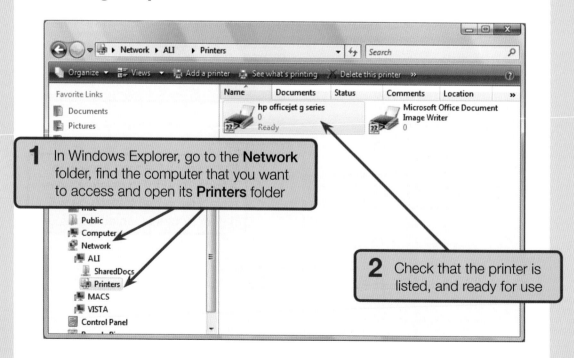

1 In Windows Explorer, go to the **Network** folder, find the computer that you want to access and open its **Printers** folder

2 Check that the printer is listed, and ready for use

Printing

As far as an application is concerned, there is nothing special about using a networked printer. So, when you are next printing from Word, and want to send the document across the network, you just need to tell Word which printer to use.

1 Open the application's **Print** dialogue box – this is Word

2 Drop down the Name list and select the networked printer – it will start with the name of its computer

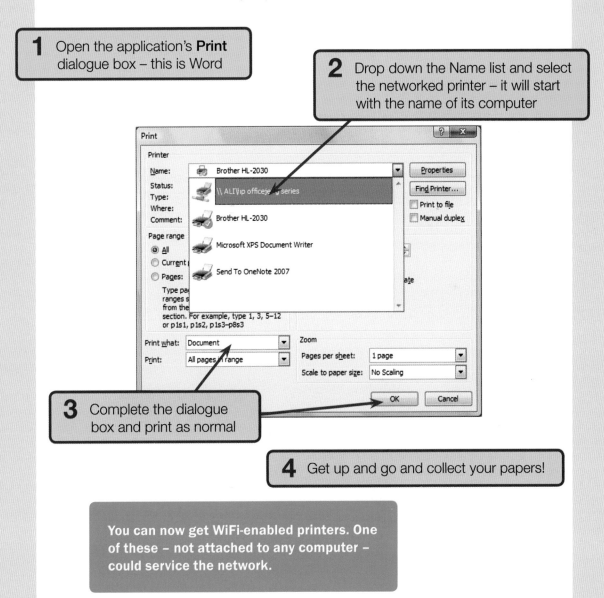

3 Complete the dialogue box and print as normal

4 Get up and go and collect your papers!

You can now get WiFi-enabled printers. One of these – not attached to any computer – could service the network.

Troubleshooting guide

The Vista Desktop and tools

File management

The Word screen and tools

Working with text

Formatting text

Music

Videos and movies

Calendar and appointments

Excel screen and tools

Formulae and working sheets